It has long been assumed that large-scale industry was one of the pillars of support for the Vichy regime, which ruled France – under the German aegis – from 1940 to 1944. In particular it has been assumed that business used Vichy to reverse the advantages that labour had secured after the election of the Popular Front government in 1936. Richard Vinen argues that this assumption is false. In *The politics of French business 1936–1945* he suggests that large-scale industry, mostly based in northern France, was geographically and psychologically isolated from the preoccupations of a government which was based in the south. Furthermore, business soon became aware of the probability of an allied victory and was consequently eager to distance itself from a government that it saw as doomed. Most importantly of all, the Popular Front legislation of 1936 had already been undermined by the rearmament programme that preceded the fall of France in 1940. For this reason most industrialists saw Vichy as a superfluous reactionary regime whose *raison d'être* soon disappeared.

The politics of French business 1936–1945 has much to say on the nature of post-war French modernization, and on the whole relationship between capitalism and the state: it will be of interest to a broad constituency of historians and political scientists specializing in the recent history of France and Western Europe.

The politics of French business 1936–1945

The politics of
French business
1936–1945

Richard Vinen
Trinity College, Cambridge

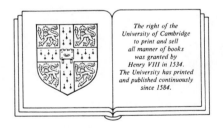

CAMBRIDGE UNIVERSITY PRESS
Cambridge
New York   Port Chester
Melbourne   Sydney

Published by the Press Syndicate of the University of Cambridge
The Pitt Building, Trumpington Street, Cambridge CB2 1RP
40 West 20th Street, New York, NY 10011-4211, USA
10 Stamford Road, Oakleigh, Melbourne 3166, Australia

First published 1991

Printed in Great Britain at the University Press, Cambridge

British Library cataloguing in publication data

Vinen, Richard Charles
The politics of French business 1936–1945.
1. France: Industrial Development
I. Title
338.0944

Library of Congress cataloguing in publication data

Vinen, Richard Charles
The politics of French business 1936–1945/Richard Charles Vinen.
    p.   cm.
Includes bibliographical references and index.
ISBN 0 521 40440 1
1. Business and politics – France – History.   2. Industry and state –
France – History.   3. Industrial relations – France – History.
4. Employers' associations – France – Political activity – History.
I. Title.
HD3616.F82V56   1991
338.944 – dc20   90-19803   CIP

ISBN 0 521 40440 1 hardback

UP

To my parents

Contents

Preface

In writing this book I have incurred a number of debts. Christopher Andrew supervised the thesis on which this book was based and nurtured my researches from very unpromising beginnings. Patrick Fridenson directed my researches when I was in Paris; his helpfulness was equalled only by that of the staff at the Bibliothèque Nationale. Three very loyal and tolerant friends – Alison Henwood, Joel Felix and Kevin Passmore – took time off from their own work to act as text editors, critics and psychotherapists. I am very grateful for the advice and encouragement given to me by M. Jean-Noel Jeanneney, Dr Julian Jackson, Professor Douglas Johnson, Professor Robert Paxton, Dr Adrian Rossiter, M. Henri Rousso and Dr Robert Tombs.

I am grateful to The British Academy for the award of a Research Studentship and to Trinity College for a number of grants that have enabled me to visit Paris.

Abbreviations

AIAF	Association de l'Industrie et de l'Agriculture Françaises
AICA	Association Industrielle Commerciale et Agricole de Lyon
AICMR	Association Internationale de la Construction du Matériel Roulant
APCC	Assemblée des Présidents des Chambres de Commerce
APM	Association Professionnelle Mixte
CA	*conseil d'administration*
CCOP	Comité Central de l'Organisation Professionnelle
CEPME	Comité d'Etudes de la Petite et Moyenne Entreprise
CGII	Confederazione Generale dell'Industria Italiana
CGPF	Confédération Générale du Patronat Français (Confédération Générale de la Production Française before August 1936)
CGPME	Confédération Générale des Petites et Moyennes Entreprises
CGT	Confédération Générale du Travail
CGTU	Confédération Générale du Travail Unitaire
CIE	Centre d'Information des Employeurs
CII	Centre d'Information Interprofessionnelle
CNE	Comité National d'Entente
CO	Comité d'Organisation
COH	Comité d'Organisation de l'Industrie des Combustibles Minéraux Solides (an acronym inherited from the Comité des Houillères)
CPAS	Comité de Prévoyance et d'Action Sociale
CSE	Comité du Salut Economique
CSEIC	Conseil Supérieur de l'Economie Industrielle et Commerciale
FAR	Fédération des Associations Régionales
GIMMCP	Groupement des Industries Métallurgiques Mécaniques et Connexes de la Région Parisienne
JO	Journal Officiel

MATFER	Agency representing the rolling stock industry in the Nord and Pas-de-Calais during the occupation
OCM	Organisation Civile et Militaire
OCRPI	Office Central de Répartition des Produits Industriels
OFK 670	German high command in the Nord and Pas-de-Calais
PME	*petite et moyenne entreprise*
PMI	Section for Petite et Moyenne Industrie of GIMMCP
PMIC	Section for Petite et Moyenne Industrie and Petit et Moyen Commerce of CGPF
PPF	Parti Populaire Français
SFIO	Section Français de l'Internationale Ouvrière
STO	Service du Travail Obligatoire
UIE	Union des Intérêts Economiques
UIMM	Union des Industries Métallurgiques et Minières
X	Graduate of the Ecole Polytechnique (the name derives from the cross guns in the school's insignia)

Chapter 1

Introduction

One of the most heavily worked seams of modern historiography is the study of the relationship between capitalism and the authoritarian anti-Marxist regimes that arose in Europe between 1922 and 1945.[1] Debate on this subject has been especially lively among historians of Germany. Indeed the study of the relationship between industry and politics in the Weimar Republic has become an industry in itself, and a highly politicized one at that.[2]

There has been far less study of the relationship between business and the Vichy regime that was installed in France after the defeat of 1940. One of the reasons for this apparent neglect is that historians have simply taken the links between business and Vichy for granted. By comparison with the Third Reich, Vichy looks like an open and shut case. It was headed by an ex-General not an ex-corporal; it was clearly a regime of the elites. The businessmen who thronged into the Hôtel des Ambassadeurs in July 1940 were in no danger of being jostled by drunken brownshirts. Vichy indulged in anti-capitalist rhetoric, but there were no assaults on the rights of property.

Business did well during the Vichy period. Work was provided for certain industries by the German war economy; labour organization was

---

[1] Daniel Guerin, *Fascism and Big Business* (London, 1973); Nicos Poulantzas, *Fascism and Dictatorship* (London, 1974); Jane Caplan, 'Theories of Fascism: Nicos Poulantzas as Historian', *History Workshop*, no. 3 (Spring 1977): 83–100; Stuart Woolf, 'Did a Fascist Economy Exist?', in idem (ed.), *The Nature of Fascism* (London, 1968).

[2] David Abraham, *The Collapse of the Weimar Public* (Princeton, N.J., 1982); Gerald Feldman, 'Big Business and the Kapp Putsch', *Central European History*, 4 (1971), 99–130; idem, *Iron and Steel in the German Inflation 1916–1923* (Princeton, N.J., 1977); Gerald Feldman and Ulrick Nockeu, 'Trade Associations and Economic Power: Interest Group Development in the German Iron and Steel Industries, 1900–1933', *Business History Review*, 49 (1975), 413–45; Henry A. Turner, 'Big Business and the Rise of Hitler', *American Historical Review*, 75 (1969), 56–70; idem, 'Hitler's Secret Pamphlet for Industrialists, 1927', *Journal of Modern History*, 40 (1968), 348–72; idem, 'The *Ruhrlade* Secret Cabinet of Heavy Industry in the Weimar Republic', *Central European History*, 3 (1970), 195–228; idem, *German Big Business and the Rise of Hitler* (Oxford, 1985).

1

suppressed; industrial organization often amounted to state-sponsored self-regulation. Not surprisingly, all this has led historians to assume that business was one of the pillars of Vichy support. In particular, it has been assumed that business used Vichy in order to reverse the defeat that had been inflicted on it by the Popular Front government and the strikes of 1936. There is some evidence for this. It is true that the business mobilization against the Popular Front involved a good deal of rhetoric directed at the *classes moyennes* and especially at small businessmen. Vichy claimed to represent precisely these classes. It is also true that during the mobilization against the Popular Front many business associations adopted the ideology of corporatism which was the official ideology of the Vichy regime. Finally, several of the leaders who rose to prominence in the business movement after 1936 went on to play important roles at Vichy.

But few historians have investigated in any detail the link between the business mobilization against the Popular Front and business support for Vichy. Scholars such as Fridenson,[3] Kolboom[4] and Bourdé[5] focus their research on the Popular Front and then make assumptions about the Vichy period that are founded on far less extensive knowledge. Similarly, historians like Paxton[6] and Kedward[7] rely on other historians to paint the Popular Front background to their brilliant portraits of Vichy. More recently historians have become increasingly inclined to explain the transition from the Third Republic to Vichy in terms of continuities, but 1940 remains a frontier that is rarely crossed in a single book or article.

The consequences of this division of scholarly effort are exacerbated by two factors. Firstly, the history of France between 1936 and 1945 is a history of constantly changing social alliances. Some of these alliances – such as that between the leaders of heavy industry and those who claimed to represent small business in 1936/7 or between the Gaullist state and the organized working class in 1944 – were highly awkward. Each of these alliances was therefore underwritten by a considerable body of myth that helped to make it more palatable by obscuring its real nature. Each time an alliance changed, the history of previous alliances was rewritten to suit the new alignment. This means that historians who focus on a short time-span are vulnerable in two ways. On the one hand, they may accept the views of previous periods presented within their own period. On the other, they may unconsciously absorb assumptions about their own period that were generated by the political circumstances of a later period. Thus the view of

---

[3] Patrick Fridenson, 'Le patronat français', in René Rémond and Janine Bourdin (eds.), *La France et les Français 1938–1939* (Paris, 1978), pp. 139–58.

[4] Ingo Kolboom, *La revanche des patrons: le patronat français face au front populaire* (Paris, 1986).   [5] Guy Bourdé, *La défaite du front populaire* (Paris, 1977).

[6] Robert Paxton, *Vichy France: Old Guard and New Order, 1940–1944* (New York, 1972).

[7] H. R. Kedward, 'Patriots and Patriotism in Vichy France', *Transactions of the Royal Historical Society*, 32 (1982), 175–92.

labour relations during the occupation presented by many historians has more to do with the circumstances of 1944 than those of 1940 to 1944. Similarly the view of the Matignon accords as a tacit collaboration between heavy industry and the Popular Front owes much to the political circumstances of 1940.

Secondly, historians of the period after the Popular Front and historians of Vichy ask different questions about their subjects. The study of business and politics is highly developed among historians of the Popular Front. But historians of Vichy rarely grant the subject more than a walk-on part in studies that concern other matters. Indeed, much of the study of Vichy has been approached from angles that actually impair an accurate view of business attitudes. In particular, many historians draw their evidence primarily from leaders of the left and the working class,[8] while others write local studies that ignore regional variations in business attitudes to the regime.[9] Even among historians who do concentrate on business attitudes there is a sharp divide between those working on the Popular Front and those working on Vichy. The former focus on business relations with organized labour,[10] while the latter focus on the role of the state and on the extent to which Vichy industrial organization anticipated post-war developments.[11]

Henry Ehrmann's *Organized Business in France* (1957) was the last work that attempted to deal with business throughout the period from 1936 to 1945. Ehrmann's book is full of insight, first-hand knowledge and sceptical common sense. But it was based on published material and testimonies that could not be cited. In the last few years an avalanche of documents concerning the period from 1936 to 1945 has become available. This book

---

[8] The studies undertaken by Etienne Dejonghe, 'Les houillères à l'épreuve: 1944–1947', *Revue du Nord*, 227 (1975), 643–67, Darryl Holter, 'Miners against the State: French Miners and the Nationalization of Coalmining 1944–1949' (unpublished PhD. thesis, University of Wisconsin, Madison, 1980), and Monique Luirard, *La région stéphanoise dans la guerre et dans la paix 1936–1951* (Saint-Etienne, 1980), all depend heavily on the testimony of working-class leaders.

[9] The problems of local studies are exacerbated by the fact that many historians study areas in the political heartland of Vichy (i.e. the south) rather than the industrial heartland of France (i.e. the north). The studies of the Nord and Pas-de-Calais undertaken by Dejonghe, and J. Thullier, 'Aspects de la crise industrielle dans la région Nord/Pas de Calais sous l'occupation allemande', *Revue du Nord*, no. 2 spécial hors de série (1987), 419–67, do concentrate on an area that contained much of French industry but, because of their limited scope, these works say little about the relations between industry in this area and the rest of France or that between industry and the Vichy government.

[10] Kolboom, *La revanche des patrons*; Fridenson, 'Le patronat français'; Bourdé, *La défaite du front populaire*; Adrian Rossiter, 'Corporatist Experiments in Republican France, 1916–1939' (unpublished D.Phil. thesis, University of Oxford, 1986).

[11] Henri Rousso, 'L'organisation industrielle de Vichy', *Revue d'histoire de la deuxième guerre mondiale*, 116 (1979), 27–44; Philippe Mioche, *Le plan Monnet: genèse et élaboration, 1941–1947* (Paris, 1987); Richard F. Kuisel, *Capitalism and the State in Modern France: Renovation and Economic Management in the Twentieth Century* (Cambridge, 1981).

will examine the politics of business in the light of these documents. Special attention will be paid to the apparent continuities between the politics of business during the Popular Front and the politics of business under the Vichy regime. Attention will also be devoted to the lowland that lies between the two peaks of scholarly interest: the period between the suppression of the general strike of November 1938 and the fall of France. It is in this period that the answers to two key questions are to be sought: firstly, what relationship did the 'réorganisation des patrons' of 1936 and 1937 have to the 'revanche des patrons' of 1938 and 1939; and secondly, to what extent had business achieved its objectives before the fall of France. It will be suggested that there was indeed a continuity in rhetoric between the employers' mobilization against the Popular Front and the Vichy regime, but that the social alliances that underlay that rhetoric had changed.

Chapter 2

Sources and methodology

Sources

Almost every work on the history of French business begins with a lament about the paucity of sources and the unwillingness of French industrialists to open their archives.[1] It is true that the archives of many major companies are unavailable. It is also true that the archives of some of the most important industrial associations of the 1930s, the UIMM, and the Comité des Forges, remain closed. The archives of the main employers' association, the CGPF, have recently been opened, but they are sparse and have obviously been thoroughly 'weeded'. It is claimed that the archives of most of the Comités d'Organisation that were established under Vichy have been irreparably damaged. However, none of these facts presents an insuperable barrier to research. Many business archives are open; furthermore, a recent wave of *glasnost* in the Archives Nationales has opened many official sources concerning the Vichy period. Business organization was hardly a private matter. No organization could make a major decision without consulting half a dozen companies, and no company could make a decision without consulting half a dozen managers. For this reason almost nothing could be done without leaving some trace in an archive accessible to historians.

Sometimes the need to approach the subject by devious archival routes is a positive advantage. Many agreements within the French industrial organizations were fixed up outside official meetings with a telephone conversation or a hasty meeting in a corridor. The frigidly formal official minutes leave no trace of such chicanery. But when business leaders reported back to their boards of directors or to their managers in the provinces they also gave an account of current rumours. For this reason hearsay evidence

[1] Jean-Noel Jeanneney, *L'argent caché: milieux d'affaires et pouvoirs politiques dans la France du XXème siècle* (Paris, 1981), p. 11.

can be more revealing than official documents. Thus the historian reading the UIMM official archives – if they were open – would be given no clue about the identity of the business leader who ejected Lambert Ribot from the social committee of the CGPF. But if he read the reports on UIMM meetings compiled by Pont-à-Mousson he would learn that 'everyone knew' this individual to be Colonel Brenot. Similarly, the official transcripts of the CNE record merely that Dalbouze was succeeded as president by Manceau in September 1936. But, in his unofficial reports to the Lyon Chamber of Commerce, Morel Journel revealed that Manceau had been fourth choice for this post (see chapter 3).

Sources not used

Historians studying French history between 1936 and 1945 – and especially the history of economic life – have depended heavily upon oral evidence, German archives and statistical studies. All of these forms of evidence are conspicuous by their absence in this work. In part this absence is explained by the very fact that so much work has already been done in these areas. However, these sources also pose particular problems which have not been fully appreciated by historians. Since these problems account for some of the distortions of previous historiography, it is worth pausing to examine them.

German archives

Ever since the seminal work of Robert Paxton, historians studying the Vichy period have drawn much of their information from the captured archives of the German authorities that operated in occupied France.[2] The use of such material was an ingenious expedient that allowed Paxton to circumvent the paucity of French sources and to undermine the previous orthodoxy, which had been constructed on the apologias of those involved in the Vichy regime. However, Paxtonite history has now become something of an orthodoxy in itself. Not surprisingly, Frenchmen who had dealings with the Germans sought to appear co-operative to their interlocutors. This has led historians to draw a picture of a nation falling over itself to collaborate, and to neglect the study of anti-German attitudes that fell short of organized resistance.

[2] Robert Paxton, *Vichy France: Old Guard and New Order, 1940–1944* (New York, 1972); Alan S. Milward, *The New Order and the French Economy* (Oxford, 1970); Ebhard Jackel, *La France dans l'Europe de Hitler* (Paris, 1968); Jacques Natali, 'L'occupant allemand à Lyon de 1942 à 1944 d'après les sources allemandes', *Cahiers d'histoire*, 22 (Lyon, 1977), 441–64.

German sources pose special problems for historians studying the political attitudes of business. For the Germans viewed the French economy in brutally practical terms. They were concerned with how many tonnes of coal or bauxite could be extracted; they did not greatly care about the subtle political distinctions within the *patronat*. Indeed German sources can be highly deceptive because those industrialists who collaborated most with the Germans at a business level were often most hostile to the efforts of the Vichy government to collaborate at a political level.

Oral history

One feature of the Vichy economy was the considerable power exercised by very young men – Lehideux became minister of industrial production while still under forty. One consequence of this is that historians have been able to interview men who played important parts in the regime. However, oral evidence of this kind is very different from oral evidence of the kind used by historians studying, say, peasant communities or criminal subcultures. The subjects are highly articulate and educated men. Many of them have already described their impressions of events in writing. Even those who have not written autobiographies have given interviews to more than one historian. Because of this they have highly developed interpretations of their own role. The historian who confronts a man like Alfred Sauvy now will simply see a performance that has been rehearsed over a period of twenty years;[3] it is hard to imagine that he will get any new information.

The use of oral evidence also presents a number of more specific problems for the historian of business attitudes. Firstly, the men alive in the 1980s do not form a representative sample of those who held power at Vichy. The men who achieved high positions very young tended to be the 'jeunes cyclistes'. They had idealistic hopes of Vichy which were often not shared by their older colleagues. Secondly, French history between 1936 and 1945 contains some highly sensitive areas. It is not surprising that men who give interviews to historians may lead them away from certain subjects. Thus the Lyonnais business leader Aymé Bernard gave testimony to Claude Paillat that took up over 120 pages in its transcribed form. But this testimony concentrates almost exclusively on the least interesting part of Bernard's career: the 1920s. It says little about his part in the suppression of the labour victory of 1936, and nothing about his role at Vichy. The fact that French business organizations were founded upon constantly shifting alliances can

---

[3] Sauvy has been interviewed by Henri Rousso, Julian Jackson, Patrick Fridenson, Philippe Mioche, Richard Kuisel and Michelle Volle. Sauvy's presentation of written accounts of his activity must be providing work for half of the French publishing industry.

also introduce more subtle distortions into testimonies. For example, when Léon Gingembre spoke to Henry Ehrmann in the 1950s, he was in violent conflict with the organizations representing large-scale business. At this time he explained that his departure from the CGPF in 1939 had been a protest at the resurrected power of the 'trusts'.[4] But when describing the same events in 1985 – after having patched up many of his differences with big business – Gingembre simply said that his departure had been caused by his call-up to the army.[5]

Statistical studies

A number of historians studying the organization of industry under Vichy have indulged in statistical studies of office-holding in the Vichy industrial system.[6] Such studies produce an impression of certainty that is especially gratifying for historians who are constantly confronted with the confident assertions of economists and political scientists. However, their value is open to considerable doubt. For, in order to prepare such studies, historians are obliged to sort their material into neat and simple categories. Vital qualitative distinctions are discarded. This is especially important because the apparent neatness of the Vichy industrial system masked huge variations. Not all bodies exercised the same powers – the committee controlling the coal industry was more important than that which controlled the wholesale potato trade.

Historians who use statistical studies are obliged to classify industrial leaders according to 'objective' criteria: the company that employed them, the organizations to which they belonged, etc. But this kind of classification is simplistic. For one of the central points about Vichy was that a whole generation of leaders arose who were not simply expressions of their backgrounds (see chapter 8). The limitations of statistical studies as tools to investigate these leaders are shown up by the case of François Lehideux. Lehideux is classified by the studies of Jones and Rousso as a representative of industry, especially the automobile industry and especially Renault. But in fact Lehideux's power aroused fear in industry as a whole, resentment in the automobile industry, and almost hysterical hatred in Lehideux's former company (see chapter 7).

---

[4] Henry Ehrmann, *Organized Business in France* (Princeton, N.J., 1957), p. 53.
[5] Sylvie Guillaume, 'Léon Gingembre défenseur des PME', *Vingtième siècle. Revue d'histoire*, 15 (1987), 69–81.
[6] Henri Rousso, 'Les élites économiques dans les années quarante', *Mélanges de l'Ecole Française de Rome*, 95 (1982–3), 29–49; Adrian Jones, 'Illusions of Sovereignty: Business and the Organization of Committees in Vichy France', *Social History*, 2 (1986), 1–33.

Defining the subject

It might be helpful to start by saying what this book is not about. It is not an account of relations between capitalism and the state. The actions of the state frequently defined the limits within which business acted, and the motive forces behind state action will frequently be touched on, but our main aim is to examine the motives of businessmen and their representatives, not those of politicians and civil servants. Secondly, it is not a book about labour relations. Once again business politics responded to strikes and union activity, but our concern is not with the reality of the working class but with business's perception of it.

Even when these provisos have been made, writing the history of business politics between 1936 and 1945 sounds like a tall order. Almost 8 million French people ran their own enterprises in 1936. All the numerous, and sometimes highly eccentric, political movements that existed in France during this period included businessmen in their number. There were communist, socialist, fascist, conservative and royalist businessmen. Most of all there were a large number of shopkeepers and artisans whose main concern was to make a living and to maintain good relations with their neighbours and clients. Understanding the politics of all businessmen is a task that could really only be undertaken in the context of a local study encapsulating the whole pattern of social relations. But, the task of this book is less ambitious. For the public expressions that were accepted as the voices of business tended to come from certain organizations that were in fact controlled by a small number of large enterprises, generally employing over 500 men, and generally concentrated in certain areas and in certain kinds of production. It is therefore on these enterprises that our study focuses. The nature of French political life often meant that it suited big business to ally with those who claimed to represent small business. But, as will be suggested in chapter 4, the links of these men to their supposed constituency were, in reality, rather weak. It is therefore possible to examine the 'leaders of small business' without becoming involved in all the contradictions and complexities of small business life.

If business, for the purposes of this book, is defined in a fairly narrow sense, politics is defined fairly widely. What is examined here is the attitude of French businessmen to the broad issues that preoccupied most of their compatriots: the strikes of 1936; the social and labour policies of the Popular Front government; the threat posed by Nazi Germany; the defeat; the establishment of the Vichy government and the questions raised by collaboration; resistance and liberation. What is not discussed much are specifically business interests – tariffs, cartels and so on. Such issues may well have absorbed industrial organizations in less turbulent times but, in the conditions that prevailed from 1936 to 1945, they were forced to the bottom of the agenda.

It might well be objected that the very idea of business politics is a contradiction in terms. Some theorists suggest that businessmen are so divided by rivalry and so preoccupied by short-term considerations that they are incapable of arriving at any overall definition of their political interest (see chapter 14). This kind of theory has developed in the United States, an area where business interests are so well protected by the general political culture that businessmen themselves rarely need to act in their own defence. But the position of French business was far less privileged. They lived in a political culture where hostility, or at least rhetoric hostile, to big business was commonplace. Under these circumstances business could not afford the luxury of not being organized. Furthermore, the business organizations brought professional leaders to the fore who were not submerged under the day-to-day pressures of running a business and who were therefore able to take a detached and far-sighted view of business interests. Robert Pinot, the secretary of the Comité des Forges, was described by his biographer in these terms:

He was not an engineer...he was not even a technician...around him, everyone was...absorbed in the myriad particular intellectual and commercial problems of industrial production. Him, he had to command an overview, to be the look-out and the guardian. He had to watch the horizon, in order to watch for dangers approaching so that they could be headed off and dealt with before it was too late.

Of course in ordinary times, when there was no immediate threat to capitalism, business organizations in France were very divided and often ineffective (see chapter 3). As the description of Pinot cited above implies, business leadership might be seen more as a question of diagnosis and preventive medicine than day-to-day treatment. But, when faced with events such as those of 1936, 1940 and 1944, business organizations came into their own. Big business in these conditions did focus its attention on certain issues and it did, on the whole, display a remarkable degree of unity. This makes the task of writing a history of business politics between 1936 and 1945 very much easier. The fact that business responded to events with a relative unanimity means that business politics can be reconstructed from the archives of certain organizations and well-placed firms without the need for an exhaustive study of every sector or every company. But the fact that business was most united and most politically active when under threat also creates certain problems. For it means that it is hardest to trace business opinion at times when business was most satisfied. This creates special problems for the period 1938 to 1940 after industry had seen the threat posed by the Popular Front labour victory dispelled and before the problems of the defeat. To some extent satisfaction on the large political questions during this period is something that can only be inferred from the resumption of old divisions in the business movement.

It seems only fair to give some advice to readers whose time, or patience, is limited. The central parts of this book are those concerned with Vichy. I believe that some understanding of events between 1936 and 1939 is essential for an understanding of business under Vichy, but my own interpretation of this period is simple: I do not believe that the employers' movement underwent fundamental changes in the aftermath of 1936. However, other historians have advanced highly sophisticated and ingenious suggestions about the new ideologies that they believe to have taken hold among the *patronat* between 1936 and 1939, and in responding to their theories I have, in chapters 4 to 7, used complicated arguments to defend my simple conclusion.

Chapter 3

Background

The life of the Third Republic, 1871–1940, coincided with a period of economic upheaval. During the last quarter of the nineteenth century technological change occurred on such a scale that historians have talked of a second industrial revolution. Industries associated with chemicals, automobiles and electrical goods grew up, and companies like ICI, Ford and IG Farben became household names throughout the world. These changes were matched by changes in the international balance of power. Russia became an industrial nation. Germany overtook Great Britain. Most of all the economic strength of the United States began to awe the world and the financial capital of the world moved from London to New York.

France was not immune to these changes. Between 1871 and 1940 the proportion of her population working in industry increased and that industry became more concentrated and more productive. But in France these developments were less dramatic than they were in her principal industrial rivals. For example the gross domestic product of France increased by an average of 1·6 per cent per annum between 1870 and 1913, and by 1·8 per cent per annum between 1922 and 1937; the comparable figures for Germany were 2·8 per cent and 3·2 per cent.[1] Most of all the relative social and economic stability of France was reflected in demography. During the entire lifetime of the Third Republic France's population hovered between 36 million and 40 million. Stability was also strikingly reflected in the lives of individual Frenchmen. There was none of the great geographical and social mobility that shook the rest of Europe. In an age when a man might be born into a starving family in the Lithuanian Pale and die as a millionaire in Chicago, a French peasant, who moved to the nearest small town and founded a business as a shopkeeper, would regard himself as having led an adventurous life.

France was not underdeveloped in technological terms. On the contrary French industrialists, formed by the engineering *grandes écoles*, were often

[1] Maurice Larkin, *France since the Popular Front* (Oxford, 1987), p. 390.

12

highly innovative. France led Europe in the manufacture of automobiles and aeroplanes before 1914. In 1929 alone 22,000 new industrial processes were patented.[2] What France lacked was a large and homogeneous market. The obsession with novelty, quality and diversity of product may actually have distracted French business from the tasks of uniform production and mass marketing that were being undertaken by their American rivals. Indeed Philip Nord suggests that as French business became more large scale and 'modern' during the late nineteenth century it became less market orientated.[3]

Historians have advanced a number of explanations for France's lack of economic growth. David Landes, drawing heavily on the example of the textile industry, focused on the conservatism of entrepreneurs. More recently, studies of other more dynamic sectors and the spectacular growth of the French economy after 1962 have encouraged historians to move away from explanations based on entrepreneurial failure.[4] Now stress is laid on inherent restrictions such as the smallness and fragmentation of the French internal market and France's inadequate reserves of energy. Examining the causes of French industrial retardation is beyond the scope of this book. What will be provided in this chapter is a brief, and purely descriptive, sketch of the mood, structure, leadership, organization and political links of French industry during the Third Republic as a backdrop to the account of its political manoeuvres that will be given in the succeeding chapters.

The psychological impact of retardation

At first France's relative economic retardation was not seen as a problem. Before 1914 France enjoyed a standard of living that was superior to that of any other European country except Britain. Frenchmen living in the 'belle époque' could hardly be expected to feel envious of the disruption, class conflict and suffering that was being caused by industrial growth in other countries. However, after the First World War this attitude began to change. What had been seen as stability was now seen as stagnation. There was an increased awareness of the industrial power of other nations and especially of the United States. Indeed France began to suffer what might be described as a national inferiority complex with regard to the USA. Not only did French industrialists, like Renault, look to the Ford works as models of

[2] Ingo Kolboom, *La revanche des patrons: le patronat français au front populaire* (Paris, 1987), p. 43.

[3] Philip Nord, *Paris Shopkeepers and the Politics of Resentment* (Princeton, N.J., 1986), p. 497.

[4] David Landes, *The Unbound Prometheus* (Cambridge, 1969). For the 'optimistic' interpretation of recent French economic history see F. Braudel and E. Labrousse (eds.), *Histoire économique et sociale de la France*, vol. IV (Paris, 1979–80).

production line efficiency, but French politicians, like Tardieu, looked to the American constitution as a provider of strong government, and even the readers of French women's magazines were convinced that American film stars were more beautiful than French ones.[5]

Concern over the state of the French economy reached an especially acute level during the mid 1930s – a concern reflected in the proliferation of discussion groups such as X crise and the *Nouveaux Cahiers* circle. There were three main reasons for this concern. Firstly, France was now confronted by the resurgence of German military threat – a fact that was brought home by the reoccupation of the Rhineland in March 1936. Secondly, the problem of low population was now exacerbated by the demographic shadow of the First World War. In particular the number of young men due to be called up for military service during the years 1937 to 1940 was lower than in previous years. Finally, France proved slower than other countries in recovering from the world depression sparked off by the Wall Street crash of 1929. The year 1935 marked the trough of this depression and France was not to recover her 1929 level of production until after the Second World War.

The structure of French industry

The French economy was subject to considerable regional variations. The level of male unemployment in 1936 varied from 3·5 to 12 per cent; the average income of workers in Paris exceeded that of workers in the provinces by 50 per cent.[6] Even the intensity of the *dénatalité* problem varied from one area of the country to another. Generally speaking birth-rates were lowest in the south of France and highest in the north-east. Low birth-rates in Paris were balanced out by provincial migration into the capital. Certain areas also received large numbers of foreign immigrants principally from Poland, Italy and Belgium.

As far as large-scale industry was concerned the effect of regional variation is relatively easy to describe. Such industry simply did not exist in most regions of France, but was concentrated in certain geographical enclaves. Heavy industries like iron, steel and the manufacture of railway rolling stock were confined to areas where raw materials, especially coal, could be obtained. Initially this meant the Rhône coal basin and the Nord

[5] Marie Genevie Chevigard and Nicole Faure, 'Système de valeurs et de références dans la presse féminine', in R. Rémond and J. Bourdin (eds.), *La France et les Français en 1938–1939* (Paris, 1978).

[6] André Straus, 'Le financement des dépenses publiques dans l'entre deux guerres', in P. Fridenson and A. Straus (eds.), *Le capitalisme français 19ᵉ–20ᵉ siècle: blocages et dynamismes d'une croissance* (Paris, 1987), pp. 97–118, at p. 111.

and Pas-de-Calais. As coal production in the Rhône became more difficult the northern field came to dominate the industry. After 1919 France also reacquired the heavy industry, particularly iron and steel production, that was based in the eastern areas of France. In 1936 the regional concentration of certain industries in France was so great that the Nord and Pas-de-Calais produced 60 per cent of her coal, 10 per cent of her pig iron and 17 per cent of her steel; the Meurthe and Moselle produced 51 per cent of her iron ore, 39 per cent of her steel and 43 per cent of her pig iron while Alsace Lorraine produced 42 per cent of her iron ore, 36 per cent of her pig iron, 33 per cent of her steel and 100 per cent of her potash.[7] Even industries that did not depend on supplies of raw materials tended to be centred in certain areas. The textile industry was largely confined to the north and the Lyon region. Paris was the centre of the light metallurgy and engineering industries – industries that were often the most dynamic and technologically advanced in France. In terms of management, as opposed to production, French industry was even more concentrated. Many companies had their headquarters or *sièges sociales* in Paris, a tendency that was reinforced by the German occupation of much of northern France during the First World War.[8]

Large and small enterprises

The size of a French enterprise was defined in terms of the number of workers employed. Generally speaking, companies employing more than 200 or sometimes 500 people were defined as large; the boundary between medium-sized and small business was usually fixed at 50 employees. Matters were complicated by the existence of a further category of artisanal enterprises. Strictly speaking this category contained only self-employed individuals; in practice it was often stretched to include all enterprises employing a very small number of people. The practice of defining business in terms of numbers of employees rather than in terms of capital, and the fact that being defined as a small business might bring such advantages, produced some strange anomalies; one business leader pointed out that 'small businessman' was a term that might cover anything from a pastry chef to the owner of a medium-sized merchant bank.

French industry became more concentrated during the Third Republic. In 1906 only 18·5 per cent of the workforce was employed in enterprises with

---

[7] Robert Young, *In Command of France. French Foreign Policy and Military Planning 1933–1940* (Cambridge, Mass., 1978), p. 15.
[8] Lévy-Leboyer, 'Le patronat français 1912–1973', in idem (ed.), *Le patronat de la seconde industrialisation* (Paris, 1979), pp. 137–68, at p. 144.

Table 3.1 *The distribution of enterprises by size in 1936*

Category (by no. of employees)	Industry		Commerce	
	Enterprises	Employees	Enterprises	Employees
0 employees	54,260		160,901	
1–10	414,421	983,413	302,716	645,455
11–20	22,924	338,676	9,263	134,337
21–50	16,668	530,651	4,696	144,859
51–200	9,188	871,187	1,947	169,930
201–1,000	2,473	949,914	319	119,036
1,001–5,000	254	464,036	27	57,594
Over 5,000	25	266,147	7	51,398

Source: Ingo Kolboom, *La revanche des patrons: le patronat français face au front populaire* (Paris, 1986).

over 500 employees; by 1931 this figure had risen to 26·6 per cent. However, overall the French economy remained dominated by small businesses. Only 25 companies employed more than 5,000 men in 1936. The largest enterprise in France was Renault which employed 30,000 people; an average coal-mine employed about 8,000; Pont-à-Mousson, the manufacturer of pipes, employed 8,000 at its peak but by 1936 this figure had dropped to about 4,000. Such industrial concentration as there was often occurred in the loose framework of a holding company that left individual firms within it considerable autonomy. Saint-Gobain, with 150 subsidiaries, was such a company but even it was less than one-tenth the size of its German rival IG Farben.[9]

Perhaps because of its very scarcity, and because of its geographical and cultural isolation, large-scale business was regarded with considerable suspicion. Descriptions of how large-scale industry exploited *la petite et moyenne entreprise* played a considerable role in French politics. In reality, however, relations between enterprises of different sizes varied from one industry to another. Large-scale heavy industries such as coal-mining and iron foundry tended to buy their raw materials and sell their products to other large enterprises or to the state. In the purely economic arena they had little to do with small business. In retailing, on the other hand, large and small businesses were in direct competition. Small shops felt threatened by the *prix unique* and sought government protection against the threat. In

[9] Richard F. Kuisel, *Capitalism and the State in Modern France: Renovation and Economic Management in the Twentieth Century* (Cambridge, 1981), p. 87.

industries like textiles, light engineering and metallurgy the situation was far more complicated. For here small- and large-scale businesses existed side by side. In 1936 the Parisian metallurgy association the GIMMCP contained the giant Renault company but it also contained a further 5,000 companies that employed an average of around 50 men. In this situation it would be wrong to assume that small business was simply archaic. Large firms like Renault had themselves often started life in back-yards. Furthermore, large firms often subcontracted work to smaller enterprises. Small firms could often provide an element of flexibility that was lacking in large production lines; they also found it easier to evade labour legislation.

Size was not the only factor that marked off certain sections of French business. Some industries were protected from the full rigours of the market by the fact that they sold the bulk of their products to the state. Manufacturers of armaments, rolling stock and water pipes were in this protected sector or *secteur abrité*. Certain industries were also protected by the existence of cartels that carved up markets between firms and fixed prices; the northern coalfields and the steel industry were governed by such arrangements. The existence of such sectors raises interesting questions for it is frequently suggested that business politics consists largely of a struggle for power between different fractions of capital. More specifically certain historians of business politics in France have argued that the *secteur abrité* exercised disproportionate influence within French business organization, and that industries rising up in more technologically modern areas were seeking to challenge that influence (see chapter 4).

However, when the firms operating within the *secteur abrité* are examined closely it seems increasingly unlikely that they functioned as a political unit. For the greatest suspicions of companies were usually directed not at other industrial sectors but rather at their own immediate competitors. Individual industries were rent by feuds between companies that were passed from one generation to another like family heirlooms. Cartelization did not necessarily make relations any easier; open commercial competition could be transformed into acrimonious squabbles about quota shares. Rivalries were especially acute within the *secteur abrité*. For companies were keenly aware that, firstly, certain elements of their production could only be sold to the state and that, secondly, overall state spending was limited. This made them especially resentful of other companies competing for government con-tracts.[10]

---

[10] Blois, Pont-à-Mousson (P-à-M) 41604, letter of 16 March 1937 to M. Morin responding to complaints from rolling stock manufacturers about government spending on water pipes.

The *patronat*

The most striking feature of French industrial leadership, when compared to that of other countries, was the continued role of companies owned by families. It was a feature that was especially marked in the long-established companies of the heavy industrial sector, the sector that exercised the most influence in business politics; two-thirds of managers in the steel industry came from families that owned steel firms and 35·1 per cent of them had begun their career in the family firm.[11] This meant that there was always far more to French industry than mere money making. It would have been inconceivable for a French industrialist to retire from business and leave most of his fortune to charity, as the American Carnegie did. In France a company was a matter of flesh and blood. Industrialists regarded their factories with the same fierce pride as an aristocrat regarded his ancestral lands – indeed aristocrats often sat on the boards of families and industrial dynasties often intermarried with the aristocracy. Like aristocrats, industrialists became local notables. They had power that extended well beyond the factory gate: they controlled the local employers' associations; they built hospitals, churches and houses for their workers; they drew up files on the political opinions and even the sexual habits of their employees. Under these circumstances it is not surprising to find that decisions about business were rarely made in terms of pure and cool calculation. Company traditions and family honour could be as important, sometimes more important, than profits.[12] The idea of distinguishing between business and personal life would have been meaningless to many *patrons*: Camille Cavalier, the founder of Pont-à-Mousson, disinherited his son after a business dispute.[13]

However, not everyone running a business was a member of an industrial dynasty. There was also a large class of professional managers. Who were these men? Lévy-Leboyer's statistical study of industrialists who became prominent between 1912 and 1973 suggests that a certain kind of education was perhaps the single most important characteristic common to French managers. Of his sample 87·8 per cent were graduates; 93·4 per cent of these had graduated in either law or engineering.[14] They were also likely to have

[11] Lévy-Leboyer, 'Le patronat français', p. 143.
[12] Pont-à-Mousson's desire to maintain a tradition of involvement in coal-mining appears to have lost the firm considerable amounts of money: see Alain Baudaint, *Pont-à-Mousson (1919–1939): stratégies industrielles d'une dynastie lorraine* (Paris, 1980).
[13] Alain Baudaint, 'Culture d'entreprise valeurs et pouvoirs à Pont-à-Mousson (1856–1939)', in P. Fridenson and A. Straus (eds.), *Le capitalisme français 19ᵉ–20ᵉ siècle: blocages et dynamismes d'une croissance* (Paris, 1987), p. 373.
[14] Lévy-Leboyer, 'Le patronat français', p. 141. It may seem somewhat perverse to cite Lévy-Leboyer so heavily in this context when he himself is seeking to illustrate the emergence of a new managerial class. However, it should be stressed that most of the changes in the structure of French managment to which Lévy-Leboyer alludes occurred after 1945; he

been educated at the same *grandes écoles*, especially the Ecole Polytechnique. It is almost impossible to overestimate the role of the Polytechnique in French business life. Half of its 7,200 graduates were working in private industry by 1929; 48·3 per cent of the graduates studied by Lévy-Leboyer were polytechnicians (16·5 per cent came from the slightly less prestigious Ecole Centrale).[15] The Polytechnique nurtured an intense *esprit de corps* and pride: former polytechnicians even put details of their educational achievements on their gravestones in Père Lachaise cemetery. It also nurtured contacts; networks of 'X' were key in the recasting of the Comité des Forges[16] on the eve of the First World War and in the administration of the coal industry during the Second World War.[17]

It is often suggested that managers operate differently from those who own their own businesses, that they are more rational, more detached and less aggressive when dealing with labour relations. Such differences were not very marked in France. Managers rarely clashed with proprietors; industries run primarily by managers do not seem to have handled their affairs very differently from those run by owner *patrons*. Indeed the main difference between managers and owners was simply that the former tended to reach positions of authority later in life than the latter (in 1913 the average age of managers in firms owned by their own families was 49 while those without such an advantage had an average age of 58).[18]

There are several obvious reasons for this harmony of approach. Firstly, finance for French industry still tended to come from the reinvestment of past profits rather than from bank loans. It is true that certain new industries were springing up, for example hydro-electrical production, that required such huge amounts of capital that they were bound to depend on outside sources. But the growth of investment was held back by the depression of the 1930s. Indeed some companies, such as Renault, were actually seeking to increase their financial autonomy during the period before the Second World War. Not surprisingly families that were still paying the piper continued to call the tune.

Secondly, managers and owners hardly came from different social strata. Most company owners were not parvenus who had come from nowhere. More usually they were second- or third-generation industrialists. Such people had often been educated in the elite engineering schools alongside future managers: Robert Peugeot and R. Delauney Belleville attended the Ecole Centrale; Edmond Gillet, of the chemical dynasty, had been trained at the chemical engineering school in Lyon; the two sons of Henri de Wendel

himself points out that the restricted opportunities of the depression years impeded democratization of the managerial class before 1939.
[15] Ibid. p. 151.   [16] Ibid. p. 155.
[17] Richard Vinen, 'The French Coal Industry during the Occupation', *Historical Journal*, 33 (1990), 105–30.   [18] Lévy-Leboyer, 'Le patronat français', p. 164.

were qualified mining engineers.[19] Indeed many *patrons* described themselves on census forms as engineers. Furthermore, managers themselves were
the products of a notoriously socially restricted education system; they were
usually from monied backgrounds themselves and they were often related to
businessmen. Over 82 per cent of Lévy-Leboyer's sample came from 'well-
off backgrounds'; 65 per cent had benefited from 'useful family contacts';
45 per cent were the sons of businessmen.[20] Sometimes, dynasties of
ownership were matched by dynasties of managerial functions who passed
down a particular office in the company from father to son.[21] Sometimes,
managers became owners themselves either by setting up on their own or by
marrying the boss's daughter (Pont-à-Mousson was managed by the son-in-
law of the founder, Renault by the husband of the founder's niece).

Thirdly, and most importantly, France did not really possess an
independent ideology that might have underwritten managerial autonomy.
The education given to French managers had been designed to produce civil
servants and army officers (the Ecole Polytechnique was still ostensibly an
artillery college) not businessmen. It tended to reinforce, rather than
undermine, the traditional authoritarianism and paternalism of French
industry. Books advising engineers on how to run factories made much of
military values and looked to General Lyautey, the author of *Le rôle social
de l'officier*, as much as Henry Ford. One influential teacher at the Ecole des
Mines even suggested that his pupils should look to the Russian aristocracy
as models of 'man management'.[22]

In the 1920s the ideas of Taylorism and scientific managment reached
France and were greeted with considerable enthusiasm. It was sometimes
suggested that these ideas helped to separate managers and proprietors. This
was certainly not the case in France. Many of the most conspicuous
enthusiasts for 'scientific management' – Renault, Jacques Warnier, Jean
Coutrot – were owners rather than managers. Furthermore, the new ideas
tended to be applied rather crudely; in practice they often meant little more
than a stiffening of labour discipline with the time-sheet and the stop-watch.
What they did not mean was a change in the way that bosses were expected
to behave.[23]

[19] Ibid. p. 165.   [20] Ibid. p. 146.   [21] Ibid. p. 154.
[22] André Thépot, 'Les ingénieurs du corps des mines', in Lévy-Leboyer (ed.), *Le patronat de
la seconde industrialisation* (Paris, 1979), pp. 237–46, at p. 239.
[23] On the spread of Taylorism in France see Aymée Moutet, 'Patronat français et système de
Taylor avant 1914: le point de vue patronal (1907–1914), *Le mouvement social*, 93 (1975),
15–49, and Odette Hardy-Hémery, 'Rationalisation technique et rationalisation du travail
à la Compagnie des Mines d'Anzin, 1927–1938', *Le mouvement social*, 72 (July–Sept. 1970),
3–48.

Business organization

In theory a law of 1791 banned economic unions in France. The ban ceased to apply to syndicates representing one industry in 1884 and to interprofessional associations in 1901. In practice the law had never been much of an impediment to employers. The iron-masters were grouped in 1864 by the Comité des Forges. The Comité des Houillères, founded in 1840, served a similar function for the French coal-mining companies. In 1878 the Association de l'Industrie et Agriculture Françaises was formed to campaign for higher tariffs and in 1901 the UIMM was formed to unite all metallurgical industries. The early Third Republic also saw a variety of movements that claimed to speak for all employers but none of these movements survived past the First World War.

The Chambers of Commerce were probably the most comprehensive representative of business opinion. A law of 1898 required that a Chamber be established in every department in France. In 1899 an Association of Presidents of Chambers of Commerce (APCC) was formed to operate at the national level. There was some justice to Chambers' contention that they were the most representative forum for all business opinion in France and in particular that they gave better expression to small and provincial business than private syndicates. However, even this claim deserves to be taken with pinch of salt. Large companies tended to dominate the larger Chambers of Commerce, i.e. those of Paris, Lyon, Marseille, Bordeaux, Lille, Strasbourg, Nantes, Rouen and Cholet. In turn the larger Chambers of Commerce dominated the bureaux of the APCC. In early 1936 the smaller Chambers of Commerce made a bid to democratize the APCC by making it a permanent body and having the costs of representation distributed among all Chambers in proportion to their means but the move was blocked by the larger Chambers of Commerce.[24]

The First World War gave the organizations of large-scale industry a considerable boost. Such industries, especially metallurgy, did well in the war, and the leaders of industrial associations played a considerable role liaising with the government. The Parisian metallurgy and mechanical industry grew especially fast during the war; in 1917 the Groupement des Industries Métallurgiques Mécaniques et Connexes de la Région Parisienne (GIMMCP) was formed and in 1919 the mechanical industry was given representation in the UIMM. In 1919 the minister of commerce Etienne Clémentel sought to continue wartime organization of industry by encouraging the formation of the Confédération Générale de la Production Française (CGPF). The new movement was divided into twenty sections to

[24] Lyon, archives of Chamber of Commerce transcript of the meeting of 14 May 1936.

represent various branches of industry and trade, a number that had expanded to twenty-eight by 1936. It claimed to represent all employers. In reality certain activities, such as banking and commerce, were notably under-represented. Furthermore, the CGPF was based in Paris and had few offices in the provinces. The Fédération des Associations Régionales (FAR), an organization founded in 1919 and dedicated to the representation of provincial business, was absorbed into the CGPF in 1923 but until 1936 it remained just one section of the peak association. Inevitably this arrangement tended to give a high degree of influence to large firms that had *sièges sociales* in Paris. It was also widely believed that metallurgy exercised a disproportionate influence over the CGPF. It was certainly true that the metallurgists had a longer tradition of organization than their new colleagues. In the early years they provided the secretariat for the CGPF; they also provided its first leader.

Alongside the CGPF a whole range of business organizations sprang up during the 1930s. Kolboom calculates that there were 6,683 such organizations in 1930. A single parliamentary enquiry (into the textile industry) heard evidence from 156 organizations.[25] However, all this did not mean that industry was well represented. The larger syndicates had great resources at their disposal but, unless business as a whole was confronted by some major threat, they tended to be too divided to arrive at a coherent position on most issues; the atmosphere that reigned at meetings of the Comité des Forges was described by one participant in these words: 'We splutter and argue, conversations go on for ever and everyone talks at the same time.'[26] Small syndicates often represented ludicrously restricted sections of industry – there was a union of pencil importers and an association of artificial flower manufacturers; they failed to attract large memberships even within their supposed constituencies and they had considerable difficulty in getting members to pay their dues. In 1940 Pierre Pucheu, who had considerable experience in this matter, wrote that before 1936 most business organizations had only been active during the brief annual scramble to obtain the legion of honour for their members.[27]

Politics and business

Industrialists and Third Republic politicians often seemed to inhabit different worlds. Large-scale industrialists wielded enormous power in

[25] Parliamentary papers, 1935, annex 4642.
[26] Jean-Noel Jeanneney, *L'argent caché: milieux d'affaires et pouvoirs politiques dans la France du XXème siècle* (Paris, 1981), p. 31.
[27] Archives Nationales (AN), F 37 77, Pucheu to Barnaud dated 6 September 1940.

industrial organizations and in the areas around their own factories but they had very few votes. The political basis of the Third Republic lay outside the industrial regions in small towns and in the countryside. This divide was reflected in the adage 'c'est le nord qui travaille, c'est le sud qui gouverne'; it was also reflected in the backgrounds of parliamentarians and especially members of the lower house: the chamber of deputies.

Very few deputies were large-scale industrialists themselves. The chamber was dominated by the chattering professions: teachers, journalists and lawyers. Those few deputies who were industrialists, such as François de Wendel, the president of the Comité des Forges, were generally to be found in the Fédération Républicaine. However, the influence of industry was limited even here and some Fédération deputies were violently hostile to big business; Xavier Vallat attacked 'the dictatorial rule of a financial oligarchy'.[28] Big business was especially under-represented in the Radical party. Only 2 of 120 Radical deputies elected in 1932 were business executives.[29] This was significant because the Radicals often provided the central pivot around which Third Republic politics revolved; coalition with the Radicals provided the means by which parties of both the right and left hoped to enter government.

Not surprisingly the social make-up of parliament and the electorate dictated the pattern of political debate. Economic discussion almost invariably revolved around the interests of small business or agriculture. When bad weather damaged crops, deputies clamoured to have the affected area declared a 'région sinistrée'. When competition damaged small shops measures were enacted to restrain it. Even when France was at war the chamber spent hours earnestly discussing how to prevent small businessmen who had been drafted into the army from losing their trade.[30]

The favour shown to small business in French politics was matched by the hostility shown to large business. Hostility came from all parts of the political spectrum; for example, attacks on 'the two hundred families', the families whose shareholdings gave them control over the Bank of France and who were alleged to control the rest of the economy, came from Henry Coston,[31] on the extreme right, from Daladier in the political centre[32] and from the film-maker Renoir on the extreme left.[33] Conspiracy theories that attributed enormous power to business circulated widely. It was, for example, alleged that certain iron-masters had used their influence to

[28] Parliamentary papers, 1938, annex 3639.
[29] Peter Larmour, *The French Radical Party in the 1930s* (Stanford, Calif., 1964), p. 31.
[30] Parliamentary papers, 1940, annex 6913.
[31] Coston, *Les deux cents familles au pouvoir* (Paris, 1977).
[32] Daladier used this phrase at the congress of the Radical party held at Nantes in 1934.
[33] Renoir's 1936 film *La vie est à nous* contains a sequence dealing with the two hundred families.

prevent their factories, located behind enemy lines, from being bombed during the First World War.[34] Allegations about the abuse of power by big business had a ready audience among French politicians for several reasons. Firstly, they appealed to an electorate made up of resentful and hard-pressed small businessmen. Secondly, the idea that big business was exerting influence 'dans les coulisses' was encouraged by its very lack of overt political representation. Thirdly, the sheer ignorance of large-scale business in political circles encouraged suspicion. Politicians usually drew such information as they had on this sector of the economy not from the evidence of expert witnesses but from secondary accounts – often lurid pieces of journalism.[35]

The intensity of the attacks on big business increased during the 1930s. This was due to the adoption of the Popular Front strategy by the French Communist party. The strategy hinged around the idea that it would be possible to ally with bourgeois parties against 'fascism'. It was accompanied by ever more vigorous efforts to distinguish between small business, part of the bourgeois electorate, and big business, which was seen as having been responsible for the rise of fascism. In an attempt to fight off this new challenge the right sought to outdo the left in its appeals to small business and its hostility to large-scale capitalism. The owners of large companies sometimes felt near-hysterical resentment at the abuse that was being thrown at them; in March 1936 Marcel Paul of Pont-à-Mousson wrote: 'we are described as bandits, thieves, members of the two hundred families, feudal barons, and other courtesies of that ilk'.[36]

However, as the more sober leaders of the *patronat* recognized, the political attacks on big business were often more a question of bark than bite. The attacks were largely symbolic; the institutions that drew the most fire, the two hundred families and the Comité des Forges, were no longer real centres of political power. Indeed the attacks on the two hundred families continued after the nationalization of the Bank of France, and the attacks on the Comité des Forges continued after its dissolution in 1940. Furthermore, the importance of the small business electorate dissuaded politicians from attempting to translate anti big business rhetoric into concrete policies. For small businessmen and their representatives were intensely attached to the rights of property, and hostile to any measure – higher taxes, nationalization, increases in trade union power – that might threaten those rights. The consequent economic and social conservatism of the French political system protected big business as much as small. Big business was thus in a paradoxical situation. On the one hand it was

---

[34] Parliamentary papers, 1936, annex 6453.
[35] Ibid. 1935, annex 4587, an enquiry into the arms industry cited a number of such books.
[36] Blois, Pont-à-Mousson archives (P-à-M), 41721, M. Paul to Henri Cavallier, 20 March 1936.

socially, geographically and politically isolated from the rest of French society. This isolation was accompanied by great expressions of hostility to big business. Yet the very social structure that led to this isolation also provided big business with considerable security. It was this security that was to be shaken by the strikes that followed the election of the Popular Front government in 1936.

Chapter 4

The mobilization of French business

Introduction

Formal organization of French business dates back to at least the middle of the nineteenth century. But most historians – and many businessmen – argue that the birth of the modern business movement in France occurred in 1936 after France had been swept by the wave of strikes that followed the electoral victory of the Popular Front government. In a bid to end the strikes, the main business associations signed the 'Matignon accords' with the unions under the aegis of the government. After these agreements had been signed the employers' movement was itself swept by changes. Historians have made a great deal of these changes and suggested that their reverberations were still being felt for many years after 1936, especially under the Vichy regime. This chapter will examine firstly relations between business and the Popular Front and secondly the reforms in the business movement that came after the summer of 1936. The interpretation suggested will be, in historiographical terms, reactionary. It will be argued that the same group remained in control of the employers' movement throughout the period, and that the activity of the movement can be explained in terms of the strategy of this group. Negotiation with the government was a short-term strategy designed to parry the threat of strikes and disorders in the summer of 1936. This was succeeded by a medium-term strategy designed to overthrow the settlement that had been imposed by these negotiations. This strategy hinged around a reform of the employers' associations and a search for new social allies. However, the reforms and new alliances were both frail and impermanent. They could be abandoned when they had served their purpose. The long-term aim of the ruling clique of the business movement was simply the restoration of the *status quo ante* Matignon.

Business opinion and the arrival of the Popular Front

The Popular Front was an alliance of left and centre parties against fascism. It began partly as a response to the internal threat that was supposedly posed to French democracy by the right-wing leagues, and particularly to the attacks by those leagues on parliament during the riots of February 1934. In part it was also a response to the international threat posed by Nazi Germany. The Soviet Union soon came to regard this threat as its major foreign policy concern; it therefore encouraged Communist parties in Western Europe to suspend their 'class against class' tactics and seek alliances with bourgeois parties in order to bolster and rearm the democratic states. The result of these events was increasing co-operation between the Socialist and Communist parties – a co-operation that gradually broadened to include most of the Radical party. The French trade union movement also became united when the Communist 'unitaires' rejoined the Confédération Générale du Travail in March 1936. The effect of this new unity was felt in the general election that took place on 26 April and 3 May 1936. In the second round of this election leaders of the Communist, Socialist and Radical parties agreed to unite their electorate behind single candidates in each constituency. As a consequence, 345 of the 598 deputies returned by mainland France were supporters of the Popular Front.

The greatest beneficiaries of this election victory were the Communists, who increased their representation in parliament from 10 deputies to 72, and the Socialists, who increased their representation from 97 to 147. The Radicals, on the other hand saw their representation in parliament cut from 150 to 106, of whom about 81 supported the Popular Front. However, the gains won by the parties of the left did not mean that the new government was intent on social reform. On the contrary, election manifestos stressed the desire of the Popular Front to unite the country in defence of democracy and to gain the support of groups that would not normally vote for the left, such as practising Catholics. Rather than emphasizing social claims the Popular Front leaders sought to arouse enthusiasm with an appeal to patriotism and to the traditions of the Revolution, the Paris commune and the defence of Dreyfus. Indeed, though the Radicals had lost importance in electoral terms, the programme of the new government bore more resemblance to their canon than to that of the Marxist parties.

Business leaders were aware of the government's cautious attitude to social reform and initially they seemed to think that it posed no threat to their own interests. The Popular Front seemed even more innocuous after the Communists confirmed, on 15 May, that they would not take posts in the new government. Léon Blum, the prime minister-elect, was a reassuringly bourgeois figure, who had been at school with the president of Paribas and in the Conseil d'Etat with the secretary of the Comité des Forges. He went out of his way to observe the proprieties of the constitution; he stressed that 'We do not aim to transform the social system', and that his government would operate 'within the capitalist framework'.[1]

The calmness of the French *patronat* after the Popular Front election victory was illustrated by the meeting of the *conseil central* of the CGPF on 15 May 1936. At this meeting the discussion focused on minor administrative matters. Only one member of the *conseil*, Aymé Bernard, wished to discuss the general political situation. Bernard did express considerable fears about the consequences that the Popular Front government might have for business:

I do not think that we are on the eve of disturbances in the streets, but M. Blum is going to take power sooner or later and I think that, while not despairing of the fate of our country, we must know what we are going to do…In practice one of two things [will happen]: either the socialist experiment will succeed and it will be a matter of knowing what we can do to avoid passing completely under the absolute control of a totalitarian state, or this experiment will not succeed, and then, it will end up with bloodshed…in either case, it will be necessary to reduce the damage to a minimum, I do not say avoid it.

But the very terms in which Bernard phrased his intervention made it clear that he was isolated. He remarked: 'I am stunned to see the spirit of cheerfulness with which this experiment is accepted among those groups most affected', and he complained about the absorption of his colleagues in what he saw as trivial matters: 'I saw the agenda with interest and I waited for "other matters" thinking that M. de Lavergne would, under cover of his discreet formula, talk about the only important problem, for it seems inappropriate to be debating the sex of angels while the enemy is at our door.'[2]

The meeting of the Chamber of Commerce in Bernard's own home town, Lyon, on 14 May 1936 illustrated once again how unusual his fears were, and how keen most business leaders were to avoid conflict with the new government. It was agreed that no public statement would be made which would imply criticism of the new regime. The president recalled the British Labour government of 1924 as an example of moderation adopted by socialists in government. He pointed out that the electoral slogan of the Popular Front – 'bread, peace and freedom' – merely reflected the legitimate

---

[1] Ingo Kolboom, *La revanche des patrons: le patronat français face au front populaire* (Paris, 1986), p. 53.
[2] Paris, Archives Nationales (AN), 72 AS 6, p-v of *conseil central* meeting of 15 May 1936.

desires of all citizens. Above all it was stressed that 'We need to show that we are willing to co-operate with the administration.'[3]

Business and the strikes

The honeymoon between business and the Popular Front did not last long. For though the leaders of the left had turned their back on social radicalism their working-class followers had not. Throughout 1936 Paris metallurgy workers had been holding a series of strikes in support of their demand for collective contracts with their employers. In the month between the Popular Front election victory and Blum taking office these strikes spread to other areas and industrial sectors. They also began to change their character; three aeronautical factories at Toulouse, Le Havre and Courbevoie were occupied by their own workers. Soon this practice spread to other factories. Formally the strikes were in support of demands to be given union delegates, higher wages, shorter hours, paid holidays and rights of collective bargaining. However, it was also clear that the strikes and occupations involved something more than this. They were explosions of emotion: workers revelled in their temporary escape from the discipline of the factory whistle and the foreman's watch; they organized games and pantomimes in the factories. Workers also revelled in the control that they now had over their workplaces; bosses were sometimes forced to obtain passes from union leaders to enter and leave their office; some workers even set their machines running again.

The extent of the strikes in June 1936 reached unprecedented proportions: 1,800,000 workers were involved in 12,142 plants; 8,441 factories were occupied. The strikes were not ended even when union leaders signed agreements with employers' leaders, on 5 June and 7 June, nor when the Communist leader Thorez urged a return to work on 11 June. Indeed in many parts of the country strikes reached their peak towards the end of June when all the workers' demands seemed to have been met, and the atmosphere only began to calm after 14 July as workers departed on their first paid holiday. Though the strikes had their origins largely outside the framework of official union organization they brought considerable benefits to the CGT. In many factories the barrier of fear that had prevented unionization broke down; in the Renault factory the membership of the CGT increased from 700 to 25,000 in a fortnight. Overall CGT membership at the end of the strikes was two-and-a-half million, three times its 1935 level.

[3] Lyon, Chamber of Commerce archives (Lyon, C de C), p-v, 14 May 1936.

It is hard to assess the mood of the French *patronat* during this period,[4] but it does seem generally accepted that the strikes evoked considerable anxiety among employers. There were two reasons for this. On the one hand the strikes were seen to pose a threat to the political order. On the other hand they posed a more immediate threat to the power of the employer in his workplace. The threat that the strikes posed to the political order is a key part of the justification used by the members of the employers' delegation to Matignon for their apparent capitulation. It is not entirely clear what form this threat was seen to take. Sometimes the prospect of outright revolution is mentioned. Neuflize, speaking to the Chamber of Commerce of Paris on 24 June 1936, said: 'We were convinced, and the government was certainly convinced, that this was the only means of avoiding revolution.'[5] The head of the Etablissements Arbel factory at Douai also claimed that the local sub-prefect had suggested that 'We find ourselves faced with an occupation of a revolutionary nature.'[6] However, Dalbouze, speaking about the same meeting as Neuflize and addressing the same body, referred to disorder on a more limited scale: 'troubles in the streets'. François de Wendel painted a lurid picture of the threat posed by the strikes in Lorraine: '25,000 men, of whom at least a third are foreigners, are on strike, exposed to all the agitations that might come from inside the country or from abroad...it was clear that the forces of order were entirely absent from the streets'; but the remainder of the article suggests that he saw this as a localized threat, not as one to the whole regime: 'In Paris, the public services held firm. Can we be certain that it would have been the same story here? And, if there had been an incident, have we taken full account of the consequences that that might have for the image of France in the regained provinces?'[7] Even the term revolution could clearly mean more than one thing. Sometimes the word was used in its most obvious sense to mean that the strikes were the prologue to more violence that would ultimately overthrow the government. Lehideux, Louis Renault's nephew-in-law and chief lieutenant, subscribed to this view; he believed that on 10 June the occupiers of the Renault plant were preparing to use the tanks stored in the factory.[8] But sometimes the term revolution is used more loosely to refer to the strikes themselves. Thus the Union des Syndicats Patronaux des Industries Textiles de la France

---

[4] Most of the accounts that exist are retrospective; furthermore, the very desire to write an account is evidence of a degree of thoughtfulness which alone makes the author's testimony unusual. For example, many of those who recorded their impressions of this period were socially concerned Catholics such as the one whose account is cited in Kolboom, *La revanche des patrons*, p. 114.

[5] Paris, Chamber of Commerce (C de C), p-v, 24 June 1936.

[6] AN, 70 AQ 300, note from Jacquier to Paris head office, 4 June 1936.

[7] *Débats*, 2 July 1936, cited in Jean-Noel Jeanneney, *François de Wendel en République: l'argent et le pouvoir, 1914–1940* (3 vols., Paris, 1975), p. 1334.

[8] Bertrand Badie, 'Les grèves du front populaire aux usines Renault', *Le mouvement social*, 81 (1972), 69–109.

wrote to Blum of 'a revolutionary movement that is characterized by the occupation of workplaces, carried out in defiance of all legality, and by numerous assaults on the right to work'.[9]

There was similar ambiguity about the nature of the strikes. Sometimes dark forces were seen to be operating behind the scenes. Sometimes the strikes were characterized as spontaneous movements running beyond the control of unions and political parties. Thus Dalbouze spoke of 'a movement that is undoubtedly concerted, but a movement that is out of the hands of the leaders of the working class – and by leaders I mean the Socialist party as much as the Communist party'.[10] This ambiguity must, in part, be attributed to the strangeness of the events which the *patronat* were confronting. Though recent research has tended to stress the planning and calculation behind the strikes,[11] there is no doubt that there was a good deal of 'kermesse' in the events of the summer of 1936. Some sections of the *patronat* did appreciate that the strikes were not entirely rational, and that they had, in part, to be explained by 'a popular mystique'.[12] But others concluded that, in the absence of any clear demand, the strikes were explicable only in terms of outside political agitation and hidden agendas: 'The development of these illegal acts, in spite of the announcement of a draft law that should, to a great extent, satisfy the demands of the workers, suffices to reveal that it is really not a labour dispute.'[13]

Even when strikers did have rational objectives these were often linked to internal struggles in the CGT. Once again the capacity of the *patronat* to appreciate the role of these internal struggles varied, and again failure to understand often led to explanations founded upon the idea of a revolutionary conspiracy. Thus Lehideux and Thiriez assumed that the hardening of the attitudes of strikers around 10 June, which was in fact a product of power struggles within the CGT, was an attempt at revolution.[14] On the other hand the Lyon Chamber of Commerce, which generally kept a cool head during the strikes, did appreciate the importance of divisions within the CGT.[15] But ambiguity on this issue was not uniquely a product of the special circumstances of 1936. The French *patronat* was always rather confused about what specific kind of threat was posed by working-class disorder (they were never quite clear what form the 'red menace' of 1939/40 took). Perhaps this was because, unlike his German counterpart, the average *patron* had never lived through a revolution. His knowledge of such events was second-hand and abstract. Words like Soviet, Marxism and revolution

[9] AN, F 22 1587, letter to Blum of 5 June 1936.   [10] C de C, p-v, 8 June 1936.
[11] Badie, 'Les grèves du front populaire aux usines Renault'.
[12] Lyon, Chamber of Commerce archives, p-v, 11 June 1936. The words were used by Morel Journel.
[13] AN, F 22 1587, Roubaix Chamber of Commerce letter to minister of work dated 6 June 1936.   [14] Badie, 'Les grèves du front populaire aux usines Renault', p. 99.
[15] Remarks made by Weitz in Lyon C de C, p-v, 22 June 1936.

were thrown about in moments of crisis without any consensus existing about what such words meant.

The *patrons'* reactions to disorder during the strikes were often closely connected to their attitude towards the local authorities. The capacity of authority to maintain order was seen to vary from one area to another. In Lyon the attitude of the Chamber of Commerce was conditioned by the trust that they felt for the prefect, Bollaert.[16] In the north things were very different. The Syndicat des Fabricants de Tissus de Roubaix Tourcoing complained of 'the incompetence of the public authorities faced with the flagrant violation of the right of property'.[17] The managers of Etablissements Arbel, a metallurgical firm based in Douai, specifically blamed the sub-prefect for their predicament, and hostility to the sub-prefect was to colour their attitude to labour relations for the next three years.

The second fact that made the strikes so shocking was the threat that they posed directly to the employer's authority in his own factory. For the first time factories were occupied. The workers seemed to be establishing an alternative power with their own leaders and discipline. As has been shown, these occupations were sometimes described as revolutions in themselves. It is often suggested that the strikes were especially galling for owners of small businesses. Small businessmen are thought to have particularly valued their paternalistic control over their own men. Furthermore, owners of firms large enough to have a separate *siège social* were partially insulated from the shock of seeing their own offices occupied.[18] These assumptions are questionable. A paternalistic and authoritarian attitude was by no means confined to small business. France's largest employer, Louis Renault, had an almost feudal image. His attitude was not unique. Etablissements Arbel was a large firm, and it had a separate *siège social* in Paris, but Arbel management in Paris took a detailed interest in the personnel of their plant at Douai – sufficiently detailed to notice the conduct of individual workers.

It is also often assumed that the challenge to employer authority posed by the strikes of 1936 was resented for reasons that were, in large part, 'irrational' and non-economic. Such a view fits in with the idea of a 'pre-industrial' *patronat* more concerned with status and position in society than with economic rationality.[19] But there were sound economic reasons to be worried by the breakdown of factory authority. It will be suggested in the next chapter that the employers were concerned to maintain labour discipline because they saw it as closely linked to productivity. This does not

[16] Lyon C de C, p-v, 11 June 1936.
[17] AN, F 22 1587, letter dated 6 June 1936 to minister of work.
[18] Henry Ehrmann, *Organized Business in France* (Princeton, N.J., 1957), p. 8.
[19] For a discussion of the pre-industrial values of French business see Stanley Hoffmann, 'Paradoxes of the French Political Community', in idem (ed.), *In Search of France* (Cambridge, Mass., 1962). The portrait that he draws of the psychology of French business is now very unfashionable among economic historians.

mean that employers' views on this matter were lucid and fully worked out. But there was rationality mixed with their confused and often hysterical fears. Sometimes the two elements can be found in the same document. Thus a letter from M. Valley of Lyon to Etablissements Arbel starts off in an apocalyptic tone – 'we are sliding rapidly into the abyss into which Spain has fallen, for these strikes are nothing less than attempts at sovietization and civil war' – but then goes on to make a hard-headed assessment of losses in productivity: 'They cannot be calculated right now, but they will certainly be very significant... following the erosion of the will to work in a labour force that is still unhappy, bitter and ill-disciplined.'[20]

The Matignon accords

Initially the employers greeted the strikes with a blank refusal to negotiate. However, on 3 June Lambert Ribot, the secretary of the Comité des Forges, received a note suggesting that the policy of 'outright resistance' was no longer viable. The author of this note proposed that negotiations should be initiated, not by individual business associations, but by 'the whole of the *patronat*'.[21] He wished to see two or three representatives of business meet a similar number of union leaders to negotiate an end to the strikes. On 5 June Lambert Ribot converted these words into actions. He telephoned Blum and suggested that a meeting between representatives of workers and employers be arranged. A delegation of employers was duly drawn up, consisting of Lambert Ribot himself, Dalbouze, president of the APCC, Richemond of the GIMMCP, and Duchemin of the CGPF. The meetings took place on 7 June and 9 June and produced the so-called Matignon accords. These accords accepted the principle of collective contracts, union recognition and the institution of workers' delegates in any factory employing more than ten people. They also accepted that wages should be raised by between 7 and 15 per cent (the total wage bill in any factory was not to be increased by more than 12 per cent). Government legislation imposed the forty-hour week, paid holidays and collective contracts.

The backgrounds of the Matignon negotiators reflected the control of the employers' movement by certain sections of industry. All of them came from large-scale industry; three were metallurgists; two led specifically Parisian associations. This led many to allege that the Matignon accords had been drawn up to protect the interests of certain industrial sectors, a view that has been accepted by some historians. Indeed the most recent work on the subject suggests that the concessions imposed by the Matignon accords were in fact acceptable to the ruling clique of the business world, and that this

---

[20] 70 AQ 300, letter, dated 17 September 1936, to M. Brochard.
[21] See appendix 2 for an account of this note.

clique only turned against the accords when their nature was changed by further government legislation in the autumn of 1936.[22]

The motives of the Matignon negotiators

It is true that all the Matignon negotiators represented large-scale industry. But did this fact make them more willing to accept the concessions given in the accords? It might be argued that large enterprises would find the loss of authority implicit in collective contracts and the recognition of worker delegates more acceptable than small ones. But this is open to doubt. It has already been suggested that large firms were often passionately concerned with employer authority. Certainly in the aftermath of Matignon big business waged an unrelenting campaign against the power of workers' delegates.

More plausibly it might be argued that big business found the institution of the forty-hour week and paid holidays easier to bear than small business. It was suggested that large enterprises had wider profit margins to absorb the losses entailed by the measures; they had the possibility of reducing their dependency on expensive labour through mechanization;[23] they also tended to be located in areas where there was a plentiful supply of spare labour to fill gaps in production left by the new regulations.[24] But whatever advantages large-scale enterprises may have possessed in *principle*, in *practice* it was small business that survived these measures better. For the forty-hour week proved unenforceable in many areas of small business (see below).

It was also alleged that the Matignon negotiators had been willing to accept the accords because they represented the 'sheltered sector', that is to say that sector of the economy which was highly organized into cartels and which obtained much of its business from state contracts. The Fédération Nationale des Syndicats des Industriels Indépendants de l'Electricité, du Gaz et de l'Eau put this charge to the Minister of Labour:

It is now no secret to anyone that the convention established on 7 June, and currently known as the MATIGNON ACCORD, was established in very special conditions by people who were not wholly independent, and who were inspired solely by the

---

[22] Adrian Rossiter, 'Corporatist Experiments in Republican France, 1916–1939' (unpublished D.Phil. thesis, University of Oxford, 1986), p. 281. 'As far as metallurgy was concerned the concessions which had been made were quite acceptable, provided that the social disorders ceased.'

[23] J. Barnaud suggested that larger enterprises were better able to absorb rising costs in an article in *Nouveaux Cahiers*, 2 April 1937.

[24] One of the most overlooked aspects of modern French history is the regional variation in the severity of the *dénatalité* problem. The birth-rates were higher in the north and east of France than in the south-west.

directives of industries and enterprises which we describe as protected, because they live in large measure from state contracts.[25]

This interpretation of the role of the sheltered sector is open to doubt for two reasons. Firstly, the Matignon negotiators did not represent exclusively sheltered industries. The boundaries of this sector were not as sharply defined as they appeared to be from the outside. The mechanical industry, represented at Matignon by Dalbouze and Richemond, consisted of firms which were in the sheltered sector and firms which were not.[26] Furthermore, armaments accounted for an increasing proportion of state contracts after 1936. This meant that a second privileged group was arising within the sheltered sector. A company which had traditionally relied on state contracts, like Pont-à-Mousson, might actually feel the squeeze as money was pumped into armaments contracts (see chapter 7).

Secondly, it is not clear how the concessions made at Matignon were more acceptable to the sheltered sector than to the rest of industry. Some alleged that the sheltered sector was less vulnerable to the rising costs that would be imposed by the accords: 'representing industries that supply to the state, they are much less sensitive to sacrifices and price rises'.[27] But the most detailed contemporary analysis of the matter took exactly the opposite view. J. Dessirier wrote an economic study of the *secteur abrité* in 1936, in which he argued that the key characteristic of prices in this sector was their immobility. Because government was less prone to renegotiate than private enterprise this sector had benefited from the declining prices of the depression, in spite of some price-cutting by the government. But, writing a few months after Matignon, Dessirier added that rising prices would hurt the sheltered sector.[28] Indeed, since the sheltered sector had accumulated excessive profit margins during the preceding period of deflation, it must have seemed very likely that the government, which needed to save money, would let inflation erode those margins.

It has also been suggested that the unity of interests represented at Matignon and the links between the sheltered sector and the state allowed certain industries to gain specific concessions that prevented them from feeling the full impact of the accords.[29] There is some evidence for this. A

---

[25] AN F 22 1587, letter to the minister of labour dated 17 June 1936. This federation was at the root of Labeur Français: see Kolboom, *La revanche des patrons*, p. 139.

[26] J. Dessirier, 'L'économie française devant la dévaluation monétaire: secteurs "abrités" et "non abrités" retour vers l'équilibre', *Revue d'économie politique*, 50 (1936), 1527–87.

[27] Bertrand de Mun, writing to Pont-à-Mousson cited by Rossiter in 'Corporatist Experiments', p. 279.

[28] Dessirier, 'L'économie française devant la dévaluation monétaire: secteurs "abrités" et "non abrités" retour vers l'équilibre'.

[29] 'It seems certain that in the course of the negotiations Lambert managed to extract an informal promise of a special regime for metallurgy': Rossiter, 'Corporatist Experiments', p. 279.

CGPF circular, marked confidential, dated 9 June 1936 and signed by Duchemin, talked of concessions that might be made to industry:

The president of the council, being aware of the risk to the financial well-being of many firms posed by the measures suggested in the accord, said that M. Vincent Auriol...will look for means of supporting firms by allowing them credits at a considerable discount (for example through the *crédit national*). As for state markets, the 10 per cent price reduction imposed by the decree laws will be revoked; the question relating to those markets unaffected by this reduction will be considered; finally M. Blum noted the necessity to stimulate the rhythm of payments made by the state and by public bodies.[30]

It is also true that Lambert Ribot expressed the hope that permission might be obtained to continue the forty-eight-hour week in a part of the metallurgy industry: 'It might well be possible to obtain the forty-eight-hour law for factories requiring continuous working [*feu continu*].'[31]

Concessions such as these must have sweetened the Matignon pill, but it would be unwise to make too much of all this. The concessions of which Duchemin and Lambert Ribot spoke were vague expressions of hope not specific guarantees. Furthermore, considering that Blum was trying to persuade the Matignon negotiators to agree, and then that the Matignon negotiators were trying to defend the agreement in front of their own members, it is not surprising to find that efforts were made to present the agreement in the best possible light.

Furthermore, on close examination, the actual value of the concessions mentioned above seems rather limited. The possibility of a 10 per cent increase, or rather the reversal of a 10 per cent decrease, in prices paid to state industries was hardly generous in view of the losses that these industries might expect to incur as their profits were squeezed by wages spiralling upward from an initial increase of 12 per cent. The concession over the forty-hour week in the metallurgy industry was of equally limited value: it applied only to a small part of the metallurgy industry (foundries). It did nothing for the industries represented at Matignon by Dalbouze, Duchemin and Richemond. Even to the members of the Comité des Forges the value of the concession over the foundries was limited. Lambert Ribot, who had every interest in presenting the accords that he had signed in a good light, told a meeting on 15 October that there was no hope of similar concessions for iron ore mines.[32] Most importantly of all it needs to be stressed that the concessions described above did not apply uniquely to the sectors represented by the Matignon negotiators. General benefits like easy

---

[30] AN, 72 AS 6, circular signed Duchemin, marked confidential and dated 9 June 1936.
[31] Rossiter, 'Corporatist Experiments'.
[32] Blois, Pont-à-Mousson archives (P-à-M), 41952, report of Comité des Forges meeting of 15 October 1936.

credit terms and subsidies to exporters were given, or promised, to all sorts of industries after Matignon, even those, like the textile industry, that were violently hostile to the accords. Efforts were made to delay the application of the forty-hour week in almost every part of the economy (see chapter 6).

There were certain respects in which the Matignon negotiators did represent special interests. Firstly, the normal interpretation of the role of the *secteur abrité* can be reversed. It can be argued that what counted was not the leverage that this sector had with the government but the leverage that the government had with it: 'They have the reputation, sometimes well founded, of not being entirely free in their discussions...with any government, and especially with the present one which, by the nature of the industries that they represent, has formidable means of applying pressure to them.'[33]

Secondly, the geography of French industry played a large part in the willingness of some to accept Matignon. Two of the Matignon negotiators, Dalbouze and Richemond, headed specifically Parisian organizations. This area was hit first, and hardest, by the strikes. Not surprisingly, industrialists from this area were most willing to make concessions to end the strikes, especially since they believed that the strikes might spill over into more serious disorder. De Wendel was well placed, as president of the Comité des Forges, to speculate about the motives of the Matignon negotiators. He believed that geography was the key to these motives: 'De Wendel later made it clear that the very existence of the UIMM, originally set up by Pinot to balance out the metallurgists and their clients, obliged the representatives to sign accords that they could have refused to sign if they had just represented provincial steel production and not the Parisian mechanical industry.'[34]

The Matignon accords were signed, not because certain industries found them acceptable, but because certain industries viewed the consequences of *not* signing the accords (the continuation of the strikes, the possibility of disorder and the prospect of sanctions against the sheltered industries by the government) as unacceptable. The note sent to Lambert Ribot underlines this interpretation. Even though it was addressed to members of the Comité des Forges it did not suggest that agreement with the unions could be softened by special concessions or by the position of the sheltered industries. Rather it emphasized the consequences of not coming to an agreement: 'This surrender of part of the employer's authority might seem enormous today; it may be worse tomorrow if we do nothing.'[35] All this sheds some light on the way in which business viewed the accords. They were a short-

---

[33] De Mun to Fayolle, 7 August 1936, cited in Rossiter, 'Corporatist Experiments', p. 292.
[34] Jeanneney, *De Wendel*, p. 795.
[35] AN, 307 AP 83, note sent to Lambert Ribot dated 3 June 1936.

term tactic designed to parry the threats presented by the labour agitation and the Popular Front government. They were never acceptable as the foundation of a new consensus between capital and labour. It is significant that the very note that outlined the plans for the Matignon meetings also discussed the techniques by which the circumstances that had made Matignon necessary might be changed (see below).

The reform of the employers' organizations

In the wake of the Matignon accords there were great changes in the structure of the French employers' associations. The first of these changes involved the Chamber of Commerce. Dalbouze, as president of the Association of Presidents of Chambers of Commerce, summoned a number of business leaders to a meeting which took place on 20 July. This meeting led to the formation of the Comité National d'Entente (CNE) on 3 August. This committee was designed to provide a united focus for the business movement. It was presided over by Dalbouze. Duchemin (of the CGPF) and Duhem (of the Confédération des Groupements Commerciaux et Industriels) were appointed vice-presidents. Aymé Bernard of the Fédération des Associations Régionales was made treasurer.

The CGPF itself underwent a series of reforms which were made public on 4 August. A number of new federations were added to it – notably the Confédération des Groupements Commerciaux, which was known within the CGPF as the Union Commerciale Professionnelle. A greater role was foreseen for the Fédération des Associations Régionales. Commerce was to be better represented within the federations affiliated to the CGPF. Finally, the central council of the CGPF was enlarged to take in 150 rather than 90 members. The Matignon delegation, which was to continue negotiating with the unions until the end of the year, was also enlarged to include a further six full members and five 'suppléants'.[36] The title of the CGPF was changed from Confédération Générale de la Production Française to Confédération Générale du Patronat Français to symbolize a more complete representation of business. In the autumn of 1936 the CGPF established a social office to deal with labour relations. A new grouping emerged which drew its support from the Chambre Syndicale des Industries Radio-électriques (CSIR) and later from the GIMMCP. By July this had crystallized into the Comité de Prévoyance et d'Action Sociale (CPAS). Finally, on 9 October, the president of the CGPF, Duchemin, resigned and was replaced by Claude Gignoux.

[36] AN, 72 AS 6, p-v of *conseil central* for 11 September 1936.

To what extent did these changes mark a shift of power within the employers' movement? Recent historians have been rather sceptical of the claims advanced at the time that the reforms enfranchised those groups, small-scale industry and commerce, that had previously been excluded from power. But it has also been suggested that the changes marked a 'palace coup' within big business.[37] There had always been certain tensions within big business and especially within the metallurgy sector. There was a conflict of interests between the founders represented by the Comité des Forges and the mechanical industries and producers of finished metal goods concentrated around Paris. In the twentieth century the tension was exacerbated by the fact that the economic importance of the latter sector grew as modern industries such as automobile and aircraft manufacture developed.

It is possible that the modern sectors of industry did use the upheavals in the employers' movement that followed Matignon to snipe at the heavy industrial establishment. Such evidence is provided by the activity of Colonel Brenot of the Chambre Syndicale des Industries Radioélectriques. Brenot formed the CPAS which was based in the modern electronics industries and Parisian metallurgical industries. Brenot pushed hard for reform within the CGPF and was instrumental in persuading that body to form a social committee. Brenot also seems to have ensured that the arch-representative of heavy industrial power – the secretary of the Comité des Forges – was excluded from the social committee of the CGPF: 'we then discussed the CGP which has created an executive commission for social questions from which M. Lambert has been excluded at the request of a member of the CGP whom M. Lambert did not name but who we all know to be Colonel Brenot of the Chambre Syndicale des Fabricants de TSF'.[38]

However, Matignon would have been a strange *casus belli* for the producers of finished goods to adopt. Their differences with heavy industry focused around tariffs and pricing, not labour relations. Besides, the light metallurgical sector had been well represented at Matignon. Indeed, since the strikes of 1936 had centred in Parisian metallurgy industry, it might be argued that this area benefited most from the accord.[39]

Furthermore, internal business archives give very little impression of a great struggle going on between modern sectors of the economy and heavy industry. Louis Renault, a leading figure among the modernized industries,

---

[37] Kolboom, *La revanche des patrons*, pp. 243–55.
[38] P-à-M, 41952, report of Comité des Forges meeting of 17 September 1936.
[39] Indeed de Wendel claimed that Matignon had represented the subordination of the interests of foundries to those of light metallurgy (Jeanneney, *De Wendel*, p. 795). In theory it might also be argued that, since labour formed a small part of the price of finished products for highly mechanized industries, they would find the new labour regulations and pay increases more acceptable than other industrial sectors. In practice there is no evidence that this was the case.

did not see the reforms of the employers' organizations as part of an attack on heavy industry. Nor did Pont-à-Mousson, a leading heavy industrial firm, feel under attack by the modernized sector. They resented the exclusion of Lambert Ribot from the social committee of the CGPF, but they did not see it as part of the general reforms of the movement. On the contrary, they blamed the leadership of the CGPF for it: 'I thought that this confirmed the mistrust that I have always felt for that fool [*dadais*] Duchemin.'[40] Indeed there is substantial evidence that Brenot and Duchemin were working in alliance during the summer of 1936. Brenot protested against Duchemin's replacement by Gignoux, which he seems to have regarded as a plot by the 'magnates' of heavy industry.[41] This fact is hard to square with a presentation of Brenot as the leader of the 'new industrial sectors' seeking to oust the old leadership of the CGPF. Things are made even less clear by the fact that Brenot had a great deal in common with his opponent Gignoux, both men being corporatists and hard-liners in terms of labour relations, and very little in common with his ally Duchemin.[42] Perhaps this shows that the conflict between Gignoux and Brenot was part of a struggle between individuals to decide who would implement a policy rather than a struggle between industries to decide what that policy should be. Brenot's own emphasis on the importance of personality bears out such a Namierite interpretation: 'It does not matter whether they are mandated representatives; what matters is that they should be a small group of able men.'[43]

The activities of the CPAS also show that is unwise to read too much into the alignment within the CGPF of 1936. Brenot was, after all, an ambitious and enterprising man seizing the chance offered by events to advance his own career; as he pushed his way forward in the scramble for new positions it is not surprising that he should have adopted some fairly strange allies, such as the ultra-progressive Jean Coutrot (see chapter 5). Maurice Olivier drily commented on the mixture of dynamism and confusion that characterized the CPAS during its early months: 'the committee seems to have extraordinary resources and it is committed to some major undertaking, without, perhaps, knowing exactly what'.[44] In the long run it is not very important whether the skirmishes between Brenot and the leaders of heavy industry were the product of personal ambition or an attempt to

---

[40] P-à-M, 41952, report of Comité des Forges meeting of 17 September 1936.
[41] AN, 72 AS 7, p-v of *conseil central*, 9 October 1936. After Duchemin's resignation Brenot complained that 'employers' groups give the impression that they are led and inspired by the 'magnates'. For Brenot's apparent belief that he and Duchemin were working in alliance see also (AN, 72 AS 9) letter from Brenot to Duchemin dated 12 August 1936.
[42] Duchemin's opposition to corporatism was made clear in the meeting of the CGPF *conseil central* of 19 November 1937: 'corporatism... will lead to the pure and simple abolition of individual liberties' (AN, 72 AS 8).
[43] AN, 72 AS 6, p-v of *conseil central*, 11 September 1936.
[44] AN, 468 AP 8, Olivier to Coutrot dated 2 October 1936.

increase the power of new industrial sectors. Such skirmishes were just a side-show. Both sides were agreed about the strategy to be pursued with regard to the main issue of the day: labour relations. Indeed, once the short-term struggles of 1936 were over, Brenot's CPAS and Gignoux's CGPF worked together closely.

Far from being displaced by the reforms in the employers' organizations that occurred in 1936, heavy industry sponsored and supported those reforms. This support was illustrated by the reaction of heavy industry to the CNE. It is true that one of most powerful leaders of heavy industry, De Peyerimhoff, did initially oppose the foundation of this body. However, de Peyerimhoff's worries were soon soothed and indeed he was persuaded to join the CNE himself.[45] The establishment of the CNE was also vigorously supported by heavy industrialists like Pont-à-Mousson. Heavy industrialists approved of the change in leadership of the CGPF,[46] although it was not engineered by them.[47] The representatives of heavy industry were often closely linked to the new leaders of the CGPF. For example, a police report of September 1936 linked one of the new leaders, Pierre Nicolle, with two of the most prominent representatives of heavy industry: de Peyerimhoff and de Wendel.[48]

The intimacy of the relations which existed between the new leadership of the CGPF and the groups that had controlled the movement before Matignon is illustrated by the career of Aymé Bernard. Bernard was one of the new leaders imported into the CGPF after 1936. A note by the President of the Reims Chamber of Commerce picked him out as one of the most important members of this group and added 'it is said that he is more important than its [the FAR's] president M. Fougère'.[49] Bernard seems to have presented himself as a representative of a group that had been insufficiently represented in the past. When he put forward his own

[45] AN, 40 AS 95, letter from president of the Chamber of Commerce of Paris dated 4/5 August 1936. This letter was in response to a letter of de Peyerimhoff's of 30 July in which he had apparently expressed concern about the divisive effect which the new body might have. Dalbouze assured him that 'In spite of the fears that you expressed, complete agreement was achieved between all concerned.' De Peyerimhoff seems to have been regarded with special enmity by those who claimed to represent small business. On the official agenda for a meeting of the CGPF (of 4 August) in the Renault archives (AN, 91 AQ 78) a number of comments are scrawled in pencil, and one of these comments refers to attacks on de Peyerimhoff by commerce. It is especially odd that, in the aftermath of Matignon, so much fire should have been directed at a leader who had not signed the accords. De Peyerimhoff was very unpopular with large-scale metallurgists, who were annoyed by his efforts to keep up the price of coal; perhaps the attacks by 'commerce' were not unrelated to this unpopularity.

[46] See the approving comments of Pont-à-Mousson management on Gignoux cited below.

[47] The departure came as a surprise to both the president of the Comité des Forges and to Pont-à-Mousson management, who could only remark that the resignation was 'sans raison donnée' (P-à-M, 41604, report of UIMM meeting for 15 October 1936).

[48] Jeanneney, *De Wendel*, p. 564.

[49] AN, 317 AP 87/88, undated. Fougère was president of the FAR, Bernard was its delegate-general and therefore, in theory, Fougère's subordinate.

candidature for the CNE, he suggested that the FAR had waited fifteen years 'probably too quietly'.[50] Historians have accepted that Bernard was 'a regionalist in CGPF HQ who was opposed to the predominance there of metallurgy and Parisian interests'.[51] But the archives of one company paint a very different picture. Etablissements Arbel was a classic example of the industrial establishment that had controlled the CGPF. It was a large, metallurgical concern, with a *siège social* in Paris. Much of its production went to state-controlled markets. It was a member of the UIMM and the GIMMCP, organizations that had signed the Matignon accords. Yet Arbel had very close links with Bernard. The local business association of Douai, which was clearly controlled by Arbel,[52] joined the FAR in 1937. The association regularly reprinted Bernard's articles from the *Journée Industrielle*. The Arbel archives even contain a series of numbers of the journal of Bernard's local association in Lyon. Bernard's relations with the controlling establishment of the employer's movement were highlighted in 1940 when he was a member of the Comité des Forges delegation to Laval.[53]

The new leaders imported into the business movement after the Matignon accords offered three things to the old business ruling group. Firstly, they offered the prospect of unity. The big business associations had always been torn apart by internal rivalries. Yet, if they were to mount a challenge to the Popular Front and the concessions that had been imposed on business after the Matignon accords, big businessmen needed to unite. The fact that the new leaders came from outside big business, and that some of the most important of them had never worked in industry themselves, made the achievement of such unity easier. Initiatives proposed by any one company or section of industry would be distrusted by others, but an outsider might be trusted. Pont-à-Mousson management were quite explicit about the advantages that they saw in being led by someone from outside industry: 'he has the advantage of having given the CGP a president who is independent of any industry'.[54]

Secondly, the new leadership offered a more vigorous and active administration of the employers' associations. It was recognized that business needed the leadership of 'a commanding group of active and well-

---

[50] C de C, 1862, transcript of CNE meeting of 3 August.
[51] Rossiter, 'Corporatist Experiments', p. 291. Rossiter adds that Bernard 'led the textile dominated AICA'. There is no evidence that AICA was dominated by the textile industry.
[52] Lucien Arbel was president of the association, and the company provided its administrative services (AN, 70 AQ 420, report of annual general meeting of Association Douaisienne de l'industrie et de commerce, its Bulletin for March 1939).
[53] Pierre Nicolle, *Cinquante mois d'armistice, Vichy, 2 juillet 1940–26 août 1944: journal d'un témoin* (2 vols., Paris, 1947), entry for 15 July 1940, vol. I, p. 30. It is especially ironic that a man imported into the CGPF as part of a 'reaction against Matignon' should finish by being labelled by Laval as one who had 'licked the arse of the Popular Front' (see chapter 12).   [54] P-à-M, 41604, UIMM file.

paid young men'.[55] The fact that many of the new leaders were not businessmen themselves meant that they could devote all their time to the business associations. Many of them had been trained as lawyers which equipped them well to implement and manipulate the new labour legislation that had been imposed after Matignon.[56] Most of all the new leaders had personalities that were seen to be suited to the period of political and industrial conflict which was to come. The principal complaint about the former leader of the CGPF, Duchemin, was not that he represented the wrong interests or subscribed to the wrong ideology, but that he lacked backbone. The Pont-à-Mousson management described him as 'ce grand dadais' (this great lump). In his resignation speech Duchemin himself appeared to recognize that his departure was primarily a matter of personality: 'it is a question of having the right man in the right place'.[57] The new leaders were often men of notably pugnacious temperament. Gignoux was described, by Blum, as 'one of those men who bring more vigour to the defence of businessmen's interests than businessmen themselves'. Aymé Bernard had been recognized as a dominating personality when he had led the Association Industrielle Commerciale et Agricole in Lyon.[58] Prax was another leader who had won his spurs at local level. His violent response to the strikes of 1936 in Marseille had attracted admiration in business circles throughout the country.[59] Prax's attack on Duchemin at the constitutive meeting of the CNE shows how the new leadership flaunted the contrast between their spirit and the indecision of the old business leaders:

You talk about the responsibilities of groups...well, I represent the leading port in France, I represent an economic region...I, in the name of all that part of the south, and the south-east, I tell you that I am consulting no one...I am prepared to support whatever motion is passed here, I do not intend to go back to my organization like a puppet to ask permission to light a cigarette.[60]

Thirdly, the new leadership offered the capacity to mount a political campaign. Clearly large-scale industry on its own could not overthrow the Popular Front or the legislation that had been imposed after Matignon. This would require a political campaign that would attract support from other classes. It is therefore not surprising to find that many of the leaders who were recruited into the business movement after 1936 were politicians. The

---

[55] AN, 91 AQ 78, report of meeting of Comité Intersyndical de Prévoyance et d'Action Sociale on 26 June 1936.   [56] Bernard, Gignoux and Gingembre had legal training.

[57] AN 72 AS 7, p-v of *conseil central*, 9 October 1936.

[58] Claude Paillat, *Dossiers secrets de la France contemporaine, 1. 1919: les illusions de la gloire* (Paris, 1979), p. 262.

[59] Prax had arranged for the red flags in Marseille to be torn down. In the Paris Chamber of Commerce Defert said that he was 'un petit peu jaloux' of the vigorous stance taken by the Chamber of Commerce in Marseille (p-v, 24 June 1936). The Lyon Chamber of Commerce was flooded with phone calls demanding that it imitate the action taken in Marseille (p-v, 11 June 1936).   [60] Kolboom, *La revanche des patrons*, p. 202.

new leader of the CGPF, Gignoux, had been a deputy and had served in Laval's cabinet. Another of the new men brought into the CGPF, Taudière, was still serving as a deputy. Germain Martin, who ultimately became president of the CPAS, had, like Gignoux, been a deputy and an associate of Laval's. Even those of the new men who were not professional politicians were highly politicized. The prefect of the Rhône suggested that the local business association, led by Aymé Bernard, was more interested in politics than business – 'an organization with reactionary tendencies sheltering behind an economic screen'[61] – and it had been rumoured that Bernard had been proposed as a candidate for the united right in central Lyon in the elections of 1936.[62]

The mobilization of the *classes moyennes*

Demographically France was dominated by the *classes moyennes* – that is to say small businessmen, shopkeepers and the *professions libérales*. If industry wished to accomplish anything politically it needed to ally with these groups. For the *classes moyennes* were seen to lie at the electoral base of the Radical party, which played a pivotal role in the politics of the Third Republic.[63] There was nothing new about this need. On previous occasions when big business had mobilized against the threat of organized labour or left-wing governments it had sought alliances with the broad bourgeois. Thus before the First World War big business had confronted the growth of the left by allying itself with the small shopkeepers' movement and turning that movement to the right.[64] Similarly in 1919 the railway companies had sought to associate the wider bourgeois with their struggles against striking workers.[65]

The circumstances of 1936 made such an alliance even more desirable than usual. For the Radical party was seen as the prop holding up the Popular Front. Business recognized that if the Radicals could be persuaded to abandon their Socialist and Communist allies then the Popular Front could be brought down. The pre-Matignon note to Lambert Ribot had stressed that resistance to the workers' demands would only be possible 'if

---

[61] Prefect's report, 22 February 1936, reference supplied by Mr Kevin Passmore.

[62] Information supplied by Mr Kevin Passmore.

[63] It should be stressed that what is at issue here is what the leaders of big business believed about the Radical party not whether those beliefs were true or not.

[64] Philip Nord, *Paris Shopkeepers and the Politics of Resentment* (Princeton, N.J., 1986).

[65] Annie Kriegel, *Aux origines du communisme française, 1914–1920, contribution à l'histoire du mouvement ouvrier français* (Paris, 1964), p. 437. The railway companies sought to associate bodies such as the *anciens combattants* and the students of *grandes écoles* with the repression of the strikes.

one could be sure that, faced with a call to arms [*un look-out presque général*], the Radicals would leave a ministry of the left for a ministry of national unity'. The new organizations which tried to present themselves to big business as representatives of the *classes moyennes* were well aware that the key to their success was their supposed capacity to influence the Radical party. One organization which claimed to represent foremen wrote to business organizations claiming that it would encourage 'non internationalist parliamentary supporters of the Popular Front' to 'dissociate themselves from their allies'.[66] In the aftermath of Matignon big business recognized the benefits which might be derived from a mobilization of the *classes moyennes*. Jean Coutrot – who was himself an industrialist – organized the association of the *classes moyennes*. He wrote of the sympathy with which his projects had been received by the CGPF. In September 1936 Louis Renault wrote: 'the association of the *classes moyennes* should be revived and made active again'.[67]

Big business directed most of its attention to one particular part of the *classes moyennes*: that made up of small businessmen. The new leaders and institutions brought into the employers' movement after 1936 were presented as the representatives of small business. The appeal to small business reached its peak in 1937 when the Petite et Moyenne Industrie et Commerce section of the CGPF was formed. This body took in two of the new generation of employers' leaders who had risen in the post-1936 reforms of the employers' movement, Nicolle and Verger, and also included a third small business leader who was to become important: Léon Gingembre.

An example of republican synthesis?

It is tempting to present the reforms of the employers' movement after Matignon as an example of what Stanley Hoffmann calls 'republican synthesis'. Hoffmann has argued that the Third Republic was dominated by an alliance of the industrialists, small businessmen and *professions libérales*. This alliance resisted traumatic social and economic change and excluded the proletariat from power. At first glance the reforms of the employers' movement look like such an alliance in operation. Industry did appear to be allied with the representatives of the broad bourgeois, especially small business, in opposition to the proletariat. This was certainly the impression

---

[66] AN, 39 AS 941, letter dated 18 June 1936 from the Front Français Constitutionnel to the GIMMCP. The Front Français Constitutionnel was an offshoot of the Union des Agents de Maîtrise Anciens Combattants (see chapter 6).
[67] Cited in Patrick Fridenson, *Histoire des usines Renault*, vol. I: *Naissance de la grande entreprise, 1898–1939* (Paris, 1972), p. 260.

that employers' leaders sought to convey: on 11 September 1936 Fougère, presiding over a meeting of the *conseil central* of the CGPF, said: 'I hope that now that we are decided to go forward for the general protection of the interests of French employers, there will be an end to talk of divisions that have existed, of the two hundred families and sheltered industries. We are a block and we must remain homogeneous.'[68]

But there are two respects in which the Hoffmannite model fails to fit. Firstly, Hoffmann suggests that big business absorbed the pre-industrial values of its social allies and was thus locked into the republican synthesis. But the fact that industry took such an interest in its social allies at moments of political crisis like 1919 or 1936, and the fact that it was able to abandon them at other times, suggests a more calculating and manipulative relationship. Examination of the internal archives of the CGPF gives further evidence that, for all their talk of unity, the leaders of large-scale industry were perfectly well aware that their interests differed from those of small business. For example, in public, the leaders of the industrial associations made a great show of their desire to see factory-based buyers' associations, which competed with small shopkeepers, suppressed.[69] But, in private, the head of the social section of the CGPF emphasized that such a suppression would increase the cost of living for workers and therefore inflate wages.[70]

Secondly, the Hoffmannite analysis is undermined by the fact that the reforms of the employers' movement were not founded on an alliance of big business and small business. Rather they were founded on an alliance of the representatives of large-scale industry with those who *claimed* to represent small business. It was easy enough to see who was represented by a classic big business organization like the Comité des Forges. There were efficient transmission belts between it and its constituents. A firm like Pont-à-Mousson would send representatives to each meeting. These would make the views of their company known. If these views were disregarded displeasure would be expressed. Specific sanctions might even be inflicted. But small business was fragmented and dispersed. They were in no position to organize or to control organizations that spoke in their name. Often the techniques by which small business was mobilized – posters, pamphlets, the mass meeting – left little scope for participation. It is impossible to know whether small businessmen agreed with what they read in pamphlets addressed to them or with what was said at mass meetings organized in their name.

Under these circumstances it is not surprising that the credentials of some

---

[68]   AN, 72 AS 6, p-v of *conseil central*, 11 September 1936.
[69]   Lambert Ribot pointed out the extent to which the failure of the industry to suppress consumer co-operatives was affecting the confidence of small business to a meeting of the railway manufacturers on 18 June 1937, P-à-M, 41604.
[70]   AN 72 AS 7, p-v of *conseil central*, 20 November 1936.

'representatives of small business' are rather dubious. Sometimes institutions or individuals that claimed a small business mandate were really closely linked to big business. Kolboom has shown that the CPAS was such a body;[71] Aymé Bernard's Fédération des Associations Régionales was another. The presentation of Bernard as a representative of small business was especially audacious. The average enterprise represented by the local association that Bernard led in Lyon employed 103 workers – which made it, by French standards, a big business association.[72] Furthermore, Bernard had close personal associations with the Gillet dynasty, owners of a chemical empire notorious for its brutal dealings with small business. Bernard never specifically claimed to be a leader of small business. But he associated himself with men, like Duhem and Nicolle,[73] who did make such claims. Bernard also managed to imply that he was associated with small business interests. For example, in 1939 during the debate on compulsory ententes in the CGPF Bernard urged that small business opinion be taken into account. But in the relative privacy of his local association's bulletin in Lyon Bernard took a stand on the issue which was diametrically opposed to that of small business.[74]

Others who claimed to represent small business were simply opportunists who represented no one at all. Pierre Nicolle was the classic example of the type. The only office to which he was ever elected from below was that of leader of the Parisian artificial flower vendors' association.[75] However, during the taxpayer protest of 1933 he established the Comité du Salut Economique and began to style himself a leader of small business. The links which this body had with the constituency which it claimed to represent are almost impossible to assess. It issued pamphlets and posters in the name of small business and organized mass meetings.[76] But the real support that it commanded seems to have been limited to Paris and possibly to just one or two arrondissements.[77] By the time that Nicolle was drawn into the CGPF

---

[71] Kolboom, *La revanche des patrons*, pp. 242–63.

[72] Kevin Passmore, 'Conservative Politics and the Crisis of the Third Republic: 1928–1939' (unpublished manuscript), p. 112. By contrast the average member of the GIMMCP employed a little under 200 men.

[73] Bernard presented himself at the constitutive meeting of the CNE (C de C, 1862, 3 August 1936) as 'solidaire avec M Duhem'. He worked in alliance with Nicolle after 1936 (see below).   [74] See below.

[75] This post is mentioned in the CGPF annuaire for 1939. The association's headquarters had the same address as those of the Comité de Salut Economique.

[76] For an account of the activity of the CSE during this period see Pierre Nicolle, *Comité de Salut Economique. Rapport de la Commission Permanente* (Paris, 1934), p. 1834, Nicolle claimed that the Comité had succeeded in obtaining an attendance of 30,000 *commerçants* at a meeting in May 1934 and that it had organized a commercial strike on 16 February of that year.

[77] Julian Jackson, *The Politics of Depression in France* (Cambridge, 1985), p. 243, points out that in a letter to Paul Reynaud in 1933 Nicolle made great play of his capacity to mobilize the *commerçants* in Reynaud's constituency (i.e. the second arrondissement). Many bodies

in 1936 there is no evidence that the CSE even existed any more. Certainly it had shown no signs of life since 1934. Once the immediate crisis of 1936 was past Nicolle hastily attached himself to a body with more real substance: Aymé Bernard's Fédération des Associations Régionales.[78] It was typical of Nicolle's opportunism that he should begin as a representative of Parisian commerce and finish as a leader of provincial industry. The same opportunism was to lead Nicolle to hop on to the two great bandwagons of the right in twentieth-century France: Vichy and Algérie Française.

The institutions on which those who claimed to represent small business founded their power were very frail. This was widely recognized. In the Lyon Chamber of Commerce the Confédération Générale du Commerce de Détail, the body lead by George Mauss, was contemptuously labelled 'a ghost organization'.[79] The insubstantial nature of Mauss's links with the constituency that he claimed to represent were revealed three years later when small business representatives were chosen for the Conseil Commercial de la Seine. Mauss was beaten by the candidate of the Confédération Générale du Petit Commerce, de la Petite Industrie, et de l'Artisanat (a Communist-controlled organization).[80] This frailty was reflected by the fact that many of the bodies which achieved prominence in 1936 soon faded away. The CNE began to decline almost as soon as the reform of the CGPF provided big business with an alternative channel with which to mobilize small business. This decline was brutally summed up by the president of the Reims Chamber of Commerce who remarked that 'the mountain has given birth to a mouse'.[81] Even the official transcripts of the committee suggest that it produced more hot air than decisions.[82] By the time of Dalbouze's death in the autumn of 1936 the CNE was so unimportant that two men – Férasson and Morel Journel – declined its presidency.[83] The CNE was seen as little more than an annexe of the body that it had been designed to circumvent – the CGPF. Indeed vociferous small business representatives in the Paris Chamber of Commerce now asked that another body be set up to

purporting to represent 'small business in France' have drawn their support from the area between the Archives Nationales and the Bibliothèque Nationale. Nord's study of the organization of commerce before the First World War focuses on the Palais Royal. Gingembre, the post-war spokesman of the PME, has always been based on the rue des Archives. It may well be that small business in the central arrondissements, which consisted largely of luxury trades, was especially right wing. By contrast in the working-class 20th arrondissement shopkeepers and strikers demonstrated together (police report of 30 May 1936 in AN, F 7 1398).

[78] Pierre Nicolle, *Cinquante mois d'armistice, Vichy, 2 juillet 1940–26 août 1944: journal d'un témoin* (2 vols., Paris, 1947), vol. I, pp. 6–9.   [79] Lyon C de C, p-v, 9 July 1936.

[80] AN, 39 AS 862, note of May 1939.

[81] AN, 317 AP 87/88, undated note from president of Reims Chamber of Commerce.

[82] C de C, 1862. On 23 November 1936 the secretary noted drily that 'there followed a long exchange of views that allowed everyone to express their point of view'.

[83] Lyon, C de C, p-v, 17 December 1936.

circumvent the CNE.[84] Even the president of the CNE recognized that it served little purpose and in mid-1938 he tried to have it dissolved.[85] The decline of Duhem after the summer of 1936 was even more ignominious than that of the CNE. He was regarded as insufficiently important to replace Dalbouze as president of the CNE even as fourth choice.[86]

There was a fierce struggle among the would-be leaders of small business in 1936 and 1937. The Paris Chamber of Commerce insisted that the UIE be excluded from the Comité National d'Entente.[87] Bernard's FAR and Duhem's confederation confronted each other in the provinces.[88] Nicolle saw attempts to mobilize the *classes moyennes* as a whole as a threat to his own efforts to mobilize small business as a separate group.[89]

All this puts the conflict in the business organizations in an interesting light. The new wave of leaders in the employers' movement were in no position to wrest control from the ruling establishment. They were a group of political carpetbaggers jostling with each other to be recognized as the representatives of the *classes moyennes*. The ultimate key to success in this struggle was the recognition, funds and access to existing organizations that came from the ruling establishment of the business organizations: big business. It is no accident that the organizations and leaders who did best in the scramble for recognition were the ones that had, or acquired, the closest links with big business.

Though the organizations which presented themselves as leaders of the *classes moyennes* were in sharp conflict with each other, there was remarkably little conflict within them. All of them behaved as though the class which they aspired to represent was unified and homogeneous. The very unity of the demands presented on behalf of small businessmen hints at how little power they had over those who claimed to represent them. Heavy industrial associations like the Comité des Forges were constantly torn apart by conflict. This was because their members exercised real power over them. Large firms would insist that their own interests be taken into

---

[84] C de C, p-v, 10 January 1938. The president of the Chamber accepted that Brinon and Bagnaud should be added to a delegation to represent activities 'that are, perhaps, not fully represented in the Comité National d'Entente'.

[85] Lyon, C de C, p-v, 9 June 1938. Manceau was persuaded by other members of the committee not to dissolve it.

[86] Lyon, C de C, p-v, 17 December 1936. Férasson and Morel Journel had turned the job down. Prax was regarded as too controversial.

[87] C de C, 1862, transcript of meeting of bureau of APCC of 6 July 1936. Though the UIE was not an organ of small business, it was less compromised by heavy industrial associations than the CGPF – indeed some of the bodies which were brought into the 'democratized' employers' movement such as Duhem's organization had been affiliated to the UIE. It could well have played the role which the Chamber of Commerce took on briefly as a means of mobilizing the *classes moyennes*. Indeed Louis Renault's references to it during this period do suggest that big business considered the UIE as a possible instrument for such a mobilization.   [88] Kolboom, *La revanche des patrons*, p. 321.

[89] Kolboom, *La revanche des patrons*, p. 320.

account when formulating policy and these interests frequently conflicted with those of other firms. Thus for example firms producing for state markets clashed with firms that wished to cut their tax bill.[90] Metallurgical firms, which consumed coal, clashed with the mines, which produced it.[91] Sometimes such conflicts were so fierce that the Comité des Forges was obliged to produce different policy proposals on a single question in order to match the various views among its members.

In terms of real economic interest there was as much, if not more, division among small businessmen. Small business was a category which covered a whole variety of enterprises, some of which were modern and growing, some of which were declining and traditional.[92] There was conflict of interests between small businesses and artisans, who had certain legal privileges. There was a conflict of interests between businesses that subcontracted for large companies and those that did not. The conflict during the 1930s was especially sharp. Previously the fact that much of the French bourgeois drew a substantial or even predominant part of their income from *rentes* or fixed incomes blunted the clash of economic interest among them. They were all united by a common interest in sound money. But private incomes had been eroded by the inflation of the First World War.

The extent to which big business ignored divisions within the *classes moyennes* was further reflected by their attitude to the organization of engineers and foremen – the group that would become known as the *cadres*. Big business sponsorship of this group was less open than that of small business organizations. But it is clear from business archives that great interest was taken in the development of *cadres* unions. Indeed industrialists in the north even lent tacit support to a strike organized by the *cadres* unions in order to give it credibility.[93] These efforts betrayed an indifference to the divisions among *cadres*. The term was used to cover both graduates of the Ecole Polytechnique and factory foremen in greasy overalls. Furthermore, it was used at a time when engineers themselves, because of the overproduction of diplomas, were more keen than ever to stress distinctions of rank within their own profession.

Business sponsorship of the *cadres* unions also reflected a more general

[90] P-à-M, 41604, report of meeting of Chambre Syndicale du Chemin de Fer of 16 March 1937 in which Pont-à-Mousson was attacked for lobbying for higher public spending.

[91] P-à-M, 41604, report by Cavalier on speech by de Peyerimhoff of 23 March 1932. Cavalier expresses hostility to de Peyerimhoff's desire for a protected coal market.

[92] For some indication of the diversity of enterprises covered by the term 'small business' see Steven M. Zdateny. 'The Artisanat in France: An Economic Portrait, 1900–1956', *French Historical Studies*, 13 (1984), 415–40.

[93] Ingo Kolboom, 'Patronat et cadres: la contribution patronale à la formation du groupe des cadres (1936–1938)', *Le mouvement social*, 121 (1982), 71–95. It is worth noting that though there may have been collusion among industrialists in the north with the strike of the *cadres* this was not co-ordinated at a national level. Lambert Ribot told a meeting of the rolling stock manufacturers' syndicate on 18 January 1937 that the strikes were 'nullement d'origine patronale'.

insensitivity towards divisions within the *classes moyennes*. For in terms of their political value to big business the *cadres* were similar to small business. Indeed, in a retrospective account of the period, the GIMMCP described small business as being part of the *cadres*. But in terms of their real economic interests the *cadres* and small businessmen were sharply opposed. The growth of the *cadres* was a product of the growth of large-scale modern industries which threatened small business. The insensitivity that the leaders of the *classes moyennes* could show to this division within the class which they purported to represent was shown in Jean Coutrot's book *Humanisme économique*. On page 97 Coutrot praised 'the hard-working small businessman', while on page 65 he praised the technocratic modernizing ethic of the *cadre*.[94] The firm praised by Coutrot as the epitome of modernity was Bata, the Czech shoe company that played a central role in the demonology of small business.[95] All this suggests that the *classes moyennes* was what recent French sociologists have labelled a 'classe objet', that is to say a class which appears unified and homogeneous because it is defined and led from outside. As Boltanski puts it:

In literature and film ... and *a fortiori* in politics, the petite bourgeoisie seems doomed to be represented by another class. It is an object about which one speaks, an object that can be defined and defended only from outside and only to serve the interests of some other group. In other words, conflicts over middle-class issues (especially intense during the 1930s) must be viewed largely in terms of attempts by other groups and agents to mobilize and co-opt the middle classes for their own interests.[96]

Of course the agent which was seeking to mobilize the middle classes from outside was the clique of large-scale industrialists who controlled the employers' movement. It is true that the mobilization of the middle classes sometimes involved considerable degrees of rhetorical hostility to this clique of large-scale industry. For example, certain engineers' unions excluded *patrons* from membership for the first time during this period.[97] Furthermore, there was much talk of the two hundred families and the wicked machinations of big business. But this rhetoric deserves to be taken with a pinch of salt. Boltanski points out that a certain amount of anti-capitalist rhetoric was a necessary ingredient of the ideology of the 'Third Way'. In order to attack the working-class movement, while preserving an air of independence, the leaders of the *classes moyennes* had to create an apparently antithetical ogre on the other side. In practice these attacks gave big business little cause for concern. They were ritual assaults focused against the symbolic target of the two hundred families. Such attacks had

[94] Cited in Luc Boltanski, *The Making of a Class: Cadres in French Society* (Cambridge 1987), pp. 72 and 73.
[95] Bata was of course the target of the *loi Pullen* which was designed to restrict large firms in the shoe industry in order to protect artisanal producers.
[96] Boltanski, *The Cadres*, p. 42.
[97] Ibid. p. 64. The Syndicat des Ingénieurs Salariés (SIS) contained no owners.

assumed so stylized a form that they were almost meaningless – André Siegried suggested that big business had replaced the Church as the stock hate figure in republican politics. Occasionally such rhetoric was even used by people who were themselves members of the two hundred families.

This clique was concerned to undermine the Popular Front and more specifically the labour legislation imposed after Matignon. Middle-class interests were therefore presented in terms of opposition to Matignon. It was continually suggested that small business would suffer particularly from the accords. In fact it is far from obvious that small business was suffering from the accords. The total number of small businesses in France actually increased after June 1936;[98] for the new labour legislation was in practice impossible to enforce on small business. Large enterprises were often forced to subcontract work to small operators who could slip under the labour inspectors' net.[99]

Talk of small business interests was really just a political battering ram with which big business hoped to knock down Matignon; the leaders who used such rhetoric feared nothing more than the prospect that the government might cut the ground from under their feet by granting exemption from labour legislation to small business alone.[100] The presentation of big business demands in small business disguise could be almost ludicrously blatant. On 24 May 1937 an attack was made in the Comité National d'Entente upon government plans to impose controls upon hiring and firing; it was alleged that this would be 'especially serious for small industry and commerce'. The speaker who displayed such touching concern for small business interest was de Peyerimhoff,[101] the leader of France's most concentrated industry who was notoriously hostile to small business interests[102] and who had initially opposed the very formation of the CNE.

Conclusion

This chapter has suggested that the same group of large-scale businessmen, especially those connected with heavy industry and metallurgy, remained in

---

[98] Ehrmann, *Organized Business in France*, pp. 39–40.

[99] Lyon, C de C, p-v, 25 February 1937, Charbin complained that 'Quite often the collective contract will only, in practice, be obligatory for large enterprises.' Roiret estimated that the eight-hour day was not being applied by 40 per cent of building firms.

[100] Fear was expressed by the railway manufacturers that the government might give small business exemption from a new law on the control of hiring and firing on 15 November 1937 (P-à-M, 41604).   [101] Lyon C de C, p-v, 27 May 1937.

[102] De Peyerimhoff had disparaged small business at the meeting of the *conseil économique et social*, in May 1936 (Zdateny, 'The Artisanat', p. 416). Small business had apparently attacked de Peyerimhoff over the reforms of the CGPF of July and August 1936 (see above).

control of the employers' movement in 1936 and 1937. This group initiated the Matignon accords. But it did so only as a short-term defensive measure 'pour éviter le pire'. It never found Matignon acceptable in the long term. This puts the reforms of the employers' movement and the mobilization of the *classes moyennes* which followed Matignon in a different light. They did not represent an attack on an industrial establishment that had imposed Matignon. Rather they were sponsored by the industrial establishment in an effort to overthrow Matignon.

Did the efforts to mobilize the *classes moyennes* achieve the ends which big business desired? In the game plan sent to Lambert Ribot immediately before Matignon it was assumed that the mobilization of the *classes moyennes* was a long-term project that would bear fruit in the elections of 1940. In fact, of course, these elections never took place. Furthermore, the Popular Front and the labour legislation imposed by Matignon were overthrown during the period 1938 to 1939. It could be argued that the collapse of the Popular Front was itself a product of the mobilization of the *classes moyennes*. The pressure which appeared to be coming from its natural electorate persuaded the Radical party to abandon its former allies and persuaded a Radical prime minister – Daladier – to dismantle the Popular Front labour legislation. No doubt there is some truth in such an analysis. But, as will be shown in the next chapter, the overthrow of the Matignon settlement had more to do with international pressures than internal French politics.

However, it would be wrong to interpret the business mobilization of 1936 and 1937 entirely in terms of cool-headed calculation. Business leaders were driven by emotion as much as reason during this period. The atmosphere in CGPF meetings must sometimes have been close to that of a court-house in seventeenth-century Salem. Conspiracy and betrayal were seen everywhere; men like Coutrot and Olivier genuinely believed that their rivals were 'agents of the two hundred families';[103] in 1937 the head of the CGPF was obliged to deny the accusation that he was secretly working in collaboration with the leader of the CGT;[104] on 11 September 1936 Brenot solemnly told the CGPF that there was a spy in its midst 'paid by the CGT to transmit information about our conversations'.[105]

There was euphoria as well as paranoia in the *patronat* during this period. Simone Weil wrote about the spirit of 'kermesse' that spread through the working classes when the strikes of 1936 freed them from the tedium of their daily working lives. But many employers also led very tedious lives – lives in which the greatest excitement of the week was a business trip to Paris or

---

[103] AN, 468 AP 8, Olivier to Coutrot, 11 October 1936.
[104] AN, 72 AS 8, p-v of *conseil central*, 9 November 1937.
[105] AN, 72 AS 6, p-v of *conseil central*, 11 September 1936.

Sunday lunch with their mother-in-law. For some of these men the upheavals in the employers' movement may have come as a positive relief. They opened up a whole new world of mass meetings, flirtation with the political parties of the extreme right, and conspiratorial closed committees. Something of the excitement that some *patrons* derived from these activities is communicated in a novel written by one of the businessmen who was most active in seeking to mobilize the *classes moyennes* – Alain Potton.[106] In this novel the hero, who bears a striking resemblance to Potton himself, is suddenly called to Paris and asked to form a government. He brings 'social progress and economic revival' to France and peace to Europe, and achieves all this within the space of a few months. There must have been many businessmen who entertained similar fantasies during the summer of 1936. Perhaps it is this element of fantasy which accounts for the note of hysteria which sometimes creeps into business rhetoric during this period. Big business leaders may have remained in the driving seat of the employers' movement, but they were not always sure where they wanted to go.

[106]   Alain Potton, *On a trouvé un chef* (Lyon, 1937).

Chapter 5

New ideologies

Introduction

One thing that all recent historians of the business reorganization have in common[1] is the belief that the *patronat* did not just wish for a return to the *status quo ante* Matignon. It is suggested that there was a wave of new thinking among French businessmen about how to organize the economy and indeed the state. This is important because the ideologies that arose seem to anticipate certain aspects of the Vichy regime. However, it will be suggested below that the new ideologies that were discussed among employers during this period did not penetrate very deeply, except within a small and unrepresentative group. Many industrialists, who were not personally sympathetic to such ideologies, saw them as tools to facilitate mobilization against the Popular Front. But they were tools which could be abandoned when they had served their purpose.

Corporatism

It is necessary to be clear about what corporatism is, or rather what it is not. Corporatism is used here to describe organization among industrialists that had a legal basis. It is not used here to describe voluntary cartels nor is it used to describe arrangements between capital and labour. There were significant degrees of light and shade within corporatist ideology. At its most

---

[1] Ingo Kolboom, *La revanche des patrons: le patronat français face au front populaire* (Paris, 1986); Patrick Fridenson, 'Le patronat français', in R. Rémond and J. Bourdin (eds.), *La France et les Français en 1938–1939* (Paris, 1978), pp. 139–58; and Adrian Rossiter, 'Corporatist Experiments in Republican France, 1916–1939' (unpublished D.Phil. thesis, University of Oxford, 1986).

moderate it could simply mean the application of legal restrictions on entry into a profession (such as those that the *loi Pullen* applied to the shoe industry). At its most extreme it could spill over into the political sphere with projects for a chamber of corporations that would have a role in government.[2]

It is easy to see why it is assumed that corporatism should have played a role in the business reorganization of the late 1930s. The changes in the business movement that occurred after 1936 coincided with a great deal of talk about the need to organize the economy on some different basis. The Conseil National Economique discussed the issue of *ententes* in 1938. Duchemin, the outgoing president of the CGPF, attributed his departure, in public at least, to an ideological change among employers: 'men are divided less about the route to be taken than about the final destination'.[3] Gignoux, his successor, was a corporatist. A number of the bodies set up among French employers after 1936, such as the CPAS or the Comité Central d'Organisation Professionnelle, propagated corporatist ideology. Corporatism was often associated with the mobilization of small business, which became a key theme among employers after 1936. When the economic commission of the CGPF debated the matter in 1939 it was the small business section of the CGPF that proposed the motion in favour of *ententes*. So widespread was the association between the new wave of business leaders and corporatism that Gignoux was obliged to deny the rumour that the CGPF had decided to press the government to give legal backing to compulsory *ententes*.[4]

But corporatism did not start with the reaction to 1936. In fact, it had been put on the agenda for debate by the attempt to institute a system of compulsory organization for the Lyon silk industry in 1935. There does not seem to have been any particular link between the new wave of organization of the *patronat* and corporatism. Indeed two of the new men in the employers' associations were explicit opponents of corporatism. Prax was opposed to obligatory *ententes*, apparently because of the traditional liberalism of the French ports.[5] Bernard was also hostile to corporatism. He had expressed this hostility during the early debate over professional organization in the textile industry in Lyon. When the issue of compulsory *ententes* was raised in 1939, by an enquiry of the Conseil National Economique, Bernard wrote an article in the bulletin of his local business

[2] Pierre Nicolle, *L'organisation corporative* (Paris, 1934).
[3] R. Duchemin, *L'organisation syndicale patronale en France* (Paris, 1940), p. 273.
[4] Paris, Archives Nationales (AN), 72 AS 8, p-v of *conseil central*, 20 January 1939.
[5] Lyon, Chamber of Commerce archives (Lyon, C de C), p-v, 14 February 1935. Chambers of port towns were reported to be 'more worried about the interests of commerce than of industry, and in complete support of liberalism'. Prax's opposition to *ententes* was said to be more moderate than that of the Bordeaux *patronat*.

associations defending voluntary associations of primary producers (that is, cartels), but attacking the idea of *ententes* in 'industries de transformation'.[6]

Bernard's attitude to corporatism is especially revealing. Firstly, judging by the contrast that he presents in his article between syndicalism and corporatism, he seems to have realized that corporatism presented a threat to his own position. A corporatist system founded on the organization of single professions and the leadership of those professions by businessmen would be bad news for a non-businessman whose power was founded on voluntary interprofessional organizations. In fact this was potentially a problem for all the leaders who had been appointed to the employers' movement after 1936, including those who were supporters of corporatism. It was a problem that would return to haunt them during the Vichy period.

Secondly, Bernard was rather muted in his opposition to corporatism. Some of Bernard's own closest associates were corporatists. Joahannes Dupraz, the editor of the AICA bulletin, was a corporatist. Bernard's ally in the FAR, Pierre Nicolle, advocated corporatism specifically as a remedy for the ills of small business. Furthermore, though Bernard expressed opposition to *ententes* in Lyon, he took a less clear stance on the national stage. During the internal debate in the economic commission of CGPF, which was stimulated by the Conseil National Economique enquiry, he confined himself to an anodyne request that the opinions of small business be taken into account.[7] This implied that he supported *ententes*, since the small business section of the CGPF had put down a motion in favour of a more organized economy. Yet the position that Bernard took in his article (that is, the defence of cartels and the attack on *ententes* in small-scale commerce) was exactly the opposite of that advocated by the representatives of small business.

It has been suggested that modernized sectors of the French economy provided especially fertile ground for corporatist doctrine.[8] This is open to considerable doubt. It is true that the CPAS, which promoted corporatist ideology, originated in the modern sector. But not all the modern industrialists behind the CPAS subscribed to this doctrine (see below). Furthermore, corporatism was also supported by many small-scale and backward industries such as those which provided support for the Comité Central d'Organisation Professionnelle.[9]

---

[6] AN, 70 AQ 420, AICA *Bulletins et documents*, 1 May 1939. See also Lyon Chamber of Commerce meeting, 17 May 1939.

[7] AN, 91 AQ 78, account of meeting of CGPF on 27 April 1939.

[8] Rossiter suggests that corporatism was popular – 'among certain highly modernized sectors of the business world' ('Corporatist Experiments', p. 307). Kolboom also associates corporatism with modern sectors of the economy (*La revanche des patrons*, p. 238).

[9] Some notable corporatist propagandists came from the wool and leather businesses (see Henry Ehrmann, *Organized Business in France* (Princeton, N.J., 1957), pp. 49 and 50). The

The fallacy of attributing corporatism to one particular sector can be revealed by an examination of the motor industry. This was the example *par excellence* of large-scale modern manufacturing. Yet, because competition was so aggressive in the industry, manufacturers had a tradition of hostility not merely to corporatism but even to voluntary industrial organization. A note in the Renault archives recalled: 'Every time that we have been obliged by circumstances to form an *entente*, it has, for one reason or another, failed to hold.'[10] Representatives of the motor industry led the opposition to corporatism in the debates of the *conseil central* of the CGPF.[11] When the issue of *ententes* was raised by the enquiry of the *conseil économique* in 1938/9 the motor industry expressed great hostility to the idea of compulsory *ententes*. Peugeot described the proposition as 'a disaster'.[12] Petiet's reply to the CNE enquiry expressed a willingness to accept *ententes* but attacked clause 419 of the proposal (that concerned with obligatory membership).[13] The Chambre Syndicale des Fabricants des Accessoires et Pièces Détachées d'Automobiles Cycles et Appareils aériens also refused to accept compulsory membership of *ententes*.[14]

Of all the manufacturers Renault was probably the most vigorously hostile to corporatism. This hostility was expressed by the support which Renault gave to the Groupement de Défense des Libertés Economiques.[15] This case shows with particular vividness how alignment on the question of corporatism could cut across the division between dynamic and traditional industries. The association had originated among the traditional and medium-sized textile manufacturers of Lyon, who resisted *ententes* because they saw them as a means by which the modern large-scale manufacturers would swallow them: 'in the end, as in many industries, it is a few big fish who vehemently wish to defend themselves from the activities of the small and medium-sized businesses'.[16] This group then found itself in alliance with one of the largest and most modern companies in the country which resisted *ententes* because it feared they would break its policy of aggressive competition. The corporatist cause in Lyon was supported by an equally heterogeneous alliance. Large-scale modern textile manufacturers (who saw *ententes* as a means of gaining control of the whole industry) were allied

Comité Central d'Organisation Professionnelle which supported corporatist projects drew most of its support from small-scale light metallurgy firms in Paris.

[10] AN, 91 AQ 78, undated.
[11] AN, 72 AS 8, Goudard's speech at the *conseil central* of 18 June 1937.
[12] AN, 91 AQ 78, Peugeot to Petiet, dated 29 December 1938.
[13] AN, 91 AQ 78, Petiet to CGPF, dated 13 June 1939.
[14] AN, 91 AQ 78, letter from Chambre Syndicale to president of economic commission of CGPF dated 27 December 1938.
[15] AN, 91 AQ 78. See also the letter, dated 22 May 1939, to Petiet asking him to send 5,000 francs to the leader of the group. Renault subsidized this group and its leader mentioned the support which it was getting from the automobile industry in its annual report of 1939.
[16] AN, 91 AQ 78, pamphlet of the Groupement de Défense des Libertés Economique.

with very small-scale traditional metal workers (who hoped that corporatism would restrain competition).

There were some contradictions in Renault's attitude to corporatism. For although he was fiercely liberal, his own right-hand man, Lehideux, was the principal, in fact just about the only, advocate of compulsory organization in the motor industry. Furthermore, Renault was closely associated with the foundation of the corporatist Comité de Prévoyance et d'Action Sociale. Indeed the corporatist propaganda of the CPAS can be found in the Renault archives mixed in with the liberal propaganda of the Groupement de Défense des Libertés Economiques.

Corporatism was not a coherent doctrine among the French *patronat* in the late 1930s. Different groups used the word to mean different things. It is clear that the artisanal metallurgists did not want the same kind of corporatism as the modern large-scale textile industrialists with whom they were allied. It is also clear that many of those who supported corporatism, such as Nicolle or Gignoux, had in fact founded their own careers on the voluntary interprofessional syndicalism that would have been rendered redundant by corporatism. Some of these contradictions were to come into the open when attempts were made to found a corporatist regime under Vichy.

But corporatism did have a role in business thinking during the late 1930s. This was for two reasons. Firstly, it was seen as a tool which facilitated the reorganization of the business movement and the mobilization against the Popular Front. A changing ideology could be used to justify changes in personnel in the employers' associations. In particular, it was more acceptable to present Duchemin's resignation as the product of dignified ideological differences than as that of personal weakness. Furthermore, corporatism was seen as an ideological banner under which it might be possible to rally large sections of the *patronat*; in this context the very ambiguity of the doctrine was an advantage. For this reason men like Renault and Bernard, who were hostile to corporatism but vigorously supportive of the mobilization against the Popular Front, were willing to associate with corporatist leaders and bodies.

Secondly, corporatism was seen as having a purely defensive role. Industrialists were deeply frightened by the prospect of state involvement in the drawing up of *ententes*, which they feared might bring worker participation and 'indiscreet examination of the account books'.[17] In the face of a dirigist government and with the prospect of war organization on the horizon, business began to feel that it was better that it should organize itself rather than wait to be organized by the government. On 18 June 1937

---

[17] AN, 72 AS 8, p-v of *conseil central* for 18 June 1937.

Serruys insisted that it was necessary for the CGPF to discuss the issue of *ententes* in order to head off a government project that would amount to 'a real sovietization of industrial *ententes*'. He stressed that 'we gave priority to the legal status of *ententes* because there is a threat of a government solution to this problem', and that 'the *patronat* looked at the problem so that they [*ententes*] should not become instruments of domination and state control'.[18]

It was fear of government action that drove the automobile industry reluctantly to accept *ententes*. A note in the Renault archives expressed this feeling:

We run the risk of being rationalized by the ministry of economics and the troops of Popular Front civil servants who would like nothing better than to get involved with our affairs... Presenting a concrete proposal to M. Spinasse would not only avoid these dangers, it might also permit our president to get certain other advantages for the industry (the forty-hour week, exports, American General Motors).[19]

The Chambre Syndicale des Pièces Détachées (the body which represented the manufacturers of motor accessories) also seems to have seen the acceptance of *ententes* as part of defensive strategy: 'such an agreement is indispensable to avoid an action that tends to provoke state control of our enterprises'.[20] The UIMM's acceptance of some degree of corporative organization was also presented as a defensive strategy: 'the profession is better equipped to defend itself in front of parliament and the authorities'.[21]

Business and the parties of the extreme right

The membership of the parties of the extreme right had always included a certain number of businessmen. However, a great many of these men joined for reasons of personal conviction that had little connection with their business lives.[22] Some, like Pucheu, seem to have been motivated by a degree

18 Ibid.   19 AN, 91 AQ 4, undated note.
20 AN, 91 AQ 4, letter to president of economic commission of CGPF, dated 27 December 1938.
21 Comment of Marcel Paul of Pont-à-Mousson, cited Rossiter, 'Corporatist Experiments', p. 315.
22 Klaus Jurgen Muller, 'French Fascism and Modernization', *Journal of Contemporary History*, 3 (1976), 76–107, at p. 82. Muller suggests that the politics of Hennessey and Coty are to be explained in terms of personal preference. Muller's article contains a number of faults which are typical of studies of the links between fascism and business. Firstly, it is based upon very limited evidence – he only names a handful of businessmen. Secondly, it relies upon arbitrary distinctions; thus the political leanings of Hennessey and Coty are dismissed as matters of personal taste while those of Pucheu and Mercier are accepted as significant illustrations of the industrial sector from which they originated. Thirdly, the definition of 'fascism' which Muller uses is hopelessly imprecise. To describe Mercier –

of idealism that made them conspicuously different from their colleagues (see below). It may be that businessmen were disproportionately represented in the leadership of such parties. But, as active and influential men, they were bound to figure prominently in almost any bourgeois organization. The fact that many businessmen led political parties may be no more significant than the fact that many businessmen led sporting clubs or boy scout troops.

The funding of right-wing parties by business is a different matter. This practice seems to have been widespread and to have increased after 1936.[23] However, funding a party did not necessarily imply a desire to see it in power. Most industrialists funded more than one of the right-wing parties. Such funding may well have been seen as a kind of insurance policy in case such a party came to power; indeed in one, admittedly unusual, area business was said to be distributing money to parties across the spectrum including the Communists.[24] Some businessmen who feared an attempt at revolution may have seen strong right-wing parties as the basis for a 'white' army should the need arise. The fact that even businessmen who were members of the chamber of deputies subsidized the extreme right suggests that such parties were regarded not as a means of displacing the democratic system but as a tool which could be used within that system. The right-wing parties could provide businessmen with a number of immediate services.

who was married to a Jewess, who dissolved Redressement Français when he felt that it had come to be associated with parties of the extreme right, who supported an alliance with Soviet Russia against Hitler and who opposed the Vichy government from the start – as a 'fascist' involves an impressive display of intellectual contortionism.

[23] Fridenson, 'Le patronat français', p. 150, suggests that Doriot's Parti Populaire Français was funded by the textile magnates of the north, motor manufacturers, grocery chain stores, the Comité des Houillères, the CPAS and the Centre de l'Industrie et du Commerce, steel firms of the east and the seven big Parisian banks (Rivaud, Vernes, Rothschild, BNCI, Banque d'Indochine, Worms and Lazard). It is hard to say how much real proof there is of the financing of right-wing parties by business. Soucy bases much of his research upon the 'archival goldmine' of the F7 series in the Archives Nationales – R. Soucy, *French Fascism: The First Wave* (New Haven, Conn., 1986). Much of the information of these archives concerning business is little more than gossip. Even company archives yield only hearsay evidence. A letter in the Pont-à-Mousson archives refers to the organization of the PPF by industrialists in Lorraine (P-à-M, 41952), while a letter in the Renault archives talks about the funding of the extreme right in Lyon by businessmen – Patrick Fridenson, *Histoire des usines Renault*, vol. I: *Naissance de la grande entreprise, 1898–1939* (Paris, 1972), p. 260. However, so far as I know, no historian has produced the internal records of a company which was subsidizing the extreme right. The problems of evidence are exacerbated by the fact that historians working in this field have a bad habit of citing each other. This creates a scholarly hall of mirrors in which tentative suggestions and insubstantial documentary evidence is magnified into an accepted orthodoxy. For example, Muller's article, which leans heavily upon the work of Soucy and Kuisel, is cited in turn by Boltanski.

[24] AN, 317 AP 87/88, 'Many industrialists and traders... give to the PSF and the PPF, but very rare are those who give as much to the second as to the first. I have been told by several reliable sources, though without any proof, that some "big fish" give to everyone, including the Communists. Insurance against a strike wherever it comes from.'

Their members could act as strikebreakers, as thugs to beat up union militants, or even perhaps as spies on the factory floor. Most of all the parties of the extreme right were a means of applying pressure to the Radical party. For, as Muller has pointed out, these parties were seen to appeal to the same electorate as the Radicals. This suggests that right-wing politics, like corporatism, was taken up by business as a means to an end; it was 'anti-parlementarisme de circonstance'.[25] When the Radicals moved out of the Popular Front and began to dismantle the labour legislation of 1936, business support for the parties of the extreme right declined.

The *avant-garde du patronat*

Not all the *patronat* regarded projects for social and economic reform as tools to be used in the struggle against the Popular Front. Certain businessmen were interested in such projects for their own sake. Such men were often members, rather than just paymasters, of the right-wing parties. They also congregated in various think tanks and discussion groups such as Redressement Français,[26] *Nouveaux Cahiers*,[27] X crise,[28] the Centre des Jeunes Patrons, the Comité Central de l'Organisation Professionnelle. This group was never ideologically coherent. Indeed the *Nouveaux Cahiers* movement had its origins in the Comité des Intellectuels Anti-Fascistes which was set up to combat the parties of the extreme right to which much of the *avant-garde* belonged.[29] What the members of these groups had in common was a network of personal contacts and an approach to life that was marked by idealism, open mindedness and, often, naivety. Their attitudes sometimes separated them sharply from the rest of business.[30] Some recognized that their political interests conflicted with their business

[25] Muller, 'French Fascism and Modernization', p. 98.
[26] Redressement Français was founded by Ernest Mercier in 1927; it was dissolved in 1935 because Mercier believed that it had developed excessively close contacts with anti-democratic parties. See Richard F. Kuisel, *Ernest Mercier: French Technocrat* (Berkeley, Calif., 1967).
[27] The group which was behind the *Nouveaux Cahiers* first came together in 1934. *Nouveaux Cahiers* was published between 1937 and 1940. See Richard F. Kuisel, 'Auguste Detoeuf, Conscience of French Industry 1926–1947', *International Review of Social History*, 20 (1975), 149–74; and Michael Blain, 'Un aspect des idées patronales dans l'entre-deux-guerres: A. Deteouf et les "Nouveaux Cahiers"' (Mémoire de maîtrise, Université de Paris X, Nanterre, 1973).
[28] X crise was, as the name suggests, a study group of alumni of the Ecole Polytechnique. See Philippe Bauchard, *Les technocrates et le pouvoir* (Paris, 1966).
[29] It is interesting to note that personal links within the *avant-garde du patronat* did cross the ideological frontiers between *Nouveaux Cahiers* and the parties of the extreme right. See the letter from Pucheu to Barnaud cited in chapter 12.
[30] It is hard to believe that many businessmen would have enjoyed the company of Jean-Paul Sartre, who attended a *Nouveaux Cahiers* meeting on education in 1937.

activities. Pucheu, for example, felt obliged to resign from Pont-à-Mousson as he became increasingly involved in Redressement Français and the Croix de Feu.[31] Others might better be described as intellectuals or campaigners who made their living in business rather than as businessmen.

To catch the flavour of the *avant-garde*, and to illustrate the gulf that could exist between its members and ordinary businessmen, it is worth pausing to examine two examples: Jean Coutrot and Jacques Warnier. Coutrot was a graduate of the Ecole Polytechnique who worked in the firm belonging to his father-in-law. However, he does not seem to have been a particularly competent manager.[32] Indeed it is hard to believe that he was able to spend any time at all in his factory. For, when he was not attending meetings of X crise, the *Nouveaux Cahiers* group and the CCOP, Coutrot was producing books and articles or writing hundreds of letters discussing every conceivable issue, in a tone of the utmost seriousness, with correspondents who ranged from Aldous Huxley to an obscure school-teacher in Bucharest.[33] Many of Coutrot's projects verged on the absurd: Alfred Sauvy reports that he once calculated the total savings that might be made to French energy supplies if housewives could be persuaded to place their saucepans properly on their stoves.[34] Coutrot tried to persuade business to adopt his plans for increasing efficiency, but he moved in a milieu which often despised the grubby 'worldliness' of ordinary businessmen.[35]

Jacques Warnier was a textile industrialist based in Reims. Not living in Paris, and not having had the dubious benefits of a *grande école* education, he was less absorbed in the *avant-garde* than Coutrot. However, Warnier too spent increasing amounts of his time away from his factory corresponding with like-minded men and attending meetings. He became a vigorous supporter of proposals for corporatist organization of the economy and an active member of the Centre des Jeunes Patrons. Like Coutrot, Warnier seems to have regarded his participation in these movements as an alternative to, rather than an extension of, his business life. Indeed Warnier did toy briefly with the idea of leaving Reims altogether to devote himself to the Centre des Jeunes Patrons in Paris, and, in a rather touching memoir, Warnier's widow recalls that he was unhappy running the business that he had inherited until he discovered the new world opened up by business politics.[36]

---

[31] Pierre Pucheu, *Ma vie* (Paris, 1948), p. 185.

[32] According to Bauchard, Coutrot merely played a minor role in the enterprise run by his father in law: Bauchard, *Les technocrats au pouvoir*.

[33] See Coutrot's extensive correspondence in his archives in AN, 468 AP.

[34] Bauchard, *Les technocrats au pouvoir*.

[35] AN, 468 AP 8, Olivier to Coutrot, dated 15 October 1936: 'unfortunately we were joined by people who brought a tone that was wordly rather than technical to our conversation'.

[36] AN, 57 AS 28, Renseignements sur la personalité de Jacques Warnier.

The leaders of the mainstream business movement were usually well aware of the gulf between themselves and many members of the business *avant-garde*. They stressed the youth and inexperience of those involved in these movements; the Centre des Jeunes Patrons was often dismissed with the words 'Quand on est jeune on n'est pas patron, et quand on est patron on n'est pas jeune.'[37] Sometimes hostility was expressed in more fierce terms. In the *conseil central* of the CGPF, Goudard asked whether the CCOP served any useful purpose.[38] Baron Petiet, the head of the social section of the CGPF, was even more blunt. He replied to a letter from the Commission Générale d'Organisation Scientifique (CEGOS) saying 'I know almost nothing of CEGOS and, unfortunately, I have more important things to occupy me'.[39]

Some historians have suggested that, although the *avant-garde* was not representative of business as a whole, it did have special links with one particular sector of business: that made up of modernized dynamic industries. This theory has been expressed in very general terms by Müller who suggests that the modern industries turned to radical political solutions because of dissatisfaction with the limitations imposed upon economic development by the stalemate society.[40] However, the assumption that the nature of French society did provide restraints upon industrial modernization is one that deserves to be subjected to severe criticism in the light of the recent economic history of France.[41] Furthermore, Müller's theory is based upon remarkably little evidence. It is true that two modern industrialists, Mercier and Detoeuf, were prominent among those who proposed radical social and economic reforms.[42] But these movements were also supported by men from older, less technologically advanced industries; for example, Pucheu and Romier, supporters of Redressement Français, were both associated with Pont-à-Mousson, a firm noted for its resistance to industrial modernity.[43]

On a more limited scale it might be suggested that there were certain specific links between modern industries and the ideologies advanced in the *avant-garde du patronat*. Firstly, it might be argued that the enthusiasm for international co-operation at a political level displayed by men like

[37] Henri Weber, *Le parti des patrons: le CNPF (1946–1986)* Paris, 1986), p. 118.
[38] AN, 72 AS 8, p-v of *conseil central*, 17 March 1939.
[39] AN, 72 AS 9, 8 February 1938.
[40] Müller, 'French Fascism and Modernization'.
[41] For a summary of the revisionist interpretation of French economic history see Rondo Cameron and Charles Freedman, 'French Economic Growth: A Radical Revision', *Social Science History*, 7 (1983), 3–30.
[42] There were also two other industrialists from the electrical sector involved in *Nouveaux Cahiers* – André Isambert, director of the Compagnie Générale d'Electricité and Henry Davezac, director of the Syndicat Général de la Construction Electrique.
[43] Alain Baudaint, *Pont-à-Mousson (1919–1939): stratégies industrielles d'une dynastie lorraine* (Paris, 1980), p. 186.

Detoeuf and de Tarde was in part a product of their background in industries when there was a degree of international co-operation at a business level.[44] Similarly it might be suggested that the enthusiasm for good labour relations in these circles was a particular characteristic of mechanized industries where wages accounted for a small proportion of total costs. But both these suggestions run up against powerful counter-examples. The enthusiasm for international co-operation shown by Detoeuf was matched by the fierce anti-Germanism of Mercier. Similarly the liberal attitude towards labour relations adopted by some industrialists in high technology industries connected with *Nouveaux Cahiers* is balanced by the combative attitude of similar firms involved in the Comité de Prévoyance et d'Action Sociale.

Many members of the *avant-garde du patronat* felt that the events of 1936 might make it possible for their ideas to escape from the intellectual ghetto in which they had been nurtured and to gain some acceptance in the mainstream employers' associations. During this period it seemed that the *patronat* was abandoning its traditional individualism and showing an increased willingness to organize. Furthermore, the talk about the decline of liberalism and the need for compulsory organization which was common currency among the *avant-garde* was heard in the mainstream employers' organizations. Pucheu and Loustau greeted business's increased willingness to organize enthusiastically.[45] The *Nouveaux Cahiers* group followed the reforms in the employers' movement with interest.

But the very zest with which the *avant-garde* approached the events of 1936 marked their separation from the rest of business. Whereas the *avant-garde* regarded a more organized economy as a good thing in itself most businessmen merely viewed the reforms in the employers' movement as an irksome necessity. They were only interested in new economic ideologies as a means to an end. Most of all, attitudes to labour divided the *avant-garde* from the rest of business. As far as mainstream business was concerned the labour victory of 1936 was a problem to be solved, while the members of the *avant-garde* saw it as an opportunity that would open the way to healthier relations between workers and bosses.[46] Indeed union leaders attended

[44] Detoeuf was a director of Alsthom, an electrical company. De Tarde was director of the Compagnie des Chemins de Fer de l'Est. In 1922 de Tarde had proposed a system of European cartels to settle the problem of reparations (Ehrmann, *Organized Business*, p. 48).

[45] Pucheu and Loustau drafted a note on the organization of employers in September 1936. It was obvious that even by this stage they were beginning to feel disappointment at the failure of radical reform in the employers' movement – 'It is to be feared that the employers' organization will remain what it was before the June events...a powerless and incoherent mass of bodies existing in semi-lethargy (except during the period when the awards of the *légion d'honneur* are announced).' Enclosed in letter of 6 September 1940, Pucheu to Barnaud (AN, F 37 77).

[46] Courtot saw the strikes as a 'psychological cure': Luc Boltanski, *The Making of a Class: Cadres in French Society* (Cambridge, 1987), p. 71.

Nouveaux Cahiers meetings.[47] The distinction between ordinary business and the *avant-garde* was marked sharply by the manner in which they recalled 1936. Most businessmen described the period as a nightmare, while the *avant-garde* nostalgically recalled 'les beaux jours de 1936'.[48]

There was one group within the business movement with which the *avant-garde* did have something in common. This was the group of new leaders who rose in the employers' movement after 1936. Like the *avant-garde* these men had an ideological agenda that sprang from conviction rather than strategy; many of them were corporatists. The similarities between the beliefs of the two groups were to be reflected in the fact that after 1940 they both provided some of the most enthusiastic participants in Vichy's projects for a new economic organization. However, underneath these apparent similarities there were important differences. Socially and culturally the *Nouveaux Cahiers* group, who, with their connections with the worlds of big business, high finance and administration, looked like the incarnation of the two hundred families, were light years away from those who purported to represent the *classes moyennes*. The 'corporatism' of the *avant-garde* included provision for the working class, whereas that of the leadership of the CGPF dealt only with employers. Furthermore, the liberal attitude to labour relations taken by the *avant-garde du patronat* was hardly likely to appeal to the leaders of the CGPF at a time when opposition to organized labour was the main plank in their political platform. Indeed the new leadership of the CGPF seem to have been vigorously hostile to the members of the *avant-garde du patronat*. In an article published in 1940 Aymé Bernard went out of his way to describe Sweden, held up by the *Nouveaux Cahiers* group as the paradigm of social harmony, as a nation rotted by Marxism.[49]

The hopes that some members of the *avant-garde* of the *patronat* had of the new leadership that arose in the business movement after 1936, and the frail foundations on which those hopes were built, emerges from the correspondence between Jean Coutrot and Maurice Olivier during the summer of 1936. The two men did not approve of the change that had occurred at the head of the CGPF; they believed that Gignoux's appointment

[47] Fridenson ('Le patronat français', pp. 139–55) compares the meetings between workers and bosses which took place under the aegis of the *Nouveaux Cahiers* group to the meetings which had taken place during the First World War under the aegis of Albert Thomas. Nothing could be further from the truth. The meetings of the First World War had involved hard-headed businessmen who were normally unsympathetic to labour, not idealistic reformers. They had discussed immediate and specific matters, not general schemes for the reordering of society. Most of all the pattern of labour relations which prevailed in a war economy was the opposite to that which prevailed in the aftermath of 1936 (see chapter 6).

[48] AN, F 37 77, letter from Pucheu to Barnaud dated 6 September 1940. Pucheu enclosed what he described as 'quelques péchés de jeunesse commis avec Robert LOUSTAU aux beaux jours de 1936'.

[49] *Documentation*, 15 March 1940. The journal of AICA changes its title several times over the course of the next six years without any apparent change of editorial control or policy.

had been fixed by the heavy industrial power brokers.[50] However, they were more optimistic about the newly formed CPAS under the leadership of Colonel Brenot; Coutrot suggested that it might be possible for the CCOP and the CPAS to co-ordinate their efforts. On the face of it such a suggestion looks reasonable; both bodies were advocating corporatist organization of the economy. However, the kind of corporatism envisaged by Coutrot and Brenot could not have been more different. For the latter was to be one of the most vigorously anti-labour leaders of the *revanche des patrons* while the former had greeted the strikes as a 'psychological cure'. Furthermore, at the very time that he was in contact with Brenot, Coutrot was also seeking the backing of Belin and Jouhaux for a scheme of compulsory *ententes*.[51] The fact that Coutrot could have imagined that the leaders of the CGT and their most outspoken opponents could mean the same thing when they talked of 'ententes' says a great deal about the vagueness of corporatist doctrine. It also says something about the confused conditions of 1936 and the naivety of Coutrot and his associates.

[50] AN, 368 AP 8, Coutrot to Olivier, dated 11 October 1936.
[51] Ibid., Olivier to Coutrot, 30 July 1936.

Chapter 6

The counter-attack

The restoration of authority by individual employers

The previous chapter described the changes in the organization of the employers in France and the attempt to mobilize a broad current of opinion in response to the Popular Front. But in fact much of the business counter-attack was carried out on a much smaller scale, that is to say by individual employers seeking to restore their authority within their own factories. This authority had been challenged by the strikes of the summer of 1936, and the regime established after those strikes presented a similar challenge. Employers had lost a psychological advantage by their very visible defeat. Reports of disruption in the Renault archives show the effect of this loss. The atmosphere of *kermesse* that had characterized the strikes continued after their end: at one point two drunken delegates dressed up as Spanish militiamen and entertained their colleagues with a song and dance routine.[1] There were endless reports of petty delinquency.[2] Furthermore, increasing unionization and the institution of workers' delegates meant that there was an alternative hierarchy to that established by managers. Alongside the formal demands made by the unions relating to pay and conditions there was a struggle for mastery within the factory. Many conflicts sprang from the attempts of workers to influence the running of the workplace. In January 1937 the workers in the polishing shop walked out in protest at the alleged lowering of quality of the work performed.[3] On 15 February 1937 one of the delegates requested that a particular foreman be posted to a workshop. In September 1937 workshops 92 and 124 refused to do certain tasks that they claimed belonged to other sections of the factory.[4]

---

[1] Paris, Archives Nationales (AN), 91 AQ 16, report by M. Freycinet of 12 January 1937.
[2] AN, 91 AQ 16, note by Duvernoy dated 6 December 1937 about a delegate using his status to avoid searches and steal material from the factory.
[3] AN, 91 AQ 16, note dated 23 January 1937.
[4] AN, 91 AQ 16, note of Rosenblatt, 28 September 1937.

The reaction of Renault management to these disruptions is interesting. For the Renault workforce was undoubtedly highly unionized and especially influenced by the Communist party. Renault management was one of the few that had expressed fears of outright revolution during the summer of 1936 (see chapter 4). The personnel officer of Renault – Duvernoy – continued to present almost hysterical fears about the revolutionary content of worker organization in his communications with business organizations. Thus, writing to the GIMMCP on 11 August 1937, Duvernoy quoted a CGT pamphlet: 'the bosses are a cancer on the social laws, which we will cut out', and continued: 'Let us reflect on this aphorism and ask if the employers should continue their discussions with those who openly want to exterminate them.'[5] To the UIMM he painted an even more lurid picture of the threat:

M. Duvernoy ... made it known that all the shop stewards had been organized under the Communist banner, that a big conference of the Communist party had taken place eight days ago, in the course of which the following plan of action had been established, (1st) stage control of hiring, (2nd) stage introduction of shop stewards into company boards, (3rd) stage total eviction of company boards. M. Duvernoy guaranteed the accuracy of this information.[6]

Yet in its internal notes the tone in which the Renault management described these incidents was one of irritation rather than fear. They regarded them as symptoms of bolshiness not Bolshevism. That is to say, they perceived them as inconvenient impediments to production rather than as part of a wider threat to the whole regime. Certainly the obstruction of production was frequently cited as the chief problem with the atmosphere in the factories. Thus Renault spoke of 'ill will, a systematic refusal to work at the pace required'.[7]

The campaign to restore employer authority was focused on particular individuals. Once again this suggests that employers saw their problem as one of labour discipline rather than revolutionary threat; there is no point in trying to isolate troublemakers in your own plant if the whole capitalist system is likely to be brought down. The files of Renault and Etablissements Arbel contain almost incredibly detailed information on employees seen as troublemakers. Arbel suggested that such information be sought immediately after the strikes and hinted at the lengths to which it expected its managers to go in obtaining such information: 'It would even be desirable for you to use your contacts in the judiciary to get access to the special files

---

[5] AN, 39 AS 836.
[6] Blois, Pont-à-Mousson archive (P-à-M), 41604, report of meeting of UIMM, 20 January 1937.   [7] AN, 91 AQ 65, note, 8 November 1937.

containing judgements passed on individuals even when these led to an amnesty.'[8] There is evidence that some companies hired men specifically to spy on their colleagues. Interest in workers extended well beyond the factory gate. Renault received reports about what workers were doing while on sick leave: 'M. Serre was told that various people had met M. Pythoud, who appeared to be well, after all, and that he told them that he was recruiting for Spain.'[9] The Arbel management drew up a list of all the Communist members in the company. This list revealed very detailed knowledge. The Communists in factory 3 were divided into 'leading members and active members'. The opinions of individuals were cited: 'In 1936 he said "we need the Popular Front to deal with Arbel".' Even the families of militants were scrutinized: 'A man of little interest, abandoned his wife and several children.'[10] Indeed Arbel's interest extended beyond the point at which an individual left the firm (see below).

Employers sought to undermine the alternative hierarchy of union authority in the plants. Workers' delegates were the most irritatingly visible sign of this hierarchy, and employers attempted to impede the elections of these officials. Arbel's Paris office wrote with reference to these elections: 'it is vital to drag things out a bit'.[11] There was a vigorous hunt for foreign delegates or delegates with a criminal record, who could be declared ineligible. Managers struggled to limit the role of delegates as much as possible. A circular from the GIMMCP stressed that delegates should not be allowed their own offices. The Renault personnel department complained about the free movement of delegates through the factory, and, eventually, Renault tried to institute a system of identity cards to control these movements.[12] Manifestations of union authority, such as the alleged control of hiring and firing or the pressure applied to workers to join unions, were bitterly resented by employers.[13]

Foremen were an important part of the reassertion of employer authority. The detailed information about workers and factory floor incidents that fills business archives was almost invariably provided by foremen. They also provided the logical counter to the authority of the workers' delegates. Six years later an employer, giving evidence to the Riom trial, was to describe the erosion of the authority of foremen as one of the worst consequences of

---

[8] AN, 70 AQ 300, Paris to Douai, 16 June 1936.
[9] AN, 91 AQ 16, note of 15 February 1937.
[10] AN, 70 AQ 300, undated list. The interest in the family situation of employees is not as bizarre as it may seem. It was widely recognized that men with wives and children to support were more stable and disciplined workers: see Alain Baudaint, *Pont-à-Mousson (1919–1939): stratégies industrielles d'une dynastie lorraine* (Paris, 1980), p. 113.
[11] AN, 70 AQ 300, Paris to Douai, 16 June 1936.
[12] AN, 91 AQ 16, note of 3 September 1936.
[13] AN, 91 AQ 65, report dated 17 January 1938 of intimidation of Mme Clément.

the strikes of 1936.[14] Restitution of the authority of the *porion* was one of the first aims of the board of the Anzin mines after the strikes; 'with regard to the re-establishment of the chief pit deputy', it expressed its wish 'that everything be done to restore the confidence of the underground foremen and to steadily rebuild their authority'.[15] In a letter to the prefect of the Nord the management of Etablissements Arbel enlarged on the damage which a decline in the authority of foremen would entail: 'It is impossible to keep the plant working without foremen. But our foremen have suffered an intolerable reduction in authority since the strikes. They have seen the shop stewards interfering in every matter: discipline, production, organization of work, hiring, firing.'[16]

As suggested in chapter 4, business sponsorship of the *cadres* movement was not simply a part of the attempt to mobilize the *classes moyennes*. It had a much more immediate use as a means of restoring factory discipline. Thus, while employers' associations sponsored the *cadres* organizations, individual employers were increasingly interested in the mechanics of how *cadres* could be recruited, trained and used in a particular company. Agencies purporting to represent the *cadres* seem to have been aware that they appealed to employers on these two levels. When the Union des Agents de Maîtrise Anciens Combattants addressed an appeal to the CIMMCP it presented itself as part of the broad political mobilization of the *classes moyennes*, the 'Front Constitutionnel'. It stressed that it aimed to 'to prepare the organization of the *cadres* of the nation and especially foremen in industry' to encourage 'non-internationalist members of parliament to define the limits beyond which they would be obliged to dissociate themselves from their allies'.[17] But, when appealing to an individual company, the association stressed the much more direct benefit that its members could bring by acting as spies and stoolpigeons:

It is at the level of unskilled workers that foremen have already been recruited and sent all over France to the regions of their choice... UNIGMAI has set itself to search throughout France for staff who are absolutely safe, and committed to avoid political activity, chosen from among foremen to be introduced in certain factories, in order to know what is going on, to spread sound doctrine among the workers and to struggle against the CGT and the CGTU.[18]

[14] M. de l'Eauville, manager of a textile factory, cited in *Le Figaro* (11 March 1942).
[15] AN, 109 MI5, p-v of CA, 24 July 1936.
[16] AN, 70 AQ 300, letter to préfet du Nord dated 21 September 1936.
[17] AN, 39 AS 941. A letter dated 24 June 1936 from the Union claims that it is forming a Front Français Constitutionnel to oppose 'Sovietisation'. There is also a letter from Front Français dated 18 June 1936 from which the passage which I quote is taken.
[18] AN, 70 AQ 300, letter from the Union dated 17 March 1937.

Employers and the strike of 30 November 1938

The employers had their chance to restore authority after the strike of 30 November 1938. This restoration of authority was concentrated around particular individuals. In theory, the breach of contract involved in the strike gave employers the freedom to sack strikers or to rehire them with a new contract. The employers' response seems to have involved precise discrimination. Before the strike the GIMMCP had stressed the need to distinguish among employees and pick out particular troublemakers: 'precise and individual faults need to be punished immediately'.[19] This was done. Factories could weed their workforce in one of three ways. Firstly, they could simply sack all those who had struck. Secondly, they could eliminate particular strikers who were seen as troublesome. Thirdly, strikers who were rehired could be punished by loss of social security rights and privileges associated with a certain period of employment in the firm – it was of special significance that strikers no longer had the one year of unbroken service necessary to be eligible as a delegate.

The UIMM reviewed the range of options pursued by its members.[20] Bordeaux refused to rehire at all; in Cail workers were hired with the loss of privileges; in Valenciennes some workers were fired; in Mauberge workers were rehired unless they were the subject of some more specific complaint.

Individual business archives provide a more sharply focused picture of the action taken. Fives-Lille rehired all but eight of its 3,700 workers.[21] Pont-à-Mousson rehired strikers except for 'meneurs', but a formal gesture of submission was required in the form of a written request to be rehired, and new contracts were imposed so that strikers lost their privileges.[22] Etablissements Arbel explored the disciplinary possibilities opened up by the strike with relish. A list was established of all strikers, and each case was then examined by a conference of management and foremen. Employers went to some lengths to stress the role of foremen in the handling of the strikes:[23] 'We drew up together, in a conference with all the heads of department, the list of workers to be immediately rehired, those to be taken on when there was work for them, and finally those who for the moment

---

[19]   AN, 39 AS 852, p-v of CA, 29 November 1938.
[20]   P-à-M, 41952, report, UIMM meeting, 14 December 1938.
[21]   AN, 198 AQ 14, report to board meeting of 8 December 1938.
[22]   P-à-M, 41721, report to *conseil d'administration* of 14 December 1938: 'In fact we have rehired the majority of workers, other than the troublemakers, but those rehired have signed a request to be rehired and their contract dates from their reintegration.'
[23]   Some foremen at Renault spent thirty consecutive hours at work preparing the list of those to be disciplined: Bertrand Badie, 'Les grèves du front populaire aux usines Renault', *Le mouvement social*, 81 (1972), 69–109.

had to be made unemployed and would thus remain sacked.'[24] It was clear that the choice of those to be dismissed was heavily influenced by the desire to crack down on troublemakers – one of the first to be sacked was the man who had headed Arbel's list of Communist militants. The whole process was staged to provide a symbolic reversal of the *patronat*'s defeat of 1936. Arbel management stressed that it was because the workers' delegates had insisted on a notice of dismissal that workers were liable to sanctions for breach of contract.[25] Arbel responded to a request by the sub-prefect to rehire one worker with an ironic reference to the atmosphere of collaboration which the conciliation legislation of 1936 had hoped to create in the workplace: 'it seems that Waillaume disturbs this very atmosphere'.[26]

When workers were rehired it was done with an almost ceremonial gesture of submission. Arbel workers were obliged to make a formal request in order to have their jobs restored. They were then faced with the possibility of losing their social security provision. However, as 'a measure of special goodwill' Arbel management waived their right to enforce this penalty.[27] In order to regain their right to social security workers were obliged to sign a form stating that they sought no legal redress against the company. The management seem to have regarded signature of this form as an admission of surrender on the part of individual workers. Each day the names of the workers who had come forward to sign, and even a description of the manner in which they signed, were sent to the head office in Paris. The head office regarded this information with intense interest. When Douai reported that one worker had signed 'without prejudice to his legal rights', the Paris office noted: 'this confirms the opinion that we have always had of this worker'.[28]

The employers' attitude to those workers who were sacked outright was somewhat ambiguous. Fridenson suggests that in fact the employers used the strikes to effect a reduction of their personnel which was in their economic interest anyway.[29] He quotes a note written by Louis Renault in December 1938:

From this time on, had we been only concerned with the immediate interest of our factories, we would have laid off a large part of the workforce. Economic and political circumstances obliged us to wait... At the beginning of September... the undue size of the workforce was even more apparent than before. External

[24] AN, 70 AQ 300, note dated 2 December 1938.
[25] AN, 70 AQ 300, note from Paris, 3 December 1938.
[26] AN, 70 AQ 300, Arbel to sous préfet, 15 June 1939.
[27] AN, 70 AQ 300, Paris to Douai, 3 December 1938.
[28] AN, 70 AQ 300, Douai to Paris, 13 December 1938 and Paris to Douai, 14 December.
[29] R. Rémond and J. Bourdin (eds.), *La France et les Français en 1938–1939* (Paris, 1978), p. 147.

circumstances – the threat of war, the arrival of the decree laws – still obliged us to wait... The matter was still being considered when the strike of 24 November broke out. The lay-offs that we have been reluctant to make for fear of repercussions that might be engendered, because of their political importance, were now effected by the breach of contract resulting from the strike by our workers.

Presumably the political restraint, to which Renault referred, was the need to sustain the plausibility of the case against the forty-hour week, which rested on the claim that the factories were overburdened with work. The archives of Etablissements Arbel confirm that, although the choice of those to be sacked was certainly dictated by disciplinary considerations, a reduction of the labour force was economically desirable. In an internal note Arbel remarked: 'in any case we have rehired all those for whom we have work'.[30]

However, the *revanche patronale* did not end with the dismissals of November 1938. It was widely suggested that there existed a 'carnet B du patronat' of those undesirable workers who had been sacked. Bourdé also suggests that companies went to some lengths to avoid hiring troublemakers. It is true that the UIMM sought to ensure that workers dismissed by one firm were not hired by another. However, what is interesting about this measure is that it was initiated, not by a company seeking to avoid hiring activists, but by one trying to prevent its former workers from being hired.[31] Arbel also took a considerable interest in its former employees: 'It would be interesting to check up on what has happened to the other workers who broke their contracts of employment.'[32] What was the reason for this interest? It might be explained by the desire to leave troublemakers conspicuously unemployed like highwaymen hung at gibbets 'pour encourager les autres'. Such an explanation would suit the employers' obsession with their authority. Alternatively, employers might have been aware that eventually they would need to hire those that they had fired, for the sackings had occurred very largely in those firms which would benefit most from rearmament and which would therefore most need labour in 1939. In fact as the rearmament programme accelerated this was exactly what happened.[33] The Arbel archives suggest an awareness of the possibility that rehirings would eventually be necessary; the note of 12 December referred to those '*for the time being* had to be laid off'. In fact Arbel seems to have hoped that those who had been sacked on 30 November would eventually display an adequate degree of contrition and willingness to mend their ways. On 20 June 1939 Arbel management wrote a report on

[30] AN, 70 AQ 300, Paris to Douai, 12 December.
[31] AN, 91 AQ 16, letter of UIMM to Hispano Suiza acknowledging this request of 29 November 1938.   [32] AN, 70 AQ 300, Paris to Douai, 12 December.
[33] Monique Luirard, *La région stéphanoise dans la guerre et dans la paix 1936–1951* (Saint-Etienne, 1980), p. 265.

a worker who had been sacked nine months previously, and who had worked for a while for another firm. The management now seemed to be considering rehiring this worker. They seemed satisfied that he had learnt his lesson: 'Some say that this worker ought to have said that he was a victim of his own ideas but that through pride, he has preferred to say nothing.'[34]

In the eyes of the *patronat* the crushing of the strike seems to have achieved its result. It was seen as having produced a more disciplined and passive labour force. The board of Fives-Lille were told, on 22 December 1938, that 'since the dismissals, the mood of the workers had changed remarkably and overtime is performed without difficulty'.[35] A Renault note reported that 'the majority of workers, who have been asked by the foremen, seem to realize that they allowed themselves to get mixed up in a purely political strike, and to regret the loss of salary...which, in general, amounts to that of eight working days'. The note anticipated an improvement in productivity: 'Though precise figures cannot be given there seems to have been a remarkable rise in production in various workshops.'[36]

The role of the employers' organizations

It would be wrong to suggest that the *revanche patronale* can be examined entirely in terms of relations between individual employers and their workers. The increasingly strong position of employers owed much to the activities of the employers' associations. The first task of these associations in the aftermath of Matignon was defensive. For they were not confronted with the prospect of fresh legislation that would further erode the power of the employer. In particular employers feared that they would be subjected to the compulsory arbitration of labour disputes and that control of hiring and firing would be undertaken by the state. In the face of this threat some businessmen favoured a policy of outright confrontation; they suggested that employers should seek to bring down the government by boycotting work on the Paris exposition of 1937[37] or that they should organize a general lock-out.[38] But the leaders of the business associations preached restraint to

---

[34] AN, 70 AQ 300, note undated and unsigned attached to a union request of 27 July 1939 for this worker to be rehired.
[35] AN, 198 AQ 14, report to board meeting of 8 December 1938.
[36] AN, 91 AQ 16, note of 8 December 1938.
[37] AN, 72 AS 8, p-v of *conseil central* of CGPF for 25 February 1937; de Peyerimhoff argued against the project.
[38] P-à-M, 41604, report of UIMM meeting for 14 April 1937; the lock-out was proposed by Lobstein as a means of resisting a law seeking to impose control of hiring and firing. On

their members. The head of the social section of the CGPF described three employers in terms that said much about his overall strategy: 'they are very calm, not *patrons de combat* but *patrons de résistance*'.[39] The business associations wanted to resist fresh labour legislation with a slow rearguard action. They aimed, not to prevent new laws entirely, but to delay their application and to dilute their content. It was suggested that the CGPF should not break off talks with the government over arbitration but rather seek to stall them with petty objections: 'find a flaw, and our negotiators are clever enough to find one'.[40] Employers' leaders even tried to make deals with the government by offering to accept arbitration if only they were spared a law regulating their rights to hire and fire.[41] Such a tactic may have been successful for, while arbitration was introduced in December 1936, no law was passed to regulate hiring and firing, though the threat of such legislation hung over employers until the outbreak of war in 1940.

Once labour legislation was in place there was even less to gain from frontal assault. But what the *patronat* could try to do was play the system. Employers' organizations had to co-ordinate their approach and discipline their members in order to extract every possible concession. These tactics can be illustrated with reference to the forty-hour week. There was a constant petty struggle over the interpretation and administration of rules. Endless attempts were made to present special cases and extract special concessions. Practically every sector of the economy had some special reason why the forty-hour legislation should not be applied to it: for commerce it was the need to remain open when workers were free to shop;[42] for the motor industry it was the seasonal nature of demand for its product;[43] for foundries it was the need to keep furnaces running continuously.[44] The manufacturers of rolling stock recognized that their previous appeals for more work would make any request for exemption from the forty-hour week law unconvincing: 'the position is very delicate for manufacturers of rolling stock; they cannot ask for exemption because they have a surfeit of work, because they constantly claim that they do not have enough work'. They hit on the formula of claiming that they had a shortage of specialist workers: 'It was therefore necessary to link this question of the forty-hour week with that of hiring for railway workshops of specialist workers from

---

9 July 1936 Pont-à-Mousson's own representative said that he would rather close the firm than accept government control of hiring and firing.
[39] AN, 72 AS 8, p-v of *conseil central*, CGPF, 19 March 1937.
[40] Aymé Bernard in AN, 72 AS 7, 20 November 1936.
[41] Report of meeting between Lambert Ribot and Blum, in P-à-M, 41604.
[42] Paris, Chamber of Commerce archives (C de C), p-v, 14 April 1937.
[43] AN, 91 AQ 4, note from Chambre Syndicale de l'Automobile to Renault, 25 September 1936.
[44] P-à-M, 41952, report of meeting of Comité des Forges, 15 October 1936.

private industry.'[45] The shortage of specialist workers seems to have become a standard theme of business complaints. Indeed it is clear that much of the academic debate about the economic effect of the forty-hour week is founded upon the deliberately manipulated information provided by business.[46] Employers themselves recognized that their claims were sometimes balanced upon precarious foundations: 'He admitted that these arguments were hardly firm, but one has to defend one's interests all the same.'[47]

Similar tactics were applied to negotiations over pay. Once again delay was the key. The head of the social section of the CGPF advised employers to seize every opportunity to avoid immediate implementation of pay rises. On 18 December 1936 he said: 'If you are subject to demands for rises you have only to refer it to matters under discussion, which will allow you to gain time';[48] On 1 September 1937 he said: 'the enquiry into productivity will provide an excellent pause to put off this increase for a little longer'.[49]

The willingness to work within the system and exploit whatever advantages could be obtained was particularly evident in the handling of compulsory arbitration. When the arbitration system was introduced it was regarded with horror by employers: 'I believe that all the social measures of which we have talked are as nothing compared to this, that is to say the employers' loss of authority, which takes us by the nose.'[50] Though the employers resented the system of arbitration they sought to co-ordinate their activities in order to exploit it as much as possible. The new social service of the CGPF gave a great deal of advice on the handling of the new system. Employers were kept informed about its working, and details of 'a series of recent arbitration decisions with which the employers might support their case'[51] were circulated. Business journals contained detailed accounts of the latest 'sentences en cours'. The employers' organizations also advised members how to avoid arbitration at times when the process might be against their interests. The GIMMCP sought to restrain the enthusiasm of Citroën and Renault for a showdown with the unions in April 1938; Villey alerted them to the disadvantages of 'an arbitration that, in view of the precedents, would certainly occur in unfavourable circumstances'.[52] The

---

[45] P-à-M, 41604, report of meeting of syndicate, 16 November 1938.
[46] See Jean Charles Asselain, 'Une erreur de politique économique: la loi des quarante heures de 1936', *Revue économique*, 25 (1974) 672–705.
[47] P-à-M, 41604, UIMM file report meeting of 15 October. The Pont-à-Mousson representative is commenting upon Petiet's suggestion that they seek to prove the non-existence of unemployment in their industry.
[48] AN, 72 AS 7, p-v of *conseil central* of CGPF for 18 December 1936.
[49] AN, 72 AS 8, p-v of *conseil central* of CGPF for 1 September 1937.
[50] AN, 72 AS 8, Lobstein addressing *conseil central* of CGPF on 22 February 1937.
[51] AN, 39 AS 836, 13 June 1938.
[52] AN, 39 AS 852, transcript of *conseil d'administration* for 30 April 1938.

head of the social section of the CGPF stressed that 'as far as possible you must avoid dismissing people on the advice of foremen, if the foreman has made a mistake the employer is compromised'.[53] Employers were advised on how to avoid having particular cases submitted to arbitration. They were reminded repeatedly that cases involving individual rather than collective grievances were not legitimate objects for the arbitration system.[54]

The business syndicates also sought to ensure that the arbitration tribunals themselves became more favourable to the *patronat*. Thus they took a keen interest in the selection of employers' representatives on these tribunals. It was noted that 'it is up to the federation to do the impossible regarding this matter to ensure discipline among employers to match that which the workers' unions display'.[55] How successful these measures were is not entirely clear. The CGPF claimed, in a note for internal circulation, that the predicament of the *patronat* had actually worsened: 'The experience of more than a year allows us to say that the jurisprudence of the court has evolved in a manner...most unfavourable to the most legitimate interests and the least debatable rights of the employers'.[56] However, at the same time, Lambert Ribot expressed satisfaction with the way in which the system was operating; indeed in a CGPF meeting of January 1939 he remarked that arbitration committees frequently talked in terms that might have been used by the employers' representatives themselves.[57] Perhaps the best measure of the *patronat*'s success in manipulating the arbitration system was the response of its adversaries. In 1939 the CGT requested the abolition of the arbitrage system. Early on it had been the *patronat* who sought to evade the system by recourse to *prudhommes*, but in June 1939 it was the Communist party in parliament that tried to restore the *prudhomme* system.[58]

The employers' organizations and the strike of 30 November 1938

Bourdé suggests that the employers' organizations played a considerable role in the repression of the 1938 strike. He suggests that 'The CGPF carefully concerted its action in anticipation of the conflict...the employers

[53] AN, 72 AS 8, Petiet to *conseil central* of CGPF on 19 February 1937. See also Aymé Bernard's advice on 22 January 1937 that employers should avoid arbitration unless they had 'a perfect case'.
[54] AN, 39 AS 836, circular from social section of CGPF dated 24 January 1939.
[55] AN, 39 AS 836, circular from CGPF dated 6 December 1937.
[56] AN, 39 AS 836, 12 June 1939.
[57] AN, 72 AS 8, 21 January 1938. A CGPF circular of 3 May 1939 (in AN, 70 AQ 417) said that the CGPF had established a 'modus vivendi with the government' over arbitration.
[58] Joel Colton, *Compulsory Labor Arbitration in France, 1936–1939* (New York, 1951), pp. 147–9.

organized the repression in advance and in secret.'[59] It is true that a number of employers' organizations circulated advice on how to handle the strikes. As early as April 1937 an attempt had been made within the UIMM to establish a code of conduct for dealing with strikes.[60] On 26 November 1938 the UIMM gave its members a six-point checklist of actions to be taken. This list stressed yet again the employers' obsession with detailed information about their employees: 'inform yourselves very precisely on the conditions in which the movement begins, find out who is to blame (individuals or organizations)'. The circular envisaged sanctions: active participants were to be sacked, while 'Proceedings should be initiated against everyone and every organization proved to have started an industrial action or to have taken an active part in it.'[61] The GIMMCP sent a similar circular stressing the need to take carefully selective sanctions: 'It is clear that the employers' organization will pursue with the CGT and its various organizations the legal consequences of the breach of laws and conventions in operation.'[62]

However, the employers' organizations seem to have recognized that their action would not, in itself, lead to the suppression of the strike. The measures that they proposed were to be taken *after* the suppression of the strike. In the meeting of the *conseil d'administration* of the GIMMCP it was stressed that all their plans were provisional: 'the general position can only be analysed on the basis of precise information concerning (1) the pattern of events (2) the attitude of the government'.[63] Indeed great stress was laid on the need to be selective and flexible in order to avoid escalating the conflict: 'The decision in favour of a general strike on Wednesday rests on no trade dispute and is of an exclusively political nature. The employers must not lose sight of this essential fact, they must not get involved with manoeuvres that might alter the situation at their expense.'[64]

It is not clear to what extent the employers' organizations actually supported the sanctions that individual employers took after 30 November. As suggested above, the actual decision about how to set about sacking and rehiring workers seems to have been a matter for individual companies. Apart from accounts of attempts to prevent workers dismissed by one company from being hired by another, the archives of employers' organizations contain remarkably little reference to sanctions taken after 30 November. Gignoux said, as early as 3 December, that the *patronat* did not

---

[59] Guy Bourdé, *La défaite du front populaire* (Paris, 1977), p. 223.

[60] P-à-M, 41604, report of UIMM meeting of 14 April 1937. The code, put forward by Goudard, was designed to prevent employers from benefiting from strikes in rival factories. Its main provision concerned the hiring of strikers or those sacked after strikes.

[61] AN, 70 AQ 300.

[62] AN, 91 AQ 16. The circular is undated in this archive; in the Arbel archives it is dated 28 November.   [63] AN, 39 AS 852, 22 November 1938.   [64] Ibid.

intend to use the strikes to seek revenge. In February 1939 Gignoux stressed that the question of rehiring strikers was a matter for individual companies. But he also repeated a call made by the president of the *section sociale* of the CGPF for employers to recognize 'the utility of considering, with all possible benevolence, individual cases relating to the liquidation of the strike of November 1938'.[65] Gignoux's speech made it clear that there were special reasons behind his desire for 'benevolence'. For the CGPF feared that, if large number of strikers remained unemployed, the government might institute a control of hiring and firing.

The state and the *revanche des patrons*

Everything that employers and their organizations were able to do to quell working-class discontent and to undermine Popular Front labour legislation was ultimately dependent on the state. The concessions that they extracted within the labour legislation and the arbitration system could have been abolished with a stroke of a pen by a hostile government. Most of all the overthrow of the Popular Front labour legislation and crushing of working-class dissent which began in the autumn of 1938 was due to the initiative of the state. This initiative was not undertaken as a result of internal political evolution. There is no proof that it was the product of pressure on the Radical party exerted by the mobilization of the *classes moyennes*. In fact the assault made by the state upon the labour legislation of the Popular Front sprang from the financial needs of rearmament. This was the point that Reynaud stressed in his speech of 12 November: 'Do you believe that in the Europe of today, France can maintain her living standard, spend 25 billions on armament, and have two days off every week, all at the same time?'[66]

The suppression of the working-class protest that erupted around the decree laws was also a product of state action. It is true that the *patronat* had plans prepared for the subsequent purge. But all these plans were provisional; the intervention of the state was required before they could be put into effect. The intervention of the police allowed factories to be evacuated in 1938 in a manner that had not been possible in 1936. In general the authorities were far more willing to act against strikers than they had been in 1936. *Patrons* who had railed against the authorities in 1936 were content with their attitude in 1938. One employer smugly reported that 2,000 *gardes mobiles* had been provided to keep factories open in his town: 'the colonel of the *gardes mobiles* showed himself most energetic and said

[65] AN, 72 AS 8, p-v of *conseil central* of CGPF for 17 February 1939.
[66] Bourdé, *La défaite du front populaire*, p. 100.

that he took no notice of orders given by the deputy mayor, who is a member of the SFIO'.[67] The maintenance of public transport was a key element in the failure of the strikes. The government kept buses and trains running with requisitions and threats.[68]

The government's attitude to the strike of November 1938 was also closely connected to the rearmament programme. It is true that the conflict between the state and unions was not entirely clear-cut on the issue of rearmament in November 1938. The government consisted both of those who vigorously supported the appeasement policies embodied in the Munich agreement, and more bellicose figures like Reynaud. Similarly, the CGT was divided between the ferociously anti-Hitlerian Communists and a pacifist tradition exemplified by Belin. Most historians have suggested that although in theory the strike was based upon opposition to the decree laws – and thus represented an impediment to rearmament – in practice it was directed against the broad Munichois policy of the government, and was therefore indirectly in favour of rearmament. Ehrmann supports this line of argument by pointing out that the CGT was not hostile to *assouplissement* of the forty-hour law if this could be shown to be useful. Bourdé suggests that it is no accident that the Renault occupation, which began the strikes, coincided with the visit to Paris of the symbol of appeasement: Chamberlain. Certainly it is true that certain pacifist sections of the union movement rejected the strike as 'belliciste'.[69] It is also true that the opening strike at Renault was presented by its leaders as an anti-Munichois movement.[70]

But whatever lay at the origin of the strikes there can be little doubt that their suppression was closely connected with rearmament. The evacuation of the Renault factory was initiated by the most *belliciste* of the ministers who linked this action closely with the success of the rearmament economy: Reynaud told Daladier, 'If we let the country slide into the troubles of 1936 again, if the Renault factory is not evacuated tonight, my experiment is over.'[71] Furthermore, the actual techniques by which the strike was

---

[67] AN, 27 AS 4, report of René Fould of Saint-Nazaire to meeting of comité directeur of Association de l'Industrie et de l'Agriculture Françaises on 15 December 1938.

[68] Bourdé, *La défaite du front populaire*, pp. 172–83.   [69] Ibid. p. 188.

[70] Badie, 'Les grèves du front populaire aux usines Renault'. See also AN, 91 AQ 16, note headed 'Motifs de la grève'. In this internal note Renault management pointed out that the part of the Issy-les-Moulineaux plant which was nationalized had not struck. They used this to support the claim that the strikes were more connected to broad political grievances than to the immediate consequences of the new laws.

[71] Bourdé, *La défaite du front populaire*, p. 146. There is some dispute about who actually initiated the evacuation. At the Riom trial Daladier implied that he personally had made the decision to evacuate the Renault works. This apparently petty divergence is significant. It seems quite plausible that Reynaud was only concerned with the arms programme whereas Daladier might well have been motivated by the fact that the Renault strike was intended partly as a protest against the Munich agreement – and coincided with the visit of Chamberlain to Paris. But Reynaud's account is more plausible. It is hard to imagine that he had anything to gain from claiming responsibility for the evacuation twenty

suppressed owed a great deal to rearmament legislation; the legal basis for the requisition of workers was provided by the National Defence law of September 1938.

The *patronat* were conscious of the role played by the state in crushing the strikes. Business organization circulars had advised employers on how to persuade the authorities to take action against occupations of factories.[72] Indeed the *patronat* sought to shelter behind the state so that they themselves were not implicated in the suppression of the November strike; Villey remarked: 'At present the conflict is a state/worker one, at all costs it must be prevented from turning into an employer/worker one.'[73] After the strike, employers' associations were again happy to avoid being seen as too strongly associated with the repression: 'The meeting agreed, especially after the contribution of M. Davezac, on the absolute necessity of keeping the nature of the restoration of authority by the state and not transforming the situation into one in which claims affect employers.'[74]

Even after the strike of November 1938 the eyes of business leaders remained focused on the state. In the CGPF meeting of January 1939 some spoke vaguely of striking back while their opponents were weak. But most delegates recognized that their main aim was to make the government 'resume its functions'.[75] Great emphasis was also laid on the role of public opinion and the need for employers to appear conciliatory. It was recognized that the ultimate solution to the employers' problems would be a political one. This was a message hammered home by Baron Petiet in March 1939; he pointed out that the CGPF could not give money directly to political causes, but he encouraged individual firms to make such donations 'otherwise you will have the same situation as in 1936, and with the same consequences'.[76]

The state crackdown on labour dissent did not end with the defeat of the strike of 30 November. In fact the confrontation between the state and the organized working class became more clear-cut. Their clash over the economics of rearmament had initially been blurred by the fact that the Communist party was vigorously in favour of resistance to Hitler, while the government was Munichois. After August 1939 this began to change. The

years after the war (he repeated his version of events in an interview with Bordé in 1965); whereas it is easy to see why Daladier should wish to present himself as a hammer of working-class agitation at Riom.

[72] AN, 70 AQ 420, 'Procédure efficace pour faire cesser une occupation', *Bulletin d'Information de l'Association Industrielle de Douai* (10 May 1938). This suggested that the authorities could be expected to be 'inert' unless it could be shown that state contracts were involved. It revealed that an appeal had even been made to the ministry of war in order to get a bar evacuated.

[73] AN, 39 AS 852, p-v of CA of GIMMCP, 29 November 1938.

[74] AN, 39 AS 852, p-v of CA of GIMMCP, 30 November 1938.

[75] AN, 72 AS 8, Aymé Bernard in p-v of *conseil central* for 10 January 1939.

[76] Ibid., 17 March 1939.

government was now committed to war. The Communist party voted war credits in September 1939, but it was compromised by the Hitler–Stalin pact. Many of its members resigned in disgust, and on 26 September 1939 it was dissolved by decree.

Arguably this development had far more significance for the French *patronat* than the previous defeats of the unions. For key parts of French industry faced very highly unionized and largely Communist-controlled workforces. It was for this reason that the whole drama of the Popular Front and its suppression meant less for them than for the rest of the *patronat*. Their workforce had not become radicalized for the first time in 1936 and could not be crushed simply by the disappointment of 1938. This was the case with the metallurgical workers in Paris. The GIMMCP described the workforce which it confronted in these terms: 'Since 1920 the representation of metal workers in the Paris area was in fact undertaken by a "unitaire" union under Communist direction. Under this leadership union action was opposed in principle to all collaboration.'[77] For this reason the mobilization of the French working class that occurred in 1936 did not present the GIMMCP with any great change. The GIMMCP described the unification of the CGT thus: 'since in effect the unions in our industries in the Paris area are almost all "unitaire" we will hardly notice the difference'. Similarly, while the GIMMCP welcomed the increasing docility of the working class in 1938, it stressed that the change among the workers with whom it was concerned would be limited: 'it would not do to forget that the key characteristic of the metallurgy workforce is obedience to union leaders'.[78]

The suppression of the Communist party, on the other hand, did make a considerable difference to Parisian metallurgy; in a retrospective account produced by the Groupement during the Vichy period this event was seen as a turning-point: 'once the dissolution of the Communist party had freed the workers' organizations of the only obstacle that existed, until then, to collaboration between unions and bosses – collaboration was put into effect by the Groupe in its dealings with the workers'.[79] The very militancy of the workforces in metallurgy and heavy industry made them vulnerable when the Communist party was suppressed. This was, for example, the case with the miners' unions in the north. The process was watched with some glee by the *patronat*. The board of Anzin noted: 'The miners union of Anzin, of which the leadership was Communist, is completely dissolved.'[80] A week

[77] AN, 70 AQ 428, 'La politique et le programme d'action sociale du Groupe des Industries Métallurgiques Mécaniques et Connexes de la Région Parisienne'.
[78] AN, 39 AS 852, transcript of CA of GIMMCP, 22 November 1938.
[79] AN, 70 AQ 428, 'La politique et le programme d'action sociale du Groupe des Industries Métallurgiques Mécaniques et Connexes de la Région Parisienne'.
[80] AN, 109 MI 5, p-v of CA, 27 October 1939.

later it was reported to the board of the Anzin mine that all the Communist-controlled unions of the Valenciennes region had been dissolved.[81]

The authority of the *patronat* was further enhanced with the outbreak of war. As Ehrmann remarks, 'the fact that the workers were put under quasi-military rule was not mitigated by any diminution of the employers' rights'.[82] The *patronat* were handed a whole variety of weapons with which to restore labour discipline. Fines were introduced for lack of punctuality, sloppy workmanship, etc. Of those employed by companies working for the war effort 1,200,000 had some kind of quasi-military status. Of these, 800,000 were 'affectés spéciaux', who could be subjected to full military discipline for faults in their work. Conscripted workers were not free to choose their workplace. But the employer preserved his right to hire and fire 'affectés spéciaux', and in practice they preserved the right to fire 'requis civils' as well.[83] The disciplinary impact of dismissal was increased by the fact that a sacked 'affecté spécial' was liable to find himself in the army. The labour legislation of the Popular Front was torn up; the working week was extended to sixty hours; the arbitration system was scrapped.

The possibilities of working-class resistance to all this were very limited. Conscripted labourers lost the right to strike. Furthermore, all strikes in requisitioned factories were illegal; this meant in practice all strikes, since the government would requisition any factory where such an event occurred. Trade unions continued to exist and had the right to recruit among armaments workers, but the powers of trade unions were eroded by three factors. Firstly, the backbone of union organization had been broken with the dissolution of the Communist party. Secondly, union meetings were often banned by local authorities. Thirdly, many workers were moved in the process of labour mobilization, and indeed whole factories were moved away from the vulnerable areas of the north and east. All this played havoc with union powers that it had taken years to establish.

The eclipse of business leadership

The crushing of labour indiscipline had considerable implications for the organization of the *patronat*. The reorganization that had followed Matignon had been based on an alliance between the industrial establishment and a new group of leaders – men who were often not businessmen themselves. But industry had always been flexible in its

[81] AN, 109 MI 5, p-v of CA, 4 December 1939.
[82] Henry Ehrmann, *French Labor from the Popular Front to the Liberation* (New York, 1947), p. 171.
[83] Ibid. p. 173. In theory 'requis civils' could only be sacked by labour inspectors, but in practice such action was taken at the initiative of employers.

methods, and its commitment to this new leadership was only provisional. Even at the height of the mobilization against the Popular Front the CGPF had not been able to exercise unquestioned authority; it had always been difficult to persuade members to pay their dues,[84] and in 1937 Gignoux had been obliged to take the unusual step of submitting to the test of a secret ballot because of 'criticism of the action and inaction of the CGPF'.[85] Some industrialists had suggested that the CGPF was redundant, and that 'it would be better to settle things either directly with the authorities or with the workers' organizations, oneself',[86] and plans to make the CGPF into a more disciplined body were greeted with derision: 'The man who talked about a dictator of business groups is a joker. Can you imagine a dictator in the Rue de Madrid?'[87]

The reformed CGPF could only hope to contain the continual threats of division and rebellion within its own ranks for as long as it was needed to confront a hostile government and a mobilized working class. But after November 1938 these threats began to recede. Gignoux recognized the new mood of complacency among his members. In June 1939 he complained about 'the excessively widespread opinion that there is no major threat to our position'.[88] Now industry could afford to start dropping the pilots. The leaders of employers' organizations found that they were held in less respect and that they had increasing difficulty in maintaining discipline among their members.[89]

The eclipse of the post-1936 leadership of the employers' organizations was underlined by ideological differences with the government. Corporatism was the doctrine of many of the post-1936 employers' leaders, but the political sponsor of the *revanche des patrons*, Paul Reynaud, was a noted liberal and he justified his attacks on union power in 1938 with liberal rhetoric. Jacques Warnier, a corporatist textile manufacturer from Reims, remarked glumly on 5 December 1938, when most businessmen were still celebrating the union defeat: 'the Reynaud experiment will doubtless be no better than the socialist experiment of 1936'.[90]

Much of the post-1936 leadership of the CGPF recognized the increasing precariousness of their position. It was admitted in October 1939 that the

---

[84] AN, 72 AS 7, p-v of *conseil central*, 19 March 1937.   [85] Ibid., 16 April 1937.
[86] P-à-M, 41604, report of meeting of Chambre Syndicale des Constructeurs de Chemin de Fer of 4 December 1936.   [87] Ibid., report of meeting of 16 March 1937.
[88] AN, 72 AS 8, Gignoux speech to *conseil central* of 16 June 1939.
[89] In his speech of June 16 (see above) Gignoux complained of a 'loosening of links' in the employers' movement. In retrospect Gignoux talked about this slackening of discipline after 1938 in *L'économie française 1919–1939* (Paris, 1943), p. 288. During the 1950s employers' leaders told Ehrmann of a breakdown in CGPF authority after 1938 (Henry Ehrmann, *Organized Business in France* (Princeton, N.J., 1957), p. 42.
[90] AN, 57 AS 12, conference of Centre Champenois d'Etude et d'Action Corporative, 5 December 1938.

PMI section of the GIMMCP – founded as a response to the Matignon settlement – was 'on the fringes of the group, and only really attached to it as an optional extra, almost by accident'.[91] One of the leaders of small business, Gingembre, resigned in disgust from the CGPF, claiming that the power of 'the trusts' was being re-established.[92] Nicolle did not resign, but the distrust that he felt for the CGPF leadership was reflected in his talk of 'democratization' at the beginning of the Vichy period. Of all the new leaders appointed after 1936 only Bernard seems to have survived well. But Bernard was a man of exceptional talents and energy who had made himself very useful to the heavy industrial group.

By the beginning of the war even Bernard seems to have been conscious of increasing isolation. It is instructive to compare his position with a classic leader of heavy industry, Lambert Ribot. Bernard described himself as 'un homme du combat'. He owed his position to the post-1936 struggle against working-class organization. It is not therefore surprising that he was unwilling to relax his hostility to the unions even when they no longer seemed to pose a threat. In February 1940 he poured scorn on Jouhaux's expressed wish for collaboration between capital and labour.[93] Lambert Ribot was a very different kind of leader. He had risen before 1936. He was not primarily 'un homme du combat'. His functions related mainly to the co-ordination of industrial activity rather than to the direction of social conflict. Among business leaders he had always been the one most disposed to concessions to unions.[94] He was the business leader who was most receptive to Jouhaux's pleas for collaboration.

The rift between the two kinds of leadership was illustrated by the Majestic accords of April 1940. This was a general declaration of goodwill signed by a number of employers' representatives, notably Lambert Ribot, and trade unionists, notably Jouhaux. Historians have usually dismissed this agreement as belated and futile.[95] In terms of its consequences this verdict is fair. But the accords were highly significant as an illustration of changes in the employers' movement. For the large-scale industry was breaking away from the post-Matignon CGPF and dealing directly with the unions again; though this time it was dealing from a position of special strength, not special vulnerability. The leaders of the CGPF who had risen after 1936 were well aware that the rapprochement between heavy industry and labour

---

[91] AN, 39 AS 852, p-v of CA, 30 October 1939.
[92] Ehrmann, *Organized Business*, p. 53.   [93] *Documents*, 9 February 1940.
[94] Lambert Ribot's role in the International Labour Office probably increased his enthusiasm for collaboration with labour. But he was also conciliatory towards the unions on purely tactical grounds. In November 1936 he had urged that concessions to Jouhaux be made to prevent him from being outflanked by Communists in the CGT (P-à-M, 41604, transcript of meeting of Chambre Syndicale du Matériel de Chemins de Fer, 16 November 1936).
[95] Ehrmann, *Organized Business*, p. 55.

undermined their position. Bernard condemned the agreement vigorously.[96] The meeting at the Majestic was significant for the future as well as the past. The dissatisfied post-1936 leadership of the CGPF were ripe for entry into the Vichy regime; Bernard was to become a vigorous 'Maréchaliste'. But heavy industry had little reason to be dissatisfied with the Republican regime and saw little to be gained from Vichy. Dautry, who set himself as a recording angel of anti-Vichy attitudes among the *patronat*, wrote to Lambert Ribot in 1942: 'I know that you have not forgotten me and friends, who keep us in touch, have told me that you remain faithful to our ideas and that you still act as a member of the Majestic team.'[97]

---

[96] *Bulletin Quotidien*, 5 April 1940, cited Ehrmann, *Organized Business*, p. 56. Bernard's condemnation seems to have been pretty discreet. He did not mention the accords in the leader articles that he wrote for his local paper. Even Ehrmann does not mention Bernard by name, he merely refers to a vice-president of the CGPF. Presumably he had been told that the individual referred to in the *Bulletin Quotidien* article is Bernard in a confidential briefing, but he gives the game away by citing a reference to Bernard in the index for page 56.

[97] AN, 307 AP 157, letter dated 6 December 1942. It must be admitted that another signatory of the agreement – Lente – was less forthright in his hostility to Vichy than Lambert Ribot. It must also be stressed that Dautry's reference to 'l'équipe du Majestic' may simply be a reference to the group connected with the ministry of armament rather than those specifically connected with the agreement. Many of those associated with Dautry in this capacity such as Bouthillier and Jean Jardin went on to serve in the Vichy government.

Chapter 7

The *patronat* and the war

Introduction

After the liberation of France it was widely alleged that the attitudes of French businessmen had contributed to the defeat. Dautry's testimony to the parliamentary enquiry into events between 1933 and 1945 exemplified these allegations: 'with regard to war production, not everyone reacted with the vigour and spirit of 1914'.[1] Not surprisingly the claim that industry had undermined the war effort was often linked with the claim that it had enjoyed illicitly close relations with the Vichy government. For those who made such allegations believed that industry had been hostile to the Republican government. Under these circumstances it might be expected to have greeted the regime that replaced the Republic after the defeat with enthusiasm. In this chapter it will be suggested that industry was often hostile to economic mobilization, but that the assumption that there were always sinister political motives behind this hostility is naive. Furthermore, attitudes to the war exposed splits in the *patronat* – indeed the very fact that the *patronat* was now so divided is highly revealing. Those who did see the war as a political threat were often the very men who had risen in the employers' movement after 1936, but these men were now isolated. The heavy industrialists, who had always been the real power brokers in the business movement, benefited most from mobilization and had most reason to support it.

[1] Assemblée Nationale, Première Législature, Session de 1947, *Rapport fait au nom de la Commission chargée d'enquêter sur les événements survenus en France de 1933 à 1945*, vol. VII, pp. 1950–93.

Le refus de guerre

Sauvy describes the French economy in 1939 and 1940 as 'un refus de guerre'.[2] By this he means that industrialists refused to accept the sacrifices necessary to create a true war economy. There is plenty of evidence of a desire to keep 'business as usual' among the French *patronat*. Normal commercial considerations continued to govern business thinking. The war was often regarded as a passing irritation, and a great deal of business attention was devoted to the post-war period.[3] Businessmen resented the increase in controls and paperwork associated with mobilization. Etienne Mimard, an industrialist of Saint-Etienne, complained 'étatisme and its red tape stifle everything now'.[4]

However, it should not be implied that the experience of French business during rearmament was unified. On the whole those who benefited most from rearmament were heavy industrialists and metallurgists. It was also inevitable that the concentrated industries of the 'sheltered sector', who were used to dealing with state contracts, benefited most. Small business was cut out of the picture. A large proportion of complaints about the war economy came from those areas which were especially hit like the Parisian luxury trade.[5] Since the political system of the Third Republic conferred great importance (or at least appeared to confer great importance) on this kind of *petite et moyenne entreprise*, the complaints of this sector had a political resonance which was out of proportion to its economic significance.

Even within large-scale industry the benefits of rearmament were distributed unevenly. A manager of Pont-à-Mousson remarked in 1937 that industry could be divided into two classes: 'those who, directly or indirectly, benefit from war production and who have too many orders for their capacity and for the working day', and the rest of industry, which was slowing down.[6] Pont-à-Mousson itself suffered as state money was diverted into arms production and it was lamented that 'All-out arms production, which is going on everywhere now, unbalances industry and causes at least as much difficulty as the social laws themselves.'[7] Indeed the war exacerbated divisions within French industry. Companies resented rivals who appeared

---

[2] Alfred Sauvy, *La vie économique des Français de 1939 à 1945* (Paris, 1978), p. 42.
[3] Paris, Archives Nationales (AN), 91 AQ 4; in a note of 11 April 1940 Renault spoke of the undesirability of state involvement in the sale of second-hand vehicles – 'Danger of étatisization after the war'.
[4] Monique Luirard, *La région stéphanoise dans la guerre et dans la paix 1936–1951* (Saint-Etienne, 1980), p. 169.
[5] Paris, Chamber of Commerce (C de C), p-v, 12 January 1940.
[6] Blois, Pont-à-Mousson archives (P-à-M), 41604, report of meeting of Chambre Syndicale des Constructeurs de Chemin de Fer, 18 October 1937.   [7] Ibid.

to be doing well out of the war economy. Furthermore, within the sectors that benefited from the war economy there were often fierce struggles over increasingly scarce labour and raw materials; the president of the Comité des Forges and Louis Renault both complained about the poaching of their workers by aeronautical industries.[8]

It should also be stressed that opposition to a certain kind of war economy did not necessarily entail opposition to the war. Hostility to greater economic controls was underwritten by a whole strategic conception. As Robert Frankenstein has shown, academics, diplomats and politicians maintained that the liberal economy might prove to be the key to allied victory. They believed that in a long war the healthy free markets of the capitalist world would bleed to death the autarkical economy of Germany. Furthermore, French strategic thinking was based on the need to maintain the alliance with England and to secure the economic support of America. The preservation of normal economic links was seen as an essential element in this policy. These beliefs filtered down to the *patronat*. Gignoux wrote in 1939 of the instability of the German economy: 'Our duty is to let the autarkical states stew in their own juice [*se débrouiller eux mêmes*].'[9] Similarly Thèry, the delegate-general of the Association de l'Industrie et de l'Agriculture Françaises, remarked that Germany was 'one big war factory', and that such an economy lacked 'a healthy foundation'.[10] He also spoke of the dangerous effects which interruptions of 'commercial currents' could have on 'the economic potential that is represented by the close co-operation of the former allies of 1914–1918'.[11] Of course, the hostility of the average businessman to wartime controls originated with self-interest rather than with subtle strategic calculation. But the fact that grievances against specific aspects of the war economy could be expressed in a language of strategic interest meant that such grievances did not necessarily lead businessmen to translate their resentment at the economic impact of the armament programme into general hostility to the war effort.

In fact Dautry's assumption that the *refus de guerre* among the *patronat* was so marked is based upon a series of naive comparisons. Firstly, it was implicitly assumed that the attitude of business was different from that of other social groups. This was part of the general myth that contrasted a patriotic working class with treasonable capitalists (a myth that was a product of the political conditions of the liberation – see chapter 9). Secondly, it was assumed that the French *patronat* was more reluctant to enter the war economy than the business classes of other nations. But common sense alone should suggest that no businessman welcomes taxes

---

[8] Robert Frankenstein, *Le prix du réarmement français, 1935–1939* (Paris, 1982), p. 282.
[9] Gignoux speaking to *conseil central* of CGPF on 21 April, reprinted in AICA bulletin, 1 May 1939, in AN, 70 AQ 420.
[10] AN, 27 AS 2, p-v, meeting of CA of AIAF, 29 June 1936.   [11] Ibid.

and bureaucratic controls. Corelli Barnet has described a British 'refus de guerre',[12] while Overy has shown that German industrialists were persuaded of the benefits of industrial mobilization at the point of a gun.[13] Thirdly, Dautry explicitly contrasted the *patronat*'s lack of enthusiasm for mobilization in 1939–40 with the enthusiasm supposedly displayed in 1914–18. There had in fact been considerable divisions between *patronat* and state in the First World War.[14]

Ironically Dautry's own naivety may have been the principal reason for differences in the relationship between the state and business during the two world wars. Thomas, the armaments minister of the first war, had clearly been a tough and realistic operator. Like his counterpart across the channel, he was a master of the art of getting things done. In spite of his business experience Dautry was not a hard-headed man. He had a faith, typical of the graduates of the Ecole Polytechnique, in the capacity of pure reason to solve all problems. Much of the failure of the attempts to mobilize the economy sprang from this faith. Both management and unions regarded his well-meaning initiatives in labour relations as naive.[15]

The political opposition to the war

Dautry's most important post-war claim was that a section of the *patronat* had entertained a political hostility to the war effort. How justified is this accusation?

At first rearmament was compromised in the eyes of business by the fact that it was associated with the social reforms of the Popular Front. The Chamber of Commerce of Paris expressed this link in its commentary on the budget proposals of the government for 1938:

It proposes to treat the execution of the armament programme as if it was a matter of a vast scheme of public works...It has abandoned none of the economic and social pretensions on which its predecessor of 1936 sought to undertake a brutal and profound transformation of economic conditions in France...Thus the government

---

[12] Corelli Barnet, *The Audit of War: The Illusion and Reality of Britain as a Great Nation* (London, 1986).
[13] Richard Overy, 'Heavy Industry and the State in Nazi Germany: The Reichewerke Crisis', *European History Quarterly*, 3 (1985), 1312–40.
[14] See Patrick Fridenson (ed.), *L'autre front* (Paris, 1977).
[15] Villiers (a businessman and a friend of Dautry's) gives the following account of a meeting between business representatives and unions at the beginning of 1940: 'One by one we tried to show him that his plan was idealistic and would not yield happy consequences.' Villiers cites Jouhaux's remark: 'As always he has generous ideas, but it would be better not to implement them' (Georges Villiers, *Témoignages* (Paris, 1978), p. 19). Belin gives a similar retrospective view of Dautry: 'Dautry had a reputation as a strong character. I thought his reputation overblown' (René Belin, *Du secrétariat de la CGT au gouvernement de Vichy* (Paris, 1978), p. 135).

tries to hide itself behind the cost of the armament programme, not just to conceal the failure of its economic and social programme, but also to enact a whole group of measures that aim to do nothing less than cause social upheaval and prepare common ownership of goods and the means of production.[16]

To a certain extent fears about the links between rearmament and left-wing political programmes continued to be expressed up to and even during the war. Gignoux reminded the *patronat* in May 1939 that war might be used as a cover for social change: 'it provides an excellent ground for those who still seek...to promote various social and economic programmes'.[17] The Paris Chamber of Commerce stressed in January 1940: 'it should not be accepted that the common sacrifice required by the war should serve to introduce for ever into our economy the intolerable constraint of étatisme'.[18] A note in the Renault archives expressed links between wartime étatisme and peacetime socialism: 'The economic organization that the authorities are installing now in France is characterized principally, when it is compared to our peacetime organization, by the progressive and total suppression of all freedom...One cannot fail to notice that this wartime organization corresponds exactly to that proposed at other times by certain economists.'[19]

However, this kind of political hostility to the war was not universal among businessmen. As far as most of industry was concerned, especially those sections of industry that benefited most from rearmament, the Popular Front was over by 1939. The Daladier/Reynaud government had destroyed the Popular Front labour legislation and crushed the unions for them. Far from the continuation of the Popular Front by other means, rearmament was, for these industries, the means by which the Popular Front had been destroyed. Frankenstein has shown that 'le mur d'argent' did make a distinction between the rearmament of the Popular Front and that which followed its fall.[20]

Furthermore, many French industrialists had traditions and interests that ought to have made them especially prone to support the war effort. Even a hostile commentator, writing in America during the war, recognized that the section of heavy industry which was seen to control the CGPF was anti-German.[21] This anti-Germanism had been seen as far back as 1923 when

[16] C de C, travaux, 2 April 1938.

[17] Gignoux speaking to *conseil central* of CGPF on 21 April 1939, reprinted in AICA bulletin for 1 May 1939 in AN, AQ 70 420.   [18] C de C, travaux, 12 January 1940.

[19] AN, 91 AQ 78, 29 October 1939.

[20] Frankenstein, *Le prix du réarmement français*, p. 292: 'Après la levée de "l'hypothèque" consituée par le front populaire au pouvoir, la situation revient à la "normale".'

[21] David Brady, *Business as a System of Power* (New York, 1943), recognizes that de Wendel and Rothschild were anti-German. He suggests that Schneider's links with German activity in Czechoslovakia made them less belligerent – in fact of course the opposite was true after September 1938. Brady is clearly being informed by someone who was in America during the occupation of France, and who had left-wing sympathies and considerable – but often inaccurate – information on the *patronat* (Simone Weil?).

certain industrialists had opposed Briand's rapprochement policy.[22] There were a variety of reasons for this attitude. Heavy industry was in the front line of economic competition with Germany. It was also the sector of the economy that would benefit most from armaments manufacture. Major French industrialists became even more fervently anti-German in the period leading up to the war. The occupation of Czechoslovakia alienated Schneider who had considerable interests there. Perhaps most importantly of all, much of French industry was concentrated in the north and east which would be especially vulnerable in the event of German invasion. Indeed 60 per cent of French coal, 89 per cent of French pig iron and 97 per cent of French steel were produced in these areas. The experience of the First World War, when northern France had been occupied by the Germans, had rammed this message home to French industrialists. It is highly significant that the Arbel archives contain a translation of the plans drawn up by the German high command in 1916 for the economic exploitation of the Nord and Pas-de-Calais.[23]

It is hard to prove that the factors listed above predisposed a majority of heavy industrialists to look favourably on the French war effort. The political interventions of French business generally consisted of reactions against policies that they did not like – disapproval was always expressed more explicitly and vociferously than approval. However, to some extent the relative satisfaction of French big business with the political situation can be inferred from their very division; the need that had been felt in 1936 to unite against a hostile government no longer existed.

The relative satisfaction of most sections of big business is thrown into sharp relief by the attitude of its former allies who had risen in the employers' associations after 1936. The most extreme example of this attitude is provided by Aymé Bernard. Throughout the period of French participation in the war Bernard or his deputy, Johannes Dupraz, produced an article every week for the bulletin of Bernard's local association in Lyon, the AICA. Most business journals confined their commentary during the war to inoffensive uplift and factual information. Bernard's paper continued to take controversial stands. Indeed the paper was frequently full of blank spaces left by the censor's pencil. Bernard repeatedly attacked the regulations imposed by the war. He seems to have had no confidence that the new

[22] Jean-Noel Jeanneney, *L'argent caché: milieux d'affaires et pouvoirs politiques dans la France du XXème siècle* (Paris, 1981), p. 38.

[23] AN, 70 AQ 444, translation of 'L'industrie en France occupée, ouvrage établi par le Grand Quartier Général Allemand en 1916'; it seems reasonable to assume that this translation was provided by one of the business associations to which Arbel belonged. It was accompanied by a note stressing the lessons which could be drawn from the document about future German intentions – 'Although the authors prudently abstained from making assumptions about the outcome of the war, and confined themselves to facts, the reader cannot fail to be enlightened by the important information that the document reveals.'

economic conditions of the war would be temporary: 'The war economy does not just send liberalism, or what remains of it, on holiday, it puts its equipment at risk.'[24] AICA's attack on wartime controls was all the more marked because it did not associate liberalism with the overthrow of an autarkical German economy. Dupraz wrote on 10 November 1939: 'we do not...feel obliged to announce the imminent collapse of the German economy'.[25] Again it was stressed that Germany's economic situation was not desperate, and that 'la guerre blanche' was an illusion: 'attempts to localize this war are doomed to failure'.[26]

Bernard's hostility to the war economy was clearly underwritten by a belief that the war was being used as an opportunity to overthrow the whole liberal economy: 'we cannot accept that a new society should be prepared, that a new doctrine should dominate our lives, and that citizens coming back from victory should find the very regime against which they are fighting installed at home'.[27] Indeed sometimes the AICA bulletin hinted at an almost revolutionary threat on the home front: 'there are two victories to be gained: one against the enemy, the other against the Marxist experiment'.[28] Dupraz presented the same message in even more graphic terms: 'there is an intense agitation in the land...Kerenkyisme is not the best way to beat it...The present attack is focused on the home front, where Frenchmen, deserting members of parliament, fleeing traitors or fanatics are working quietly to destroy French nationhood.'[29]

Bernard's fierce hostility to the war is highly revealing. For Bernard represented, as far as he represented anyone at all, the broad French bourgeois. This alliance of liberal professions, small businessmen and *rentiers* had traditionally formed the basis of the republican synthesis. As suggested above, this group had been sought by heavy industry as an ally during the drive against the Popular Front. But, now that heavy industry's campaign against the Popular Front was over, it no longer needed allies. This split had already been marked by Bernard's condemnation of the Majestic accords. The war economy exacerbated the division between heavy industry and the broad bourgeoisie. Heavy industry did well out of armaments contracts. But the wider bourgeoisie lost out. War hit small business, and it threatened the social peace which was so important to the bourgeoisie. Perhaps most importantly rearmament and war raised the spectre of inflation. This was highly important because, until recently, the prosperity of the French bourgeoisie had been founded upon fixed incomes. The dependence upon *rentes* had provided the main, and perhaps the only, element of genuine common interest within the bourgeoisie and between the

[24] *Documents*, 27 October 1939.   [25] *Documents*, 10 November 1939.
[26] *Documents*, 19 April 1940.   [27] *Documents*, 17 November 1940.
[28] *Documents*, 27 October 1939.   [29] *Documents*, 1 December 1939.

bourgeoisie and heavy industry.[30] Although the importance of fixed incomes had been declining ever since the First World War industrialists and bourgeois leaders had still united to defend the value of the franc as late as 1933.[31] The fact that heavy industrial leaders accepted the prospect of devaluation in 1937[32] is, therefore, a very important symptom of disintegrating social alliances.

The division of interest between the broad bourgeoisie and heavy industry was neatly represented by two politicians. Daladier, with his belief in order and stability, represented the broad bourgeoisie. Reynaud on the other hand was the direct benefactor of heavy industry. It was he who had initiated the suppression of the labour movement and it was he who had begun the drive for rearmament. But in the eyes of the broad bourgeoisie he had committed the ultimate sin of attacking the value of money. It is therefore significant that Bernard was fiercely loyal to Daladier, indeed, he suggested giving him full powers to act without parliament.[33] But Reynaud's appointment as prime minister was received coldly.[34] The significance of this is underlined by the fact that the article suggested a better candidate for the leadership of France: Marshal Pétain.

---

[30] Charles Maier, *Reconstructing Bourgeois Europe* (Princeton, N.J., 1975), p. 82, compares the attitudes of French and German industrialists to devaluation. He concludes from this that the former were 'bourgeois first and businessmen second'.

[31] Julian Jackson, *The Politics of Depression in France* (Cambridge, 1985), p. 187.

[32] Jean-Noel Jeanneney, *François de Wendel en République: l'Argent et le pouvoir, 1914–1940* (3 vols., Paris, 1976), p. 887.   [33] *Documents*, 8 December 1939.

[34] *Documents*, 29 March 1940. In this article Dupraz rebuked Reynaud for comparing himself to Clemenceau.

Chapter 8

The *patronat* and the establishment of the Vichy regime

Background: the defeat, the armistice and the Vichy constitution

In the early summer of 1940 the 'drôle de guerre' turned serious. On 13 May German troops, who had evaded the Maginot line by cutting through Belgium, crossed the Meuse. The German army's advance into France proved unexpectedly successful. On 28 May French and British troops had to be evacuated from the encircled pocket around Dunkirk and on 10 June Paris fell. In the immediate aftermath of the war the German success seemed so astounding that many were inclined to attribute it to long-term social decline in France or even to the activities of fifth columnists and anti-republican conspirators. Recent historians have been more inclined to explain the defeat in terms of precise military mistakes and failures of generalship.

However, the political reaction to military disaster certainly did have roots in some of the social and political conflicts that had divided France before the war. Paul Reynaud, the prime minister, was in a weak position; his appointment dated back only to 22 March and he had won a vote of confidence in parliament by only one vote. On 18 May Reynaud appointed Marshal Philippe Pétain as vice-president of the council. The eighty-four-year-old hero of Verdun had become a figurehead for those who desired strong government during the 1930s. He was ostensibly brought in to stiffen resolve, but, in fact, he had already decided that France was defeated. The following day Weygand was appointed commander-in-chief over the head of Gamelin. Finally, in the last ministerial reshuffle of the Third Republic, the young military theorist Charles de Gaulle was made under-secretary of state for war on 5 June.

While the Germans advanced the government was confused, frightened and on the run. On 10 June it left Paris for Bordeaux, where there was an argument between ministers who wished to continue the fight from North

Africa and those who wished to remain in France and to seek an armistice with the Germans. The victory of the latter group was eventually marked by the resignation of Reynaud and his replacement by Pétain on 16 June. On 17 June Pétain formed his first cabinet and ordered the French people to stop fighting. On 22 June an armistice was signed between Pétain's government and the German occupying authorities. For our purposes the most important provision of this armistice was the division of France because, though in theory the French government retained its sovereignty intact, the Germans continued to occupy the north and west of the country.

The new government left Bordeaux, which fell into the zone occupied by the Germans, and settled in Vichy, a spa town in the Auvergne that was chosen mainly because it offered a large supply of hotel beds and because it did not, unlike Lyon and Clermont-Ferrand, serve as the political base for any figure from the Third Republic. At Vichy the national assembly was convoked in order to provide the constitutional foundation for the new regime. On 9 July the assembly voted, with only four dissenting voices, in favour of a revision of the constitution. The following day Pétain was voted full powers to do anything except declare war; 468 deputies voted in favour of this motion, 80 voted against and 20 abstained. Even among those deputies who voted against parliament's surrender of its authority there were a number who went out of their way to express personal loyalty to Pétain. Vichy's constitutional legislation was rounded off by an act of 12 July that made Laval Pétain's official heir. In its very early stages the government was highly popular; Amouroux is exaggerating only slightly when he talks of 'forty million Pétainists' – though beyond personal loyalty to Pétain himself it is not very clear what underlay that popularity. Vichy soon came to be regarded as a regime of the right but in its very early days it seemed to represent a wide spectrum of opinion. Its supporters ranged from the Socialists on the left – seventy-five Socialist deputies had voted full powers to Pétain – to the leader of the royalist Action Française on the right.

It cannot be said that business had any role in the events that brought the Pétain government to power. The Vichy government did not spring from any long-term campaign requiring support and subsidy. It was the product of manipulation by a very small cabal operating in isolation, in response to an unforeseen event, the defeat, and in circumstances of considerable confusion. Furthermore, businessmen in the summer of 1940 were rarely in any position to be pulling political strings. Many industrialists whose factories were located in the north of France or in Paris had themselves taken to the roads during the *exode*. After the armistice many of them were fully occupied trying to contact their scattered employees and organize the resumption of production.[1] However, historians who see business as one of

---

[1] The confusion of managers attempting to locate their workforces is revealed by the Fives-Lille archives in Paris, Archives Nationales (AN), 198 AQ 54, notes on meeting of northern

the pillars of the Vichy government would argue that the *patronat* regarded these events as a divine surprise: 'it cannot be denied...that the events of 1939/1940 brought about a situation in social affairs and politics that matched the wishes of the majority of the political and social elites at the time, especially those of the employers'.[2]

To understand how true this view is, it is useful to examine the reaction of the *patronat* to the Vichy regime in the months immediately following its formation. For it is in this early period that the Vichy regime can be seen in its purest form. At this time it did seem possible that a rapid peace would be concluded leaving the government free to construct a new order. As far as business was concerned this illusion did not last long; it was soon apparent that the needs of the German war economy counted for more than Vichy ideology. Furthermore, it was during the early period that the German victory, which underwrote Vichy, seemed irreversible. From as early as December 1940 doubts began to surface in the French population about the permanency of this victory. From this point on, the *patronat* became increasingly wary of association with the Vichy regime. In this section it will be shown that even during this period, when Vichy looked at its most promising, businessmen, and especially heavy industrialists, did not regard it with much favour and were not received with favour by the regime. The considerable advantages that business was to obtain between 1940 and 1944 were achieved, not because of, but in spite of, the Vichy regime.

At the beginning of the Vichy regime businessmen flocked to the new capital. Lambert Ribot, Petiet, Thiriez, Dubrelle, de Peyerimhoff, Painvin and Gillet[3] were all present at Vichy in July 1940. However, they seem to have lobbied as outsiders rather than manipulated as insiders. Their main aim was to restore the northern part of France to French administration and to install a candidate sympathetic to them as minister of industrial

industrialists chaired by Lambert Ribot, 15 July 1940. The political confusion in which Pétain came to power is revealed by Assemblée Nationale, Première Législature, Session de 1947, *Rapport fait au nom de la Commission chargée d'enquêter sur les événements survenus en France de 1933 à 1945.*

[2] Ingo Kolboom, *La revanche des patrons: le patronat français face au front populaire* (Paris, 1986), pp. 349–50.

[3] Pierre Nicolle, *Cinquante mois d'armistice, Vichy, 2 juillet 1940–26 août 1944: journal d'un témoin* (2 vols., Paris, 1947), vol. I, p. 26, entry for 12 July 1940. The individuals mentioned were respectively head of the Comité des Forges, provisional head of the CGPF and president of the motor manufacturers' association, the head of the Lille Chamber of Commerce and a northern textile leader, the head of the Comité des Houillères, the head of the aluminium manufacturers' association, and a large-scale chemical industrialist from Lyon. It should also be noted that individuals who were business leaders rather than businessmen such as Bernard and Nicolle himself were in Vichy. There were also businessmen who were not lobbying the interests of their industry but who were seeking office for themselves. Nicolle reports that Fougières – the president of the FAR – requested a post in the ministry of supply. Daum, a metallurgist, was also in the capital and was indeed a proposed candidate as minister of industrial production (René Belin, *Du secrétariat de la CGT au gouvernment de Vichy* (Paris, 1978), p. 127).

production. Vichy was unable to indulge their first request and unwilling to indulge their second. Businessmen were given a frosty reception. Dubrelle was told: 'No personal request can be tolerated regardless of the importance of the firm concerned.'[4] The arch representative of heavy industrial power (Lambert Ribot) left Vichy in despair saying 'the government understands nothing, there is no point in wasting our time here'.[5]

Historians often present Vichy as being an extension of the reaction against the Popular Front. As far as the *patronat* was concerned the relationship between the new government and the Popular Front must have looked much more complicated. The parliament that voted full powers to Marshal Pétain was the same parliament that had voted for the forty-hour week in 1936. The new minister of industrial production had been a strike leader in 1936. De Wendel recognized some of these uncomfortable resemblances. He grumbled that the government 'continues the work of the Popular Front'.[6]

On the other hand it was clear that many who had been involved in the employers' reaction against the Popular Front, such as Nicolle, resurfaced at Vichy. But it would be crude to suggest that these men were simply 'business representatives'. The men who had risen in the CGPF after 1936 had been presented as representatives of small business and of the broader *classes moyennes*. They had in fact risen with a wave of rhetoric directed against heavy industry, which was alleged to have betrayed small business by signing the Matignon accords. In 1936 much of this had been just rhetoric. The new leaders of the CGPF had in fact enjoyed close relations with heavy industry. But ironically this opposition to heavy industry had been made much more sincere by the events that had followed 1936. The new leadership of the CGPF had seen themselves dumped by their allies in heavy industry when its aims had been fulfilled by the circumstances of the war economy. Now the new government seemed to offer the representatives of the *classes moyennes* a new power base which would allow them to do without their heavy industrial allies.

The diary of Pierre Nicolle indicates the extent to which the rhetorical divisions of 1936 had become the real divisions of 1940. Nicolle had been closely allied with the ruling clique of the CGPF in 1936. But, writing in 1940, he presented the changes of 1936 as representing a real revolution: 'on 4 August it [the CGPF] became representative of all the economic activity of the country'.[7] He then described the moves against heavy industry of 1940 in similar terms: 'the democratization of the CGPF...will soon be a

---

[4] Ibid. p. 36, entry for 20 July.   [5] Ibid. p. 31, entry for 16 July.
[6] Jean-Noel Jeanneney, *François de Wendel en République: l'argent et le pouvoir, 1914–1940* (3 vols., Paris, 1975), p. 1371.
[7] Nicolle, *Cinquante mois d'armistice*, vol. I, p. 8, introduction.

reality'.[8] Nicolle and Verger, another leader who had entered the CGPF after 1936 on a supposedly small business ticket, tried to get Gignoux (like them a post-1936 appointment to the CGPF) appointed as minister of industrial production. Meanwhile the old heavy industrial faction was lobbying for its candidates to be given the job.

In short, heavy industry seems to have felt as isolated and vulnerable in 1940 as it had in 1936. It is significant that heavy industry reactivated contact with one of its allies of 1936, Aymé Bernard. He had become isolated from heavy industry during the period of rearmament. However, his alienation from heavy industry was never as great as that of his colleagues like Nicolle and Gingembre. He was therefore still available as an ally for heavy industry in 1940. The meetings of his association, the FAR, were attended by numerous prominent heavy industrialists in 1940. In a supremely ironic twist Bernard was recruited as a member of the delegation of heavy industrialists, led by Lambert Ribot, with whom he had crossed swords only a few months earlier over the Majestic accords.[9]

The isolation of much of French industry from the new government was reinforced by the geography of Vichy France. Industry was concentrated overwhelmingly in the northern zone, which was occupied by the Germans. Vichy could offer little protection and help in this area: 'French industrialists requested, with agonized insistence, the return of the government to Paris; because, to quote…M. Lamy of Citroën, industrialists were obliged to struggle with the German authorities without support.'[10]

Even more significantly a large proportion of French industry was concentrated in two areas which were placed under very special conditions in 1940: Alsace-Lorraine, and the Nord and Pas-de-Calais. Alsace-Lorraine was simply annexed by the Germans, and French industrialists were ejected from the area; this move made French industry suspicious of the Germans from the start. The Nord and the Pas-de-Calais were placed in the *zone interdite*. The area was separated from the rest of France and ruled by the military command in Brussels. In the early stages of the occupation the separation between the *zone interdite* and the rest of France was almost complete. The Vichy government seemed to offer inhabitants of this area little, even when that government was most popular in the rest of the country.

[8] Ibid. p. 37, entry for 22 July.
[9] Ibid. p. 30, entry for 15 July. It was typical of the contradictions which sprang from the alliance between heavy industry and the representatives of the wider bourgeoisie that Bernard should be a member of a delegation condemned by his own lieutenant Nicolle. Typical too that Bernard – brought into the CGPF after 1936 as part of the anti-Matignon reaction – should be part of a group accused of having 'licked the arse of the Popular Front'.
[10] Hoover Institute, *La vie de la France sous l'occupation* (3 vols., Paris, 1959), Belin testimony, vol. I, pp. 138–85.

Industrialists in the Nord and Pas-de-Calais had special reason to be disgruntled with the armistice and the government that had imposed it. The military authorities in Brussels were far rougher in their treatment of industrialists than those in Paris. Thiriez and Legrand, two of the leaders of the business community in the north, were put under virtual house arrest. Furthermore, the German authorities in the area made vigorous efforts to win the loyalty of industrial workers in the north, efforts that unnerved employers. One of the few government representatives who did penetrate the *zone interdite* in the early stages of the occupation reported the mood of industrialists in the following terms:

M. Thiriez and M. Legrand gave me the impression that the industrialists of the north were very demoralized on account of the vexations to which they were submitted in the absence of all relations with the rest of France... Their complaints, sometimes expressed in a rather violent tone, denoted a vigorous dissatisfaction with the policy followed by the government of Marshal PÉTAIN at the time of the signature of the armistice.

The delegate went on to describe the resentment inspired by German requisition policy; the 'veritable Nazification of the working population', and the separation from the rest of France. The report is concluded: 'the absence of all contact between free France [that is, the southern zone] and the departments of the north has given the latter the impression that they have been abandoned'.[11]

Heavy industrial leaders got an especially rough ride at Vichy in the first few months after the armistice because of one man: Pierre Laval. During his first five months in power Laval was exceptionally outspoken and aggressive. He had every reason to be confident. He had been the real author of parliament's abdication, and his own power seemed unchallenged. He believed that German victory over Britain would soon bring real peace and the prospect of ambitious initiatives in France. Perhaps because of this confidence, Laval was much more ideologically radical during this period than he was to be later. Bouthillier suggests that during the first government Laval wanted 'a real revolution, a sort of French fascism'.[12]

Part of Laval's radicalism consisted of a hostility to big business. This may seem strange. Laval had close connections with certain business leaders; indeed he had fairly substantial business interests of his own. The economist Charles Rist commented on this apparent contradiction: 'Laval was the hope of the bourgeois...I am afraid that they will soon be disabused...Plans like that of Bouthillier, the recent decree on companies,

---

[11] Paris, Archives Nationales (AN), F 37 39, 'Rapport du délegué', dated 16 July 1940.
[12] Yves Bouthillier, *Le drame de Vichy* (2 vols., Paris, 1950), vol. I, p. 209.

etc., are anti-capitalist demagoguery of a kind far more effective than all the communism in the world.'[13] But Rist's remarks reveal an interesting misunderstanding. For Rist, an intellectual based in the north with extensive connections in big business and the administration, was the classic representative of 'le Nord qui travaille'; for him bourgeois and capitalist meant the same thing. Laval on the other hand was the classic representative of 'le Sud qui gouverne'; his constituency was in southern provincial towns among the small businessmen and peasants who made up the electoral bedrock of the Third Republic. Laval's connections were all with those business leaders who claimed to represent the wider *classes moyennes* rather than heavy industry. He had close links with those who had arisen to represent this class in the taxpayers' revolt of 1933, like Nicolle and Lemaigre Dubreuil,[14] and with some of the post-1936 leaders of the CGPF, like Gignoux and Germain Martin. Like these leaders of the *classes moyennes* Laval seems to have been deeply suspicious of big business. He had a particular disdain for the Comité des Forges.[15] He expressed retrospective conspiracy theories linking big business and the Popular Front that were similar to those of Pierre Nicolle. This link was described with some subtlety by Bouthillier: 'It would be a mistake to think that the nationalizations, that are so dear to socialism, are considered unfavourably by capitalism. They find that these provide a means of eliminating risk and obtaining a stable profit with the constant support of the state';[16] and with brutality by Laval himself, when confronting the delegation of heavy industry on 15 July 1940: 'you and your friends licked the arse of the Popular Front; you need not have bothered to come here'.[17]

Industry and Vichy industrial legislation (the first wave)

Yet the regime which was so hostile to large-scale industry produced an economic system under which such industry flourished. It is tempting to assume that Vichy industrial legislation was a special case, and that somehow the *patronat* succeeded in colonizing this one enclave in hostile territory. But this was not so. To start with, heavy industry did not choose

---

[13] Charles Rist, *Une saison gâtée: journal de la guerre et de l'occupation, 1939–1945*, ed. Jean-Noel Jeanneney (Paris, 1985), entry for 26 October 1940, p. 101.

[14] Nicolle and Lemaigre were both members of the very select group willing to defend Laval after the liberation. See Hoover Institute, *La vie de la France sous l'occupation*, vol. III, pp. 1177–86, testimony of Lemaigre Dubreuil, and Nicolle, *Cinquante mois d'armistice*.

[15] Laval was to justify the eviction of Mireaux from the cabinet in July 1941 on the grounds that he 'représente pour les allemands le Comité des Forges et le temps' (Bouthillier, *Le drame de Vichy*, p. 176).   [16] Ibid. p. 15.

[17] Nicolle, *Cinquante mois d'armistice*, vol. I, p. 30, entry for 15 July 1940.

the man who drew up the most important pieces of Vichy industrial legislation. One of the main aims of the industrialists who gathered at Vichy had been to influence the choice of the new minister of industrial production. They were unsuccessful. They failed to get their first choice, Davezac, and failed again with their second choice, Pichon. It has been suggested that, though the new minister, Belin, was a trade unionist, he had enjoyed close contacts with big business through his participation in the *Nouveaux Cahiers* meetings.[18] But the businessmen who had participated in the *Nouveaux Cahiers* group were far from typical (see chapter 5). Of course Belin was less inimical to the *patronat* than a trade unionist of 'unitarian' tendencies would have been. But within the range of men mentioned as candidates for the job (Gignoux, Verger, Davezac, Pichon, de Vitry and Daum) Belin was the only one who did not originate in the *patronat*. His appointment seems to have been decided as a last-minute expedient by Laval. He was a surprisingly left-wing choice for Vichy.[19]

The first economic law to be drawn up by the new government was that of 16 August 1940. This set up the Comité d'Organisation system. Julliard argues that it was upon these bodies that the 'golden age of the *patronat*' was founded.[20] Once again it is important to stress that the *patronat* had no opportunity to influence the framing of this law. It was drawn up too fast to allow time for lobbying. Those who had to operate the law were struck by its almost improvised quality. Lehideux (Belin's successor) wrote that 'everything was done in haste'.[21] Belin stressed that the law was drawn up in a mere two days by himself and a small group of civil servants (Lafond, Bichelonne, Barnaud, Larroque and Lacour) working in isolation 'without systematic or obligatory consultation'.[22] Even the ubiquitous Nicolle knew nothing of the law until three days before its publication. Belin portrays the measure as a response to immediate pressures (that is, the starved economy, the need to counteract German economic organization in the northern zone, and the need to find men with industrial expertise fast).[23] He suggests that it was neither the product of any ideological predisposition nor of the interests of any powerful group;[24] it was simply what needed to be done.

---

[18] Jacques Julliard, 'La Charte du Travail', in FNSP, *Le gouvernement de Vichy 1940–1942* (Paris, 1972), p. 159.

[19] Belin, *Du secrétariat de la CGT au gouvernement de Vichy*, p. 125. The choice was surprising even to Belin himself who thought that he would be lucky to get a job as a village postmaster from the new government.

[20] FNSP, *Le gouvernement de Vichy*, p. 161.

[21] Hoover Institute, *La vie de la France sous l'occupation*, vol. I, p. 113.

[22] Ibid. p. 146.   [23] Ibid.

[24] The only ideological gloss put on the new law suggested that it was directed against heavy industry. Laval and Marquet said that the law was designed to 'faire disparaître la CGT et surtout le Comité des Forges': Nicolle, *Cinquante mois d'armistice* (the Comité des Forges was dissolved under the 16 August law).

Such an argument could be dismissed as a typical Vichy apologia. Vichy ministers frequently claimed that they had merely done what circumstances required. This line of defence was expressed in its most succinct form at the trial of Bouthillier when it was said that Vichy represented the triumph of 'administration over politics'. But in this case Belin seems to be on firm ground. For, as he suggests, the industrial system that he created was not a particularly Vichyite one. It blended in well with the law of 11 July 1938 on the organization of the economy in wartime. Even more significantly Belin's system was not scrapped by the post-liberation government. The COs were recognized by the provisional government on 22 June and again on 7 October 1944 and they were not abolished until 1946. The fact that they were retained by a government with so much reason to distance itself from the Vichy legacy suggests that they were indeed the inevitable products of a war economy.

The first wave of Vichy industrial legislation was completed with two measures that had little effect in themselves but that were significant as general indicators of the climate of relations between Vichy and industry. Firstly, three employers' organizations – the CGPF, the Comité des Forges and the Comité des Houillères – were dissolved.[25] The dissolution of the CGPF made little difference because its regional section, the FAR, was left intact and served, during the early months of the war, as an effective replacement for the CGPF. Indeed employers' leaders seem to have taken the dissolution of the CGPF rather lightly. Petiet, the head of the social section of the CGPF, saw it as a necessary but unimportant consequence of the dissolution of the CGT and hoped that 'in one form or another the information and documentary services of the CGPF will survive'.[26] Probably this was because, since the suppression of the labour movement, the industrialists behind the CGPF had lost interest in it. As far as the post-1936 leadership of the CGPF (Bernard, Gignoux, Nicolle and Verger) were concerned the pill of dissolution was sweetened by the fact that the Vichy regime was opening up fresh pastures for their ambitions.

It could be argued that, in the long run, the dissolution of the Comité des Forges and the Comité des Houillères made equally little difference. After all, the UIMM, which was responsible for labour relations in the metallurgy industry, was left untouched;[27] while the Comité d'Organisation for the coal

[25] It is not entirely clear who initiated the dissolutions. Laval had certainly been agitating for dissolution for some time. Belin was to claim responsibility retrospectively for himself. But Etienne Mimard told de Wendel that the issue had first been raised in cabinet by Weygand (see Jeanneney, *De Wendel*, p. 1371).

[26] AN, 70 AQ 420, Petiet to meeting of FAR in northern zone, 12 September 1940.

[27] The fact that the UIMM should be allowed to survive while the Comité des Forges, which was not responsible for labour relations – and whose leader was in fact very liberal in his attitude to workers' demands – was dissolved in the interests of social peace is typical of the way in which the Comité des Forges served as an all-purpose scapegoat in French politics.

industry proved at least as effective in representing the industry as the Comité des Houillères had been. But the dissolution of the two heavy industrial associations did arouse genuine resentment among the employers. These were not just 'syndicats d'occasion' set up to deal with some particular crisis. The Comité des Houillères dated back to 1864, the Comité des Forges to 1846. The leaders of the Comité des Forges and the Comité des Houillères, Lambert Ribot and de Peyerimhoff, were two of the most long-serving representatives of heavy industry. Lambert Ribot had been described by the Pont-à-Mousson management as 'Le bon Lambert', a term as close to affection as a *maître des forges* was ever likely to get. It is clear that the leaders of the dissolved bodies resented their exclusion violently. De Peyerimhoff wrote a celebrated letter to Belin complaining about the dissolution of the Comité des Houillères: 'The Comité des Forges and the Comité des Houillères, alone among all primary business and worker organizations, were officially dissolved. The special place in the com-muniqué, the intended isolation of these two great associations, the press comments, all mark, in their regard, an express intention to condemn.'[28] De Wendel, the vice-president of the Comité des Forges, expressed similar resentment at the 'ugly and unjust gesture'.[29]

The second of the measures which completed Vichy's wave of industrial legislation was the law on companies of 1940. This law forbade one individual to hold the directorship of more than one company. It was designed to thwart the creation of vast interlocking industrial empires. Once again, the legislation, in itself, meant little; it was easy enough for directors to find straw men to represent them. But once again the law was important as a symbol of Vichy's hostility to a certain kind of capitalism. As almost every major company in France was obliged to rearrange its board in accordance with the new law it was a symbol that the *patronat* could not fail to notice.

The *Charte du Travail*

The *Charte du Travail* was finally acted in October 1941. It was meant to provide the framework for labour relations and industrial organization. In its intention and preparation this law presented a sharp contrast with that of 16 August. The latter had been drawn up fast by a small and isolated group of civil servants to provide a temporary solution to an immediate crisis. The *Charte* took over a year to prepare. It was meant to be the corner-stone of an economic and social new order; indeed it was a vital part of the

[28] Philippe Bauchard, *Les technocrates et le pouvoir* (Paris, 1966), p. 123.
[29] Jeanneney, *De Wendel*, p. 844.

Vichy constitution.[30] The *Charte* excited great interest from the whole political world at Vichy, especially from the Marshal's cabinet.[31] It was at the centre of a heated, often savage, argument that was to last beyond the publication of the *Charte* until the liberation. It is clear that the degree of interest which industrialists displayed in the *Charte* provides a useful gauge of their commitment to the aims of the new regime.

The background: politicians and the *Charte*

Broadly speaking, the politicians debating the *Charte* fell into two groups: corporatists and syndicalists. The former wished to see industrial organization founded on single bodies to represent both workers and employers in each industry. The latter wished to see trade unions survive. The two schools of thought originated in different political camps. The syndicalists were concentrated in the ministry of labour. The corporatist case was initially made by the *garde des sceaux* and then taken up with considerable vigour by the secretariat to the Marshal's cabinet. These origins are significant. The ministry of labour contained a large number of former unionists, notably the minister himself, who naturally took a 'conservative' line. Corporatism was the doctrine of those at the political heart of the Vichy government who wished to see the sharpest possible break with the institutions of the Republic. In purely intellectual terms, the division between the two interpretations was not clear-cut.[32] Corporatism was the officially sponsored doctrine of the regime and there was little explicit assault on corporatist ideals. Syndicalists merely argued that corporatism was premature. Similarly, few called for the elimination of unions; the dispute was a matter of degree and revolved around the level, local, regional or national, at which unions could be allowed to survive. Debate was further blurred by the repetition, pedantry and long-windedness of many of the participants.

However, the difference in tone between the two groups was unmistakable. Colonel Cèbe, one of the key figures in the debate, recognized

---

[30] Cèbe, the secretary to the committee which ultimately drafted the *Charte*, stressed the constitutional implications of the enterprise: 'S'agissant d'une oeuvre législative relative à la constitution c'est naturellement le Garde des Sceaux qui a soumis le premier projet' (AN, F 22 1836).

[31] It is worth noting that the German authorities in Paris also followed the progress of the *Charte*. Belin mentioned in a letter to Pétain of 22 December 1940 that the Germans had been shown his draft of that month (Paris, Institut d'Histoire Sociale, Belin archives).

[32] Two workers' representatives on the Commission d'Organisation Professionnelle (Savoie and Poimbeuf) stressed that 'La corporatisme n'était pas une anti-thèse du syndicalisme' (letter in Belin archives dated 18 September 1941).

the importance of the difference. 'Thus two principal tendencies confronted each other, the one giving preponderance to unionism in each category, the other substituting a common organization blending all the various categories of those in the profession...All the later debate focused around these two poles.'[33]

In 1940 the two most vigorous proponents of corporatism in the cabinet were Baudouin and Bouthillier. Baudouin accepted Belin's project of December 1940 but did so with considerable reservations: 'This project is not entirely satisfactory for the following reasons: (1) it does not bring on corporative reform, as it should. (2) In reviving unionism it risks impeding, in some measure, effective action which must be based on social reform of enterprises.'[34] Bouthillier was far more hostile: 'Far from organizing a real corporative regime, the project tends to give back to workers' and employers' unions their separate, and therefore rival, existence.'

The involvement of Baudouin and Bouthillier is very interesting. These men both came from 'technocratic' backgrounds. Vichy loyalists such as Pierre Nicolle tended to assume that such men, and especially those connected with the ministry of finances, were hostile to the corporatist new order of Vichy. Indeed the assumption that the ministry was a hive of resistance to Vichy directives was later to lead to mass arrests of civil servants by the Germans.[35]

Vichy loyalists also assumed that the ministry of finances supported heavy industrial interests. This seemed reasonable enough. The background of men like Baudouin and Bouthillier was certainly close to that of the leaders of heavy industry. But in fact these men expressed their position on the *Charte* in terms of opposition to heavy industry. Bouthillier suggested that the Comité des Houillères and the Comité des Forges would effectively be reconstituted under a syndicalist system. He also had doubts about the influence of big business in the Comités d'Organisation:

In these conditions, it is to be feared that the heads of the trusts, who have the Comités d'Organisation well in hand, will not be qualified to achieve professional organization in its social dimension...It seems, rather, that such a task should be entrusted to the leaders of medium-sized businesses who represent better the real structure of French industry, and are better prepared for a fruitful collaboration with the workers.[36]

The extent to which Vichy reversed traditional alliances is reflected by the

[33] AN, F 22 1836, Cèbe report.   [34] Belin archives, Baudouin note (undated).
[35] AN, 2 AG 1927, De Brinon to Laval: 'the German authorities are sure that senior officials in the ministry of industrial production are acting against the policy of the French government and obviously against Germany'.
[36] Belin archives, 'Projet de loi sur l'organisation professionnelle', dated 5 December 1941. See also Bouthillier's letter to Belin of 4 December 1941.

fact that Belin, the former unionist, was now defending the heavy industrial associations against the assaults of Bouthillier:

You stress that we risk re-establishing, under the name of National Federations, the dissolved groups: the Comité des Forges and the Comité des Houillères. I beg to observe that what we have criticized in these organizations is not their professional activity but rather their political activity. We need professional organizations all the time.[37]

In classically Vichy fashion, Baudouin and Bouthillier mixed hostility to heavy industry with hostility to the organized working class. Bouthillier wrote that 'the powerful metallurgy union would be free to take up again the agitation which has only just been calmed by the events of these last months'.[38] Baudouin gave very specific reasons for his disquiet about the leaders of trade unions: 'It is worth noting that the leaders of the unions were, for the most part, chosen on the crest of the Popular Front wave.'[39] It seems clear that among politicians one of the perceived aims of Vichy labour legislation was to reverse the situation established by the Popular Front.

The clash between Bouthillier and Belin became savage: 'the secretary of state for finances replies to the draft point by point and shows that it is unacceptable'.[40] Belin retorted in similar vein, talking of 'the inanity of certain fears expressed in your letter' and adding: 'I regret to have to inform you that I must formulate the most explicit reserves about the summary of the project presented in your letter of 4 December. This summary is not just incomplete. It is also manifestly inexact. I can only express my surprise that your staff could be so imprudent in a text submitted to their scrutiny.'[41] Belin became so enraged by the opposition expressed to syndicalism that on 21 December 1940 he threatened to resign if his project was not accepted.[42]

Belin did not resign, in spite of the fact that Pétain did not grant him the concession that he demanded. However, the conflict between corporatists operating from the Marshal's cabinet and syndicalists based in the ministry of labour continued. Belin seems to have been deliberately excluded from the Commission d'Organisation Professionnelle, which drew up the final

---

[37] Belin archives, Belin to Bouthillier, 7 December 1941. The origins of an unspoken alliance between industrialists and Belin can be traced back to August 1940. Nicolle wrote: 'the employers' organizations rush to his office to ask for help and protection' (*Cinquante mois*, vol. I, entry for 27 August 1940).

[38] Belin archives, Bouthillier to Belin, 5 December 1941.

[39] Belin archives, Baudouin note.   [40] Belin archives, 5 December 1941.

[41] Belin archives, Belin to Bouthillier, 7 December 1941.

[42] Belin archives, Belin to Pétain, 21 December 1941: 'But if you feel obliged to follow the suggestion of one of my colleagues, that is to say draw up a special commission to examine for final approval an urgent text, already adopted by the *conseil des ministres* and counter-signed by the majority of its members, then, in the interest of the government and in the interest of the reform itself, I must ask you to get someone else to see it through.'

draft of the *Charte*. There was a dramatic struggle over this draft right up to the last moment. Belin threatened resignation again and the text of the *Charte* was snatched back from the printing presses for further alteration.[43] Belin demanded the resignation of certain members of the commission designed to implement the *Charte* on the grounds that they were openly opposing his own policy (see below). Indeed the conflict lasted beyond Belin's resignation. Belin's successor (Lagardelle) intervened at a meeting of the *conseil supérieur* in 1943 in terms which revealed how much of the heat of the conflict had survived: 'The text of the *Charte* was a compromise between two tendencies; since its publication there is conflict between the two positions every day. It seems that now the Marshal's entourage, want more than ever, to see *syndicalisme* disappear.'[44]

Industry and the *Charte*

During the preparation of the *Charte* interested parties were specifically asked to express their opinions on the proposed legislation. Cèbe analysed the response that this had produced by March 1941. He suggested that initially opinion was very much in favour of corporatism: 'All the other drafts and suggestions, forming a considerable majority, stressed the inconveniences, the dangers and the useless duplication of parallel organizations in each category; consequently the fusion of workers' and employers' unions in a single body was foreseen.' However, Cèbe's interpretation deserves to be regarded with a certain amount of scepticism; he was, after all, an enthusiastic proponent of corporatism himself. Once the Comité d'Organisation Professionnelle was set up, the analysis of submissions on the *Charte* became more systematic. Of 300 which were considered relevant 76 came from employers, and, of these, 42 were from employers' associations and 34 were from individual *patrons*. According to Cèbe these opinions were now dividing more or less evenly between corporatism and syndicalism.[45]

In fact, much of the significant correspondence from employers is still available in the Belin archives. Furthermore, in March 1941 the government set up the Commission d'Organisation Professionnelle to draw up the final draft of the *Charte*. Seven of the twenty-nine members of this commission

---

[43] For an account of these events see Julliard, 'La Charte du Travail', in FNSP, *Le gouvernement de Vichy 1940–1942*, pp. 157–211.

[44] AN, 2 AG 586, transcript of *conseil supérieur de la Charte* meeting of 14 September 1943. Lagardelle apparently regarded his speech as so potentially sensitive that he requested the stenographers to stop recording the meeting. But there is a full transcript of his intervention in the archives??

[45] AN, F 22 1835 Cèbe report to Commission d'Organisation Professionnelle.

came from the *patronat*.[46] The transcripts of the debates of this commission are still available. The study of these sources makes it possible to analyse the attitudes of different sections of the *patronat* with some precision.

Heavy industry and the *Charte*

The representatives of heavy industry were not, on the whole, interested in a corporatist new order. Many important industries made no contribution to the debate whatsoever. For example, the influential Parisian metallurgy association was aware of the debate over the *Charte*, but did not bother to submit any proposals of its own.[47] Those who did submit proposals were often indifferent or hostile to corporatism. The Groupement Interprofessionnel of Roubaix wrote: 'As for the corporatist system, we believe that at the moment it is impracticable.'[48] Lente, the head of the Union des Industries Métallurgiques et Minières, expressed support for corporatism as a long-term aim, but added: 'it does not seem to me that present conditions allow the generalization of the direct and intimate form of collaboration right now'.[49]

What were the reasons for this lack of enthusiasm? Firstly, it was a symptom of a general reluctance on the part of industrialists to become involved in grand schemes for economic reform at a time when immediate problems were so pressing. Lente expressed this reservation with reference to the *Charte*: 'the social problem today is less a matter of building corporative institutions without delay than of practical work to allow enterprises to survive'.[50]

Secondly, heavy industrialists had never been enthusiastic about corporatism. As suggested in chapter 5, they had used it as a short-term tactic to rally small business and the bourgeois against the Popular Front.

---

[46] These were Bardet, a manufacturer of machines, Pierre Laguionie, administrator of the Printemps Department Store, Jacques Lente, president of the UIMM (one of the three vice-presidents of the commission), Georges Painvin of the Union des Industries Chimiques and of the firm Ugine, and Jules Verger, the electrical businessman and the president of the Confédération Nationale des Associations Professionnelles Mixtes. By contrast the Commission contained five representatives of the *cadres*, two of the *artisant*, six official delegates from the administration and seven workers' representatives. For these purposes I have chosen to define representatives of the *patronat* fairly narrowly. I have not included representatives of the *artisanat* like Huguet (a locksmith) or Jeannin (a plumber). It should also be stressed that some members of the Commission delegated by the administration such as Dauvergne (an Inspector of Mines) or Lucien may have had close links with the *patronat*.

[47] AN, 39 AS 852, *conseil d'administration* meeting of 8 April 1941. De Canisy gave the meeting an account of the latest developments in the Comité d'Organisation Professionnelle.

[48] Belin archives, letter from Roubaix Groupement Patronal Interprofessionnel.

[49] Belin archives, UIMM submission, dated 22 January 1941.   [50] Ibid.

But it had merely been a means to an end. The Popular Front was now destroyed. Trade union power had been ended. Lente admitted that industry had little objection to unions now that the principal subject of dispute between employers and workers – pay – had been removed from the agenda by government controls. Indeed far from wishing to see trade unions destroyed employers were often concerned to appease labour in order to secure a more harmonious atmosphere in which to exploit the opportunities of the war economy. They saw the abolition of labour unions under these circumstances as a futile provocation. The Roubaix Groupement Inter-professionnel (which had been noted before the war for its aggressively anti-union attitude) suggested that corporations were 'frankly to be rejected' because 'the workers see in them a means to be used by employers to separate them from their fellow workers in other professions'. For this reason it was admitted that 'the employers in our area have never sought to create such associations, which we actively discouraged'.[51]

Thirdly, many of the leaders of industrial associations saw the *Charte* as a potential threat to their own position as well as to the prosperity of the industries that they claimed to represent. Since many leaders founded their power on associations that incorporated more than one industry it was clear that corporatism would cut them out of the picture. The Roubaix Group displayed particular concern that the role of local interprofessional bodies (like itself) should be recognized.[52]

The *avant-garde du patronat*

There had always been a recognizable section of the *patronat* that had an interest in social and economic reform for its own sake, rather than as an instrument of business advantage. Such men took a considerable interest in the *Charte* and especially in the corporatist elements of the proposed reform.

The *avant-garde patronale* had always been closely linked to the tradition of the French *grandes écoles*. Cèbe recognized that much of the interest in the *Charte* was coming from the graduates of the *grandes écoles*.[53] Furthermore, many who expressed interest in the *Charte* had belonged to various pre-war study groups and think tanks of the type described in chapter 5. Lefaurichon was a member of the Comité Central des Classes Moyennes and the Centre de Réforme Economique; he sent a copy of the

---

[51] Belin archives, submission of Roubaix Groupement.
[52] The element of institutional self-interest in submissions to Belin was also revealed by the insistence of the Roubaix Groupement that Chambers of Commerce were not appropriate bodies to operate within the framework of the *Charte*.
[53] AN, F 22 1835, Cèbe report. See also Belin archives, note on *organisation professionnelle* by A. Garnier, president of the Association Amicale des Anciens Elèves de l'Ecole Centrale.

corporatist project of this latter body to Pétain on 20 March 1941.[54] A number of members of the Commission d'Organisation Professionnelle had been connected to the *avant-garde patronale*. Mersch was the head of the Centre des Jeunes Patrons and a member of the Comité Central d'Organisation Professionnelle; Painvin had been a member of the *Nouveaux Cahiers* movement.

The involvement of these men is significant for two reasons. Firstly, it shows once again that the modernizing ambitions of the 'technocrats' and the corporatism that was so dear to the Marshal's entourage were by no means mutually exclusive. Secondly, the involvement of these men highlights once again the distance of ordinary industrialists from the corporatist schemes. For, as has been stressed, the preoccupations of these men were very different from those of ordinary industrialists; indeed Vichy gave many such men the chance to lose all contact with ordinary business life and devote themselves full-time to the study groups and commissions that the regime established. Of course it would be wrong to suggest that an absolute division can be made between 'real industrialists' and the 'avant-garde'. Bardet was an obvious example of a man who fitted neither category. In his later incarnation, as head of the Centre d'Information Interprofessionnelle, he stood halfway between being a representative of industry and a Vichy functionary. Perhaps his own refusal to endorse either syndicalism or corporatism reflected this ambiguous position, although his opponents had no difficulty in labelling him a representative of big business and a 'syndicalist'. Other figures were clearly separate from the concerns of ordinary industrialists. The most clear evidence of how sharp such a separation could be is provided by Painvin. His public activities as president of the Paris Chamber of Commerce, as president of the Comité d'Organisation for the chemical industry, and president of the Crédit Commercial de France, did not leave him time to administer his own company, a task which was undertaken by Eugène Matthieu.[55]

Small and declining business

The attitudes of businessmen to the *Charte* reveal significant rifts in French society. The heavy industrialists who were primarily based in the north of France were generally indifferent or hostile to the prospect of corporatism. By contrast, the supporters of corporatism came from the southern zone and

---

[54] Belin archives, Lefaurichon to Pétain, 20 March 1941. The Comité Central des Classes Moyennes also submitted the same project on the same date.
[55] Henri Rousso, 'Les élites économiques dans les années quarante', *Mélanges de l'Ecole Française de Rome*, 95 (1982–3), 29–49, at p. 35.

especially from Lyon, which seems to have become a powerhouse of corporatist thinking during the occupation.[56] They also came from industries that were small scale and declining. In particular great interest in corporatism was expressed by the Lyon textile industry. It was also claimed that the northern textile industry was on the verge of organizing itself in corporatist fashion.[57] These industries often presented their claims in terms of anti-big business rhetoric: 'For this sector [is] in...in conflict with the great Lyonnais trusts.'[58]

A great deal of the support for corporatism came from those who had been brought into the leadership of the employers' movement after 1936. Johannes Dupraz, a colleague of Aymé Bernard in Lyon, submitted a corporatist charter.[59] Pierre Nicolle, the leader of the Comité de Salut Economique, who had been brought into the CGPF after 1936, submitted the same corporatist project under three different aliases.[60] Jules Verger, the leader of the CPAS, was indefatigable in his promotion of the benefits of the Association Professionnelle Mixte. The fact that such men were involved in the *Charte* is hardly surprising. Corporatism had been their creed in the late 1930s, and indeed it had been a large part of the justification for their accession to power in the employers' movement.

However, as has been stressed, men like Verger and Nicolle were operating in a changed context during the Vichy regime. They had been allied with heavy industry in the aftermath of the Popular Front. But, with the Popular Front legacy destroyed, heavy industry abandoned not only corporatism and anti-unionism but also the men who had propagated those

[56] The Belin archives contain notes from the Union des Syndicats de la Teinture de l'Impression et de l'Apprêt de Lyon et de la Région, from a Groupement Corporatif in Lyon (actually the project of Pierre Nicolle), and from the Centrale de l'Industrie et du Commerce in Lyon.

[57] AN, F 22 1835, Cèbe report, p. 13. Cèbe is probably referring to the efforts of Jacques Warnier and his associates in the Association Textile in Reims (see AN, 57 AS 3, 'essai d'organisation textile'). However, Cèbe's assertion would have surprised the Roubaix Groupement which was heavily influenced by textile interests but hostile to corporatism.

[58] Cèbe account, pages 6 and 13. See also the voluminous note of the Union des Syndicats de la Teinture de l'Impression et de l'Apprêt de Lyon et de la Région, dated 30 April 1941. There are a variety of caveats to be added to any presentation of the textile industry as the foundation of corporatist power. The textile industry did not have a unitary interest in the question of professional organization, and medium-sized textile manufacturers had often been very hostile to corporatism (see chapter 5).

[59] Belin archive, pamphlet from the Centrale de l'Industrie et Commerce de Lyon, received 5 April 1941. No author's name is given on the cover but Dupraz is mentioned as being the author in the text. The pamphlet suggested that the Centrale's enquiry had begun in May 1940 (i.e. before the establishment of the Vichy regime). It also stressed that corporatism was a long-term aim which might take ten or twenty years to achieve.

[60] Ibid., 'Projet Nicolle', 8 January 1941. The same project was also submitted as *projet d'une organisation corporative à Lyon*, and as the project of the Allier Chamber of Commerce. In a covering note Nicolle implied that his note sprang from a recent meeting of the southern zone of the FAR. But in fact Bernard, the president of the FAR, submitted a quite different project.

creeds. Nicolle and Verger were isolated from their former allies. Furthermore, in 1936 such men had supported their claims to represent small business with a certain amount of rhetorical hostility to heavy industry. In their new isolation this rhetorical hostility became real. Typically, indeed, they began to rewrite the history of 1936 in terms of conspiracy theories about relations between heavy industry and the left-wing government. Jules Verger's comments upon Bardet's proposed *Charte* reveal this tendency beautifully: 'The draft is essentially *syndicaliste*...the natural product of the collusion between the representatives of big business who prefer, as in 1936, to move ahead with their traditional, but secret, friends, the CGT unions, rather than to run the risk of a corporatist organization with all its possible consequences.'[61]

Business and the *Charte* after publication

The *Charte* was always meant to be a framework for a new regime rather than a complete structure. After publication, the debate about how the *Charte* was to be implemented continued in the Conseil Supérieur de la Charte. A number of employers who had been members of the Commission d'Organisation Professionnelle were appointed to the *conseil supérieur*. Many of the debates that had dominated the work of the Commission continued in the *conseil*. In particular, Jules Verger persisted in his near obsessive promotion of the Association Professionnelle Mixte (APM), and continued to express extreme hostility to both the ministry of labour and the representatives of heavy industry. Once again, these latter two seem to have found themselves in alliance against the APM. The issue came to a head when Verger sent a letter to Belin demanding that the APM be given representation on the *conseil* equal to that of the syndicalists and artisans. Belin demanded his resignation in especially vigorous terms – 'his letter shows a lack of respect for the simple truth, and is also insulting to me personally',[62] which was apparently supported by his colleagues on the *conseil*. Nicolle interpreted the exclusion of Verger from the *conseil* as the final victory of the alliance of syndicalists and industrialists against corporatists: 'the triumph of marxist trade unionists supported by the representatives of big business'.[63]

The reception of the *Charte* by ordinary employers was unenthusiastic. Julliard characterizes the reaction of the business press as polite indifference. Most significantly, the mechanisms for establishing corporations were

---

[61] Belin archive, criticism of projet Bardet dated September 1941.
[62] AN, F 22 1836, 4 February 1942.
[63] Nicolle, *Cinquante mois d'armistice*, vol. I, p. 407, entry for 6 February 1941.

simply left unused. In 1944, of twenty-nine *familles professionnelles* previewed by the *Charte* only twenty-four had formed a provisional committee and only three, mining, clothing and wool, had formed *comités sociaux*.[64]

Conclusion

Superficially the debate on the *Charte du Travail* seems to confirm the view that Vichy was the *revanche des patrons* for the Popular Front. Politicians presented the *Charte* as a response to the crisis of 1936. Many of the keenest supporters of the *Charte*, and especially of the corporatist version of the *Charte*, came from that section of the employers' movement that had arisen after 1936. But in fact the *Charte* exposed divisions in both the Vichy government and the business movement. It also exposed alignments which had been reversed since 1936. Heavy industrialists, who had been so hostile to the trade unions, were now allied with the trade unionists in the ministry of labour. Meanwhile the post-1936 leaders who had arisen in the employers' movement claiming to represent small business and the *classes moyennes* vigorously supported the corporatist projects of the Marshal's cabinet. But the alliance that had existed between heavy industry and the post-1936 leaders was now broken. Indeed heavy industry was now opposed to the corporatist projects of its former allies and consequently opposed to a central part of the Vichy regime.

[64] Henri Rousso, 'L'organisation industrielle de Vichy', *Revue d'histoire de la deuxième guerre mondiale*, 116, (1979), 27–44. Of course clothing and wool were the kind of industries likely to be sympathetic to Vichy. The progress of the *Charte* in the mining industry was much more surprising – the coal industry was the classic example of heavy industry which did well out of the war economy but displayed great hostility to the Vichy government.

Chapter 9

Labour relations during the occupation

Introduction

The occupation is remembered among the French working classes as a grim period: pay and rations were reduced almost to starvation levels, work rates were increased, labour discipline was fierce, strikes were crushed and unions dissolved. Historians have tended to approach the study of labour relations during the occupation through the eyes of the workers and more particularly through the retrospective accounts of union militants.[1] Under these circumstances it is not surprising that the Vichy government has been seen as the revenge of the French *patronat* for the Popular Front.[2] However, when examined through the eyes of the employers, the situation looks far less clear. As far as they were concerned the labour victory of 1936 had already been reversed before the establishment of the Vichy regime. The Majestic accords had marked the end of this process. Under Vichy three factors disposed the *patronat* to seek better relations with their workers. Firstly, the growing intervention of the state meant that workers and employers no longer confronted each other directly. Secondly, the labour famine that afflicted certain industries disposed employers to concessions. Thirdly, as the prospect of allied victory loomed on the horizon, employers were keen to avoid conflict with an organized working class that was associated with the Resistance. In this chapter it will be argued that the view of labour relations between 1940 and 1944 enshrined in previous historiography springs more from the myths of the liberation than from the realities of the occupation.

---

[1] This tendency is especially marked among local historians. The accounts of Dejonghe, Gillet, Holter and Luirard all depend heavily on interviews which they conducted with former union militants.

[2] H. R. Kedward, 'Patriots and Patriotism in Vichy France', *Transactions of the Royal Historical Society*, 32 (1981), 175–92, at p. 178. '1940 is less the death of the Third Republic than the final death of the Popular Front... Vichy labour legislation, culminating in the Charte du Travail was heavily weighted towards the employers.'

The division of France and the role of the occupying authorities

It was obvious from the very beginning that the occupation would radically alter the pattern of labour relations. In the Third Republic politics had been conditioned by the electoral preponderance of the *classes moyennes* which was especially pronounced in the south of the country; the proletariat had been confined to what Hoffmann has labelled 'a social ghetto'. The occupation separated 'le Nord qui travaille' from 'le Sud qui gouverne'. Industry was concentrated in areas under German administration, and especially in the Nord and Pas-de-Calais or *zone interdite*, which was, in the early months of the occupation, entirely outside the control of the French administration. In these circumstances the social ghetto in which the proletariat had been confined was replaced by a geographical ghetto in which industrialists and workers were confined together.

German administrators in France imported their own set of social attitudes. The proletariat was far more politically significant in Germany, and especially Nazi Germany, than it had ever been in France. At the beginning of the occupation the Germans courted the workers in the *zone interdite* assiduously. A train bringing extra rations was sent to the area, and special offices of the German labour organization were set up.[3] Throughout the occupation the Germans continued to display concern about the plight of the working class, even in private.[4] On the whole German initiatives were greeted coldly by the workers themselves, but they impressed, and startled,[5] many French industrialists. It may well be that the efforts that employers made during the occupation to obtain better relations with their workers were, in part, designed to counter and pre-empt advances which the Germans might make to the proletariat.

[3] For an account of German efforts to win over the working classes in the *zone interdite* see Etienne Dejonghe, 'Les problèmes sociaux dans les entreprises houillères du Nord et du Pas-de-Calais durant la seconde guerre mondiale', *Revue d'histoire moderne et contemporaine*, 18 (1971), 124–44.

[4] Paris, Archives Nationales (AN), F 37 46. The German economic authorities wrote to Barnaud on 26 May 1942 complaining about the disparity between industrialists who were benefiting from the war economy and workers who were suffering. When shown the final draft of the *Charte du Travail* on 22 October Dr Michel complained that it did not do enough for the workers (Paris, Institut d'Histoire Sociale, Belin archives).

[5] Industrialists in the *zone interdite* talked of 'une véritable Nazification ouvrière': see previous chapter.

The effect of official intervention in the economy

The increasing role in the economy that was played by the authorities, both German and French, had a considerable impact on labour relations. Before the mobilization of the French economy that preceded the Vichy regime industrial relations had been a game with only two players; whatever the employers lost the workers gained and vice versa. Mobilization meant an increasing role for the state. One consequence of this was that the major issue that had divided employers and workers before the war, pay, was simply removed from the agenda, Lente, the president of the UIMM, recognized this: 'If the fixing of salaries is excluded from discussions between workers and bosses, then the source of conflict has been removed. But fixing salaries, in present circumstances, can only be one part of the overall economic system.'[6]

Under Vichy, state economic controls became more extensive and this gave both sides in industry issues on which they could make common cause. Indeed workers and bosses were united in their alienation from a government that was both geographically and psychologically separate from the industrial areas of France. Many of the demands of the workers were addressed to the state rather than to the employer. Whereas in the Republic the well-being of workers had depended principally on the pay that they could extract from the employers, it now depended largely on the rations that could be extracted from the government. The Paris metallurgy association recognized the significance of this shift: 'It is clear that now the relief of the difficult situation of the workers depends much less on the level of wages than on problems of food supply. Furthermore, it is impossible to get a sensible level of wages when the cost of living is affected by so many irregularities and uncertainties in supply.'[7] On the issue of rationing the employers could support their workers' demands. Indeed the situation that had prevailed before the war was now reversed. Previously workers had addressed their demands to the employers and had often been supported by the authorities. Now demands were addressed to the authorities and often supported by employers. There were even occasions on which *patrons* seemed to be playing the part which in normal times would have been taken by a trade union. Thus the *conseil d'administration* of the Blanzy mine explained a recent strike as the inevitable product of the problems induced by reduced rations 'that have frequently been drawn to the attention of the authorities'.[8] Indeed the Germans complained that employers were lending

[6] Paris, Institut d'Histoire Sociale, Belin archives, note of Lente dated 22 January 1941.
[7] AN, 39 AS 853, GIMMCP, p-v of CA, 20 June 1941.
[8] AN, 92 AQ 27, p-v of CA of Blanzy company, 18 December 1941.

tacit support to strikes: 'some of the mining companies make it obvious how little interest they have in a settlement of this strike'.[9] As the demands of the Vichy government and the occupation authorities increased there were more and more issues on which workers were supported by the employers. This support was sometimes expressed in extravagant terms. The Mines de Cessous wrote of an 'incredible but true situation' in which its workers were being forced to guard railway lines during their free time:

These things are very prone to annoy a staff who are already subject to rather extraordinary treatment, that is to say losing a large part of their salary and not even paid for months at a time, they are obliged to undertake guard duty at night...the obligation is really a matter of coercion...One wants to avoid the worst for the stout chaps who remain at work and continue to do their duty.[10]

The Vichy labour market

The role of the Vichy state explains the fact that it was possible for employers to support workers' demands without damaging their own interests. But why should employers have wanted to support workers' demands? To understand this concern for the welfare of workers it is necessary to examine the economic circumstances of the occupation. At first it seemed that unemployment might be the major problem of the occupation. In the immediate aftermath of defeat one million Frenchmen were unemployed, in spite of the fact that two million workers had been removed from the labour market into German prison camps. However, as order was restored and as the requirements of the German war economy began to make themselves felt, this situation was reversed. It did not change in a uniform or regular way. Certain industries began to suffer from a severe lack of labour at a time when the rest of France was still concerned with unemployment. The industries which began to feel the need for labour first were those that were of most use to the Germans. These were initially heavy industries that provided the infrastructure for armaments manufacture and troop movement. The demands of the war economy were especially pressing because the French heavy industrial sector had always been relatively small. The situation was illustrated by the predicament of the coal-mines. Before the war France had imported about one-third of its coal, and an even higher proportion of coke which was of special use to industry. During the occupation this was lost. At the same time France lost the production of the

---

[9] AN, 40 AS 78, letter from Oberfeldkommandur 670 to the prefect at Lille, quoted in a note dated 11 October 1943.   [10] AN, 40 AS 44, letter to COH dated 28 April 1944.

Lorraine coalfield. In these conditions the mines could sell anything that could be produced: 'As long as the coal shortage lasts, the mines are certain to be able to sell all their produce.'[11] Soon there was a terrible labour famine in the coalfields. As early as November 1941 the Comité d'Organisation for the coal industry (COH) remarked that it needed an extra 48,000 workers. In April 1942 the COH's section of the Loire wrote of 'the dangers risked by industry in the Loire basin on account of labour shortage'.[12] They sought to extract workers from the Chantiers de Jeunesse,[13] and to have workers freed by the scaling down of public works or agriculture;[14] they requested the release of miners who were being held as prisoners of war; they struggled to get extra foreign labour;[15] they were even prepared to sue workers who went voluntarily to Germany.[16]

As the war continued the labour famine extended to other sectors of the economy. The general need for labour was exacerbated by two factors. Firstly, the French economy was drained by the transfer of labour across the Rhine, a transfer that began in 1941 and became obligatory, for men of certain ages, after February 1943. Secondly, the productivity of labour was greatly diminished by the ageing of plant which, under the circumstances of the occupation, could not be replaced. The minister of industrial production pointed out in 1943 that the problem of ageing plant in the mines was so severe that a 15 per cent increase in the labour force would only produce a 3 or 4 per cent increase in production.[17]

A sharp competition developed among heavy industries to obtain and keep labour. A note of one of the supply agencies recorded in October 1943: 'the mines and naval construction are damaged by hiring in the mechanical electrical and chemical industries, mines and steel production'. Maurice Sartiaux and company complained in early 1944 that their labour was being poached by the mines.[18] The committee controlling the coal-mines did not try to restrain such activity; on the contrary it wrote to the Mines de Roche la Molière specifically telling them that they were entitled to hire workers from other industries, even from those whose labour forces enjoyed the

---

[11] AN, 68 AJ 130, note of 26 March 1942.
[12] AN, 40 AS 43, dated 22 April 1942.
[13] AN, 40 AS 43, letter, dated 10 June 1943, from Lepercq to Bichelonne.
[14] AN, 40 AS 43, note of 9 June 1942.
[15] AN, 40 AS 43, note of 24 February about the hiring of Poles; letter, dated 15 May 1942, to the Loire Chamber of Mines about attempts to assimilate foreign workers; and note of telephone conversation of 18 February 1942 about attempts to get access to groups of foreign workers.
[16] AN, 40 AS 43. The COH wrote, of the company de Bethune's proposal to sue workers who had broken their contracts to work in Germany: 'Dans ce cas particulier les poursuites seraient absolument justifiées' (letter dated 2 June 1943).
[17] AN, 72 AJ 1926, Bichelonne speaking in Speer-Bichelonne meeting, 27 September 1943.
[18] AN, 40 AS 43, note from the Chamber of Mines in the Nord and Pas-de-Calais, dated 20 January 1942.

same special protection as that of the mines. By the end of the occupation the French economy had degenerated into a chaotic scramble for labour:

The situation of the labour market is very confused on account of, on the one hand, the diversity of need and on the other hand the fragmentation of agencies…Each agency, French as well as German, looks for men on its own account, the Secrétariat Général à la main d'oeuvre and the Arbeitseinsatz are more registries of demand… than real coordinators…'S' factories receive ever greater workloads, and the mines…push production to a maximum, the German army, navy, airforce and the Todt organization all require an ever larger workforce.[19]

The survival of labour power

The labour shortage affected the balance of power between workers and employers. It would be wrong to assume that the elimination of labour's formal rights led to 'total power for the bosses'.[20] Mason has shown that, in spite of the formal suppression of the unions in the Third Reich, workers had great informal leverage because of the labour shortage that affected heavy industry.[21] The same was true in France. Workers in the key industries which were necessary to the German war economy were aware that their indispensability made coercion impossible. For example, strikes in the coal industry continued throughout the war. The authorities could not hope to arrest or deport those involved in these movements. A pamphlet circulated immediately before the strike in the northern coalfield in May 1941 mocked the prospect of reprisal: 'Deportation to Germany? That's a good one. Will Hitler and Mussolini's generals come and dig coal in our place?'[22] When 300 miners were arrested in 1943 the Germans were obliged to release them again. Even if workers did not indulge in outright rebellion, *patrons* could not stop exhausted, underpaid and underfed workers from simply working more slowly or reporting as absent. A note of the Anzin mine reveals the threat that excessive exploitation of workers posed: 'The workers suffer more and more from the physical and psychological

---

[19] 72 AJ 1929, note of 12 April 1944, 'Le problème de la main d'oeuvre en France'.
[20] This is the phrase coined by Julliard in 'La Charte du Travail', in FNSP, *Le gouvernement de Vichy 1940–1942* (Paris, 1972), pp. 157–211, at p. 170.
[21] T. Mason, 'Labour in the Third Reich', *Past and Present*, 33 (1966), 112–41. 'As the strain on the labour market increased industrial discipline decreased' (p. 131). Mason describes a situation in which certain key industries were so stretched for labour that they sought to circumvent maximum pay limits imposed by the government' (p. 137). This is very similar to the position of certain industries in Vichy France. The key difference between France and Mason's Germany is the fact that in the latter the government ruled out certain measures of coercion for political reasons.
[22] Dejonghe, 'Les problèmes sociaux dans les entreprises houillères du Nord et du Pas-de-Calais durant la seconde guerre mondiale'.

depression that affects many of them…Absence through illness and accidental injury are increasing, absenteeism continues in the pits by the Belgian frontier.'[23] After the institution of Service du Travail Obligatoire increasing numbers of young workers simply went walkabout, and joined bands of *réfractaires* in the mountains.

The employers' appeasement of labour

The need to obtain labour meant that it was in the interests of employers to provide whatever benefits they could for their workers. In fact one of the ironies of the Vichy regime was that, while Vichy talked about class collaboration, heavy industry was desperately trying to obtain collaboration from its workers. Industrialists sometimes compared their own practical efforts with the fine words of the Vichy regime. Thus the Roubaix Employers' Syndicate, famous for its fiercely combative attitude to labour relations in the 1930s, wrote with reference to the *Charte du Travail*: 'This propaganda, however well conducted, will be ineffective, and may provoke a counter-reaction, if employers are not given the means to provide their workers with the material aid that they need more than words.'[24]

The attempt to appease labour had some odd side-effects. The most conspicuous of these concerned employers' attitudes to pay. Pay control was so strict, largely because of the desire of the Germans to make work across the Rhine more attractive, that only one general pay increase was allowed during the whole of the occupation. Initially heavy industry rather welcomed these regulations (see above). But soon the labour needs of industrialists working for the war economy were so great that they began to turn the normal pattern of labour relations on its head and lobby for the right to pay their workers more. This trend originated in the coal industry. The COH appealed for higher wages as early as May 1941, and made at least two further requests of this nature.[25] The metallurgy industry was suffering from a similar labour shortage by 1943. A member of the *conseil d'administration* of the GIMMCP said in May of that year 'an increase in official wages is urgently needed'.[26] Most astonishing of all was the case of the president of

---

[23] AN, 109 MI 5, p-v of CA, 24 June 1941.

[24] Belin archives, submission of Groupement Interprofessionnel of Roubaix.

[25] AN, 40 AS 43, 1 October 1942. The COH appealed for 'une heureuse solution aux problèmes des salaires' and warned that 'if this is not done, the large-scale arrival of inexperienced workers in an atmosphere of resentment may bring about new disorders'. See also 40 AS 43, note of 7 July 1943: 'M. Daval feels that M. Perrin, of the Labour Ministry, is not really interested in the problem of wages, he is seeking a means of arousing his enthusiasm.'

[26] AN, 39 AS 854, p-v of CA, 27 May 1943, remarks of M. Chamon.

the Comité de Liaison Interprofessionnelle of the building industry; he was threatened with imprisonment for having granted an illegal pay increase.[27]

If the *patronat* could not obtain the right to bid for labour with pay increases, they tried to do so with payment in kind. Indeed the head of the Centre d'Information Interprofessionnelle (the closest thing which the *patronat* had to an official leader during the war) explicitly advocated such a strategy: 'it now seems impossible to get a general wage rise in the near future. But it is worth considering whether the same result could be obtained by increasing social supplements given to workers.'[28] Company archives are full of descriptions of special provisions for workers: gardens were set aside where food could be grown, works canteens were set up, special co-operatives where groceries could be obtained at a discount were established, companies even provided Christmas trees for the children of prisoners of war. The management of Renault (not a company noted for benevolence to its workers) gave the following report to its shareholders' assembly on 15 December 1942: 'Among our main preoccupations is the daily welfare of our staff... we have sought to ease their difficulties by developing our social activities. Deserving special mention are the construction of canteens, the setting up of a holiday camp, the creation of workers' gardens, and the opening of a social centre.'[29]

It is tempting not to pay much attention to this. One would expect to find such smug talk of good deeds in the circumstances. But these social provisions reflect a highly significant change. The first point to be noted is that only large-scale enterprises were in a position to provide such facilities. Furthermore, only companies that were of some value to the German war economy were able to obtain the provisions with which to stock special shops.[30] The apparent philanthropy on the part of heavy industry marked a highly significant shift of social alliances. Before the war the *patronat* had been part of what Hoffmann has labelled the republican synthesis. That is to say they had allied with (or rather had sought to appear allied with) the *classes moyennes*. This alliance had been perceived as especially important during the aftermath of the Popular Front. One of the key aspects of the programme which industrial organizations had adopted to appease the *classes moyennes* had been the suppression of consumer co-operatives based

---

[27] AN, 72 AJ 1931, letter from Bichelonne dated 6 December 1943. Note that the Comité de Liaison was not a Comité d'Organisation (though the Germans seem to have believed that it was).

[28] AN, 72 AJ 1931, note dated 20 December 1943. Bardet's approach is not entirely typical of the *patronat*. He suggests raising family supplements. More typically the *patronat* sought to provide food to workers at the workplace in order to deter absenteeism.

[29] AN, 91 AQ 1/2.

[30] AN, F 22 1775, 31 December 1941, Bichelonne to Inspecteurs du Travail: 'The creation of canteens has, so far, run up against difficulties due to problems of supply, except in factories working for the occupation authorities.'

in factories, since such co-operatives would naturally cut out small traders.[31] During the occupation, on the other hand, the key to big business social strategy was the appeasement of the working class (the group confined to a 'social ghetto' by the republican synthesis). The old alliance with the *classes moyennes* was broken; it is highly significant that Bernard, one of the leaders who claimed to represent the *classes moyennes*, condemned the provision of factory canteens.[32]

An exception? The strike in the Nord and Pas-de-Calais of 1941

Historians who see the occupation as a period of violent confrontation between capital and labour have devoted a great deal of attention to the strike in the northern coal basin of May and June 1941. The strike began on 27 May at the Dourges Mine and lasted until 6 June.[33] Initially the miners were protesting about the methods by which their salaries were calculated; they resented the fixing of pay to the work performed by individuals or small groups of workers, a system sometimes referred to as 'le système Bédaux'.[34] The strikers' demands soon became widened to include higher rations, the return of prisoners of war and the release of militants arrested at the beginning of the strike. The strike was a remarkable display of working-class solidarity: at its peak 80 per cent of the miners in the area had stopped work. The decision to strike appears to have been spontaneous; known militants, who were being closely watched by the authorities, played little part in the spread of the movement. Orders were spread by word of mouth and considerable support was given to the striking miners by the working-class population of the area and especially by women.[35] Not surprisingly the strike was soon enshrined in local mythology. It was presented as a confrontation between a heroically resistant proletariat and a collaborating *patronat*. In 1975 Marcel Paul, a Communist minister of 1944, suggested that the strike indicated 'the miners' refusal to accept the policy of the pseudo government installed by the enemy at Vichy'. He described a

---

[31] See the appeals of Duchemin and Lambert Ribot cited in chapter 2.

[32] AN, 70 AQ 442, transcript of meeting of northern FAR, 18 July 1941.

[33] For an account of the strike see Etienne Dejonghe, 'Chronique de la grève des mineurs du Nord/Pas-de-Calais (27 mai–6 juin 1941)', *Revue du Nord*, 69 (1987), 323–45.

[34] AN, F 37 39, note of 7 June 1941, Monique Luirard (*La région stéphanoise dans la guerre et dans la paix 1936–1951* (Saint-Etienne, 1981)) quotes Perrin Pelletier's complaint that the phrase 'système Bédaux' was used too loosely to describe any system of payment by results. No doubt this is true. However, in practice both mine managers and the COH used the phrase fairly loosely.

[35] AN, F 37 39, report of 10 June 1941: 'In the mines, women make up pickets at each shift change...the police are obliged to intervene to prevent them from turning away miners turning up for work.'

confrontation between the bosses' delegate and the miners: '"What do you want?", asked the employers' delegate. "Rifles", replied the miners', and portrays this as indicative that 'The division between managers and the miners on this matter, that is so sensitive in terms of national feeling, was absolute.'[36]

In fact the conflict between employers and workers during the strike was far more ambiguous and complicated than Paul's description implies. There was certainly no outright confrontation between the delegates of the two sides. The demands of the strikers were only made known through anonymous pamphlets. Some of these demands, those relating to rations, pay and the return of prisoners of war, touched upon matters that were governed by German ordinances, and it might be argued that these demands were a form of resistance. But over these issues there was no division between workers and bosses. The COH had requested higher rations and the return of prisoners of war; the president of the COH, Aimé Lepercq, had appealed for higher pay only weeks before the strike began.[37]

The only issue which divided strikers and bosses was the restoration of the *système Bédaux*. This restoration had been one of the mining companies' principal aims ever since 1936. They identified opposition to this system as the main motive for the strike, and it seems reasonable to assume that it was for this reason that their reaction was so violent.[38] This puts the strike in a very different perspective from that established by the post-war mythology. The conflict between the strikers and management entailed by the strike was not simply one aspect of a general battle between capital and labour during the occupation; rather it was a struggle over a very specific issue. Furthermore, the struggle over the restoration of the *système Bédaux* was an exception in the general pattern of labour relations during the period. For the suppression of the *système Bédaux* had been a product of the workers' victory in 1936. This was one of the few areas where management had not succeeded in reversing that victory before June 1940.

There may have been another motive for the violence of the coal-mining *patronat*'s reaction to the strike. For the strike coincided with an attempt by the ministry of industrial production to have the Nord and Pas-de-Calais removed from the administration of the German high command in Brussels and integrated into French administration. The coal industry had very good

[36] Marcel Paul, 'Sur l'importance de la nationalisation des houillères', *Revue du Nord*, 227 (1975), 667–9.

[37] AN, F 12 10 033, letter dated 10 May 1941 from Lepercq to the Inspector of Mines, Lepercq enclosed an article about recent pay increases in the building industry and warned that there might be trouble if these were not matched in the mines.

[38] Dejonghe points out that the mining companies worked closely with the French and German authorities to help suppress the strikes. The terms in which they described the 'purely political character of the strike' (AN, 40 AS 78, note dated 6 June 1941, to Lafond) was an effective invitation for intervention by the Germans.

reason to hope that such an initiative would succeed (see chapter 11). In its note describing the strikes the COH alleged that they were the product of similar events in Belgium.[39] It may well have been hoped that emphasis on such links and upon the gravity of the strike would strengthen the case for returning the area to French administration. There may even have been an element of genuine patriotism behind the tactics of the COH. Etienne Dejonghe remarks that the workers' response to the strike needs to be understood in terms of both self-interest and patriotism. Perhaps the *patronat* had a similar mix of motives.[40]

The transfer of labour to Germany

The most important issue that united workers and employers was the transfer of labour to Germany. Initially this unity took the form of attempts to obtain the release of prisoners of war. For example, one of the demands in 1941 of the striking miners in the Nord and Pas-de-Calais was the return of prisoners of war. At the same time the COH were lobbying for precisely this concession. Once again it was primarily those industries useful to the German war effort that were able to obtain results in this area. Thus the coal industry, though it never got the release of all miners, managed to obtain the release of engineers and foremen.[41] Renault linked the satisfaction of German orders to the return of specific prisoners of war.[42]

As the war progressed labour became scarce and the Germans sought to fuel their economy by transferring French labour across the Rhine. At first this was done by voluntary means, the Germans setting up labour offices to recruit in unoccupied France. Soon the French government became involved in the transfer, and on 22 June Laval appealed for craftsmen to volunteer their services in order to facilitate the return of imprisoned Frenchmen. On 2 July he addressed a specific appeal for industrialists 'to relay my ideas to their employees: they must explain the reasons of national and professional solidarity which will not fail to produce volunteers from among French workers'.[43] Subsequently the government enacted legislation in September

[39] AN, 40 AS 78, note to Lafond, dated 6 June 1941: 'the very general nature of these demands, and especially the fact that they appear at a time when rations are improving due to the production of vegetables reflects the purely political character of the strike which may be a simple consequence of the recent strikes in Belgium'.

[40] It is worth noting that the man who directed the COH's response to the strike, Aimé Lepercq, was to join the Organisation Civile et Militaire resistance network in December 1942 and, eventually, to be imprisoned by the Germans for his resistance activity.

[41] Darryl Holter, 'Miners against the State: French Miners and the Nationalization of Coalmining 1944–1949' (unpublished PhD. thesis, University of Wisconsin, Madison, 1980), p. 49.

[42] AN, 91 AQ 84, 11 May 1942, letter of Guerin to Daimler Benz.

[43] Luirard, *La région stéphanoise dans la guerre et dans la paix*, p. 436.

1942 to oblige workers to depart for Germany. At both stages the government's initiatives were resisted by employers.

There were two confrontations at a national level. Firstly, in June 1942 the heads of a number of Comités d'Organisation were convoked to the Matignon palace to hear an appeal for help with the *relève*. This help was flatly refused.[44] Again in 1943 Bichelonne arranged a series of meetings with de Tavernost of the Centre d'Information Interprofessionnelle in order to discuss the participation of the COs in STO. Tavernost stressed that most committees were very reluctant to become involved in such operations: 'The majority of committees feel that, already severely affected by the *relève*, their member companies can only consider their remaining personnel as essential.'[45] At a local level the authorities encountered a similarly cool reception. The prefect of the Loire reported that, when he convoked a meeting of employers in the metallurgy industry to pass on Laval's request, 'I encountered an open resistance ranging from inertia to explicit hostility.'[46] This was clearly an issue on which workers and employers had a joint interest: the workers did not want to go to Germany and the bosses did not want their workforces depleted. One of the Vichy officials trying to encourage departures to Germany, Benoist Méchin, talked bitterly about a new 'union sacrée' between capital and labour formed by the implementation of this policy.[47]

Although the policy of resisting deportations to Germany was a joint decision by the heads of all Comités d'Organisation, the willingness and the ability to implement this decision varied from one industry to another. Once again heavy industries needed labour most and therefore had most incentive to resist the *relève*. A comparison of several economic sectors is revealing. At one extreme was the coal industry, represented by the Comité d'Organisation de l'Industrie des Combustibles Minéraux Solides (COH), which had both the incentive and the means to resist the displacement of its labour.

The COH vigorously opposed the requisition of miners. After the war it was to claim that there had been a concerted campaign springing from 'the verbal instructions of our president' to resist deportations of labour.[48] Such a claim is of necessity impossible to check, but there is overwhelming evidence of resistance to STO in the industry. The COH wrote to the Chamber of Mines in the Loire: 'I remind you that the COH, in full agreement with the director of mines, intends to defend all this labour force with all its energy, and that it is absolutely indispensable to avoid any

[44] Jacques Benoist Méchin, *De la défaite au désastre* (2 vols., Paris, 1984), vol. II, p. 124.
[45] AN, 40 AS 43, Tavernost to Bichelonne, dated 13 April 1943.
[46] Report of Potut to Laval cited in Luirard, *La région stéphanoise dans la guerre et dans la paix*, p. 436.   [47] Benoist Méchin, *De la défaite au désastre*, vol. II, p. 124.
[48] AN, 40 AS 44, letter dated 14 February 1945 to Etablissements Schneider.

presentation of a list that might let it be thought that the managers are willing to abandon even a small part of this.'[49] Companies wrote to the COH appealing for help in preventing particular requisitions and warning about possible further moves. Companies that allowed requisitions were rapped over the knuckles for the damage which they were alleged to have done to the interests of the industry: 'It seems to me that the abnormal character of this measure, which contravenes the interministerial decision of 20 October 1942, should have encouraged you to inform us straight away...you have allowed a precedent to be created that may bring very severe repercussions for all mines.'[50] It is clear that the Germans too were aware that their demands were being resisted; the archives of the Anzin company contain a letter from the local Feldkommandur alleging that 'your attitude during the last requisitions confirms the impression that you are resisting the order of the occupation forces'.[51] The coal industry's enthusiasm for resistance to STO was fuelled by its need for labour. The very circumstances that gave rise to this need also gave the coal industry the means with which to resist STO. For the mines were desperate for labour largely because they were working, albeit indirectly, for the German war economy. Because of this the German central authorities were themselves willing to give the industry certain concessions. They classified all mines as 'S' plants, thus making them theoretically immune from the *relève*. It was in this knowledge that the mines were able to resist local Vichy or German authorities who wished to encroach upon the concession which they had been given by the German high command. Ironically the mining *patronat* could 'resist' by obstructing STO, just as the workers could 'resist' by striking, precisely because they realized their economic utility to the Germans.[52] The nature of the coal industry with its highly concentrated production and long tradition of discipline also made it especially easy for a unified policy of resistance to be enforced in this sector (see chapter 10).

The manufacturers of rolling stock, represented by MATFER, were in a similar economic position to that of the coal-mines. They were highly organized and disciplined, and their production was vital to the war economy. In this industry too there was a considerable need for labour that conflicted with the requirements of the STO programme. However, the political context in which the rolling stock industry operated was very different from that of the coal industry. Mining companies, especially in the Nord and Pas-de-Calais, were hostile to the German occupation, whereas

[49]   AN, 40 AS 43, note dated 16 February 1943.
[50]   AN, 40 AS 44, letter of COH to director of Ronchamps mine dated 22 February 1943.
[51]   AN, 109 MI 5, transcript of *conseil d'administration* of Anzin company. The letter is reproduced in an account of the wartime activities of the company given to the board on 29 September 1944.
[52]   See Richard Vinen, 'The French Coal Industry during the Occupation', *Historical Journal*, 33 (1990), 105–30.

the rolling stock industry, with a tradition of international co-operation, was favourable to the idea of collaboration with the Germans (see chapter 11). Thus, while the COH encouraged resistance to STO, MATFER encouraged its members to assist with the programme. In July 1942 it circulated its members with a request for such help.[53] Only gradually and reluctantly did MATFER accept that economic circumstances meant that there was no spare manpower in the industry.[54] Indeed eventually MATFER was driven to ask for extra labour.[55]

The situation of the shopkeepers' Comité d'Organisation (COGC) presented a very sharp contrast to that of the coal industry and the rolling stock manufacturers. It governed a sector that had been rendered marginal by the war economy. It was not surprising that the incentive to maintain the defences of the sector against requisitions was limited. Furthermore, the shopkeepers had no leverage with the occupying authorities. Their activity was not necessary for German purposes, and the dispersed and fragmented nature of the sector meant that they could not even be sure of exercising control over their own members (see chapter 10). In May 1943, when Bichelonne demanded that the files of the shopkeepers' CO be handed over to assist with the *relève*, the committee members did not feel strong enough to resist. With only one voice raised in dissent they voted to comply; 75,000 workers from this sector were sent to Germany.[56]

There was another motive for resistance to labour being sent to Germany: fear. Employers were terrified of the wrath that might be aroused among their workers if bosses were implicated in the dispatch of workers to Germany. The GIMMCP expressed this fear: 'This interference of employers in an essentially political matter outside the normal sphere of

---

[53] AN, 70 AQ 430. MATFER wrote to its members asking them to inform them of surplus labour which might be available to work in Germany. In view of the role which social fear had on the attitude of the *patronat* to the provision of labour for Germany, it is worth pointing out that MATFER stressed that information would be treated in confidence and that the matter should not be discussed with workers.

[54] AN, 70 AQ 430. On 12 August 1942 Etablissements Arbel replied to the MATFER circular requesting help with the provision of labour for Germany saying that in fact the company was short of labour itself.

[55] AN, 72 AJ 1929, note on 'Le problème de la main d'oeuvre' dated 12 April 1944: 'the damages caused by Anglo-Saxon raids obliges MATFER to increase its workforce; we have recently received a request for 5,000 workers'.

[56] Joseph Jones, 'Vichy France and Post-war Economic Modernization: The Cases of the Shopkeepers', *French Historical Studies*, 12 (1982), 541–63. There is a slight misunderstanding in this article. Jones assumes that the initial position adopted by the COGC – that is to say, acceptance of participation in the local bodies administering STO – represents an effective surrender in the face of Vichy demands. In fact this seems to be an implementation of the policy of participation in the overall direction of the policy by business organizations, though not specific participation by individual firms, that was outlined by the CII in its letter of April 1943: 'the heads of Comités d'Organisation seem disposed to provide all necessary information on the economic situation of their trades, to allow the best movement of manpower according to economic needs and the general interest'.

labour relations carries a danger for future social peace.'[57] Benoist Méchin was aware of the reasons behind the *patronat*'s resistance: 'If bosses make the choice themselves...they are inevitably exposed to the hostility of their staff.'[58] The letter sent by the CII to the minister of industrial production relating to STO expressed similar fears:

Very serious problems are posed, when heads of companies are obliged to distinguish, among staff regarded as indispensable, those who should be subjected to conscription first.

This responsibility cannot be undertaken by businessmen in the present circumstances without provoking unfortunate consequences. Not only is it to be feared that the employer might establish the order of preference in an arbitrary fashion, but it is also to be feared that, in current conditions, such a measure would only create an atmosphere of jealousy and even hatred in the business, and make employers responsible, in the eyes of their employees, for subsequent conscription operations. The interpretation made of the decree of 27 March in the instructions distributed to employers could thus compromise for good the unity within the workplace that is more necessary than ever, and so difficult to promote.[59]

Individual employers expressed fears about the effects of deportations on their relations with their workers. The mining *patronat* were especially worried by the fact that professional miners were being deported while new workers were being drafted into the mines. The Nessux mine wrote: 'Apart from the question of productivity, this situation cannot fail to provoke justified protests from the families of young miners who have not come back to the mine.'[60] The Carmaux mines urged the retrieval of 'real miners' in the following terms: 'this measure will bring an element of social peace, because it will silence the criticisms raised by the families who now see younger men benefiting from a concession that was refused to their husband or son'.[61]

To understand the role that social fear played in the calculations of the *patronat* it is necessary to examine the changing role of the working-class movement during the occupation. After June 1941 the Communist party, which dominated this movement in industrial areas, began to devote most of its energy to the struggle against the Germans. In May 1943 the comintern was dissolved and the Communist party presented itself in terms of national liberation, not in terms of challenge to the capitalist order. In the short term all this removed some of the heat from the class war in France; the key battles were now being fought in the mountains of Haute Savoie, not on the factory floor. While the occupation lasted it was even possible for industrialists to make contact with working-class leaders in the Resistance. Indeed some *patrons* who had been on very bad terms with the unions

[57] AN, 39 AS 853, Roullier speaking to *conseil d'administration*, 26 June 1942.
[58] Benoist Méchin, *De la défaite au désastre*, vol. I, p. 124.
[59] AN, 40 AS 43, letter of 13 April 1943, Tavernost to Bichelonne.
[60] AN, 40 AS 44, 28 June 1944.   [61] AN, 40 AS 44, 18 June 1943.

before the war, such as Lucien Arbel in the north[62] and Etienne Mimard in Saint-Etienne,[63] found themselves in this position.

However, in the long term the entry of the working-class movement into the Resistance had an even more profound effect. For the majority of Frenchmen soon became convinced that the Germans could not win the war. This conviction must have been especially strong in business circles. For businessmen had been obsessed with the inherent weakness of the Nazi economy and with the dynamism of American industry. In a contest between the two, few businessmen could have been in much doubt about the victor. In a memorandum written soon after the liberation, Laederich, president of the Comité d'Organisation for the textile industry, summed up the thinking that must have influenced many industrialists: 'the entry of the USA into the war at the end of 1941 clarified the situation and made an allied victory, albeit far off, almost certain'.[64] Of course open discussion of this matter was hardly possible under the circumstances, but Alfred Sauvy has pointed out that conclusions about the outcome of the war could easily be deduced from certain economic statistics, especially those relating to American shipping. Business journals during the occupation are full of references to such statistics, and it seems more than likely that discussion of such figures often contained a coded debate about the outcome of the war.[65]

Abstract intellectual belief in the certainty of allied victory did not necessarily translate into changes in business behaviour. However, in 1943 an alternative French government was established in Algiers. This government took a considerable interest in the behaviour of businessmen in occupied France. The *patronat* themselves were well aware of this.[66] One

[62] AN, 70 AQ 300, note by Section d'Entreprise of the PPF. The PPF was attacking the 'Gaullism' of certain *patrons*. In its note it mentioned that the Front National resistance movement had referred to the patriotism of Arbel.

[63] Luirard, *La région stéphanoise dans la guerre et dans la paix*, p. 512, testimony of Lucien Neurwith: 'it [the *résistance*] brought together, teachers, managers and bosses – notably Mimard'.

[64] Exactly how soon this conviction spread is a matter for some debate. Retrospective oral evidence shows that many claimed to have anticipated allied victory as early as December 1940 while others remained in doubt until after the allied landings of 1944 (J.-L. Crémieux-Brilhac and G. Ben Simon, 'Les propagandes radiophoniques et l'opinion politique en France 1940–1944', *Revue d'histoire de la deuxième guerre mondiale*, 101 (1976), 3–18). Even the attitudes of individuals were not unambiguous. Charles Rist's diary shows that his underlying faith in allied victory was constantly buffeted by waves of rumour: Charles Rist, *Une saison gâtée: journal de la guerre et de l'occupation, 1939–1945*, ed. Jean-Noel Jeanneney (Paris, 1982), p. 91.

[65] AN, 57 AS 3, Laederich 'note sur mon activité pendant l'occupation'. For examples of statistics relating to American economic prospects see the circular of the CII. In an article for his local business journal Aymé Bernard specifically alluded to the possibility that economic figures might be used to divine the outcome of the war (see chapter 12).

[66] François Picard (a manager at the Renault works) made the following entry in his diary on 24 November 1943: 'René de Peyrecave, the director general asked...that a dossier be composed showing that the factories only worked for the German armies as a result of compulsion and that they never proposed the slightest improvement in equipment. The

very graphic index of the extent to which businessmen wished to distance themselves from the Vichy government is provided by the value of 'aryanized' stocks on the Paris *bourse*. In 1943 it was clear that these stocks had become too hot to handle; their value halved within a matter of months.[67] Within the closely knit world of the French elite there were many channels of communication that crossed the dividing line between 'collaboration' and 'resistance'. Raoul Dautry provided such a link. He set himself up as a recording angel of business behaviour. He advised industrialists not to collaborate too closely with the occupying authorities.[68] He discussed the possibility of setting up a special court to judge industrialists at the liberation, and even drew up a scheme to mark companies on a scale of 0 to 14 according to the attitude that they had displayed during the occupation.[69] By March 1944 the desirability of acquiring resistance credentials had been impressed on even the most unreceptive *patron*.[70]

Obtaining good relations with the working-class movement was one way in which *patrons* could acquire such credentials, for it was obvious that working-class leaders would play a considerable role in the regime installed by an allied victory. The switch of the Communist party into national rather than class-based activity allowed it to enjoy a kind of renaissance. The CGT was reunified in May 1943. Labour was perceived as a key element in the Resistance. Saillant, the head of the underground CGT, was made head of the national council of the Resistance. Charles Laurent, the treasurer of the CGT, became finance minister of the provisional government in Algiers in 1943. The Communist party that had been discredited and demoralized by the Hitler–Stalin pact was recognized, even by the *patronat*, to have

purge in North Africa is bearing fruit.' François Picard, *L'épopée de Renault* (Paris, 1976), p. 218.

[67] Henri Rousso, 'L'aryanisation économique, Vichy, l'occupant et la spoliation des juifs', *YOD*, nos. 15 and 16 (1982). See also Pierre Nicolle, *Cinquante mois d'armistice, Vichy, 2 juillet 1940–26 août 1944: journal d'un témoin* (2 vols., Paris, 1947), p. 363, entry for 16–19 February 1944: 'stocks coming from Jewish property are almost unsaleable, with good reason'.

[68] Dautry was advising industrialists to indulge in 'freinage' as early as 30 September 1941 when he wrote to the secretary-general of Hispano Suiza (his old company): 'I hope that you are working with a wise moderation for every project that is not clearly in French interests' (AN, 307 AP 157). Dautry was able to fulfil such a role because he had close links with both the Vichy regime (via friends such as Jean Jardin) and with the Free French. Charles Rist was another example of bridges between Vichy and Free French. Rist was a director of Paribas (which was widely seen as a collaborating bank) and he was even offered official positions in the Vichy government. Yet he had close links with resistance organizations and his own son was killed while fighting with a resistance unit in 1944.

[69] George Villiers, *Témoignages* (Paris, 1978), p. 74.

[70] In March 1944 Picard (who was a member of the OCM resistance network) visited Renault and urged him to distance himself from the Vichy regime: Picard, *L'épopée de Renault*, p. 228.

achieved unprecedented legitimacy by its actions after June 1941: 'by a rather extraordinary combination of circumstances, the Communists now appear as the fierce, and to some extent the only, defenders of the patriotic ideal'.[71] In the long run therefore the best that the *patronat* could hope for at the liberation was a government very sympathetic to labour; the worst that they could expect was a lynch mob. Even if the *patronat* had enjoyed 'toute puissance patronale' they would have been very foolish to exploit it under these circumstances.

The clearest response to the social fear which was enveloping the *patronat* came from the Parisian metallurgical industry. In a pamphlet of 1943 the GIMMCP was very explicit about the need for social concessions in order to buy off a workers' revenge. The pamphlet recognized the compromised position of the *patronat* under Vichy: 'Following the armistice, developments have been imposed on the industrial world that, in the eyes of workers, have rendered employers guilty of both exploitation of labour and lack of patriotism.' And it discussed the possible consequences of this position:

circumstances furnish revolutionaries with a superb springboard using this triple theme: Employers enriched themselves while workers have been in almost abject poverty. Capitalists have taken profits from their collaboration with German activity proving that their patriotism can be bought and sold. The bosses have benefited from the crisis to take revenge for 1936 shielded by the repression of the working class.[72]

Among other measures, the GIMMCP envisaged immediate pay rises at the moment of liberation to appease the workers. It is also clear that metallurgists were careful to take their workers' side in conflicts with the occupier. When the workers marked armistice day 1943 with strikes the GIMMCP stressed that 'Stretching the truth a little, we have advised that, as far as possible, incidents should be recorded not as strikes but as slow-downs; this tactic, already adopted by many businesses of their own accord, makes it possible not to deduct pay.'[73]

The attempted social appeasement of Parisian metallurgists reached its climax with moves to contact trade union leaders with a view to making some kind of joint statement at the liberation. These negotiations failed because of the lack of interest displayed by the trade union side. The negotiations are also highly revealing. After all, it was metallurgy, and especially Parisian metallurgy, that had been behind a whole series of advances to working-class leaders. Why was this? Firstly, the metallurgy industry did exceptionally well out of the war economy, and it was therefore

[71] AN, 39 AS 861, *programme patronal* of 23 June 1943.
[72] AN, 39 AS 861, *programme patronal* of 23 June 1943.
[73] AN, 39 AS 854, p-v of CA, 25 November 1943.

in its interests to develop close contacts with workers in order to facilitate the exploitation of that economy (the GIMMCP had originally been formed as part of the effort to bring workers and employers together during the First World War). It was also in Parisian metallurgy that contacts had developed during the period of French participation in the allied war effort, contacts that had ultimately led to the Majestic agreement. Secondly, metallurgy had been recognized as the most powerful part of the business world for so long that it was in a highly exposed position. *Patrons* could not fail to be aware that the Comité des Forges was top of the hit list of the left and that this would put the metallurgists 'au piquet' at the liberation. Thirdly, certain metallurgical leaders had long displayed a liberal attitude to labour relations – Lente and Lambert Ribot were poring over *samizdat* copies of the Beveridge report in 1943.[74] Perhaps this was because the metallurgical leaders had been established long before 1936 and did not – unlike Nicolle, Bernard and so on – owe their rise to the class war which had followed the Popular Front.

The overtures that the Paris metallurgists made to the unions attracted attention outside Paris and outside the metallurgy industry. They also exposed old splits in the employers' movement. Jacques Warnier, a textile industrialist who was a convinced corporatist and a supporter of the Vichy government, heard of the moves afoot in Paris and described them in these terms: 'it appears that a large-scale manoeuvre is being prepared involving an agreement between business circles [de Vitry and Lente] and union circles... with a view to a return of the old state of affairs before 1940, that is to say the reconstitution of the CGPF and the CGT and the elimination of small and medium-sized business'.[75]

The myth of the 'revanche des patrons' under Vichy

All the efforts of the *patronat* to seek a rapprochement with the working class that would buy off revenge at the liberation were singularly unsuccessful. The GIMMCP's overtures towards the trade unionists were sharply rebuffed. At the liberation the bosses were widely blamed for having treated labour brutally. Why was this? Partly, no doubt, the answer is that workers simply did not care to make the subtle distinctions between employers and the state that the business leaders had hoped to promote. The GIMMCP effectively recognized that its attempts to distance itself from the

[74] Villey report in archives of Institut d'Histoire Sociale, in file marked CNPF. Villey himself claims that he found the Beveridge report insufficiently radical!
[75] AN, 57 AS 12, 13 June 1944, 'manœuvres milieux patronaux et syndicalistes'.

STO policy were not working in early 1944: 'Previous operations to send workers to Germany have brought about a disastrous social position because, in the minds of those concerned, the employers bear the brunt of the responsibility. It is essential that everything be done to avoid aggravating, and if possible to ease this mood.'[76]

However, it was also clear that in some ways the attacks levelled against the *patronat* at the end of the war did not really originate with the *patronat*'s war record. Often the attacks were motivated by a general hostility to a certain kind of capitalism. Big business was the *Reichsfeind* of French society. The Comité des Forges had a special place in the demonology of the left. In fact the Comité des Forges had been dissolved by Vichy. The two most prominent leaders of the Comité, Lambert Ribot and de Wendel, had been notably hostile to the Vichy regime. Yet almost as soon as it was reformed at the liberation the Comité was under fire once again. De Wendel and Lambert Ribot both found themselves in political exile at the liberation. De Wendel was excluded by the Committee of Twenty from the consultative assembly,[77] while Chevalme insisted to Villey that Lambert Ribot could not be a member of the *commission paritaire* because his name had 'anti-social associations'.[78] It is especially notable that another metallurgist who had been more compromised by association with Vichy but who was not associated with the magic words Comité des Forges – Lente – was accepted as a member of the *commission paritaire*. Indeed the attack on the metallurgy industry at the liberation echoed that which had occurred at the beginning of the Vichy regime. In 1944 the leaders of the Comité des Forges were attacked while those of the UIMM were spared, just as in 1940 the Comité des Forges had been dissolved while the UIMM had been allowed to survive.

One allegation about the *patronat*'s war record was expressed so specifically during the war that it requires special explanation. This is that the *patronat* used the Vichy period to reverse the workers' victory of 1936. Closon, the Commissioner for the Republic in the Nord and Pas-de-Calais, wrote in 1944: 'The management techniques of the mining companies, and their police systems, seemed ready-made to serve the policy of intensification of production during the occupation, to watch and hunt political agitators, and to seek revenge for 1936.'[79] The fact that such a claim should be made in the coalfields is especially ironic and revealing. For it was especially

---

[76] AN, 39 AS 854, p-v of CA, January 1944.

[77] Jean-Noel Jeanneney, *Francois de Wendel en République: l'argent et le pouvoir, 1914–1940* (3 vols., Paris, 1976), p. 852. It is true that de Wendel's exclusion does seem to have been based upon a misunderstanding of his war record rather than upon a simple hostility to him as a symbol of big business.

[78] Villey report marked CNPF in Institut d'Histoire Sociale, p. 9.

[79] Report reprinted in *Revue du Nord*, 227 (1975), pp. 669–71.

evident in the mines that the suppression of the workers' victory of 1936 had occurred before July 1940. The Communist party had been the backbone of working-class organization in the area, and the dissolution of the party in September 1938 had been recognized by the *patronat* as the death-knell of union activism. Vichy had enacted no further anti-Communist legislation. Furthermore, the mines had been seen as a key part of the economic mobilization and had therefore benefited considerably from the economic mobilization law of 11 July 1938. This remained their key instrument of labour discipline. In fact, far from using Vichy and the occupation to add to the law of July 1938, the coal industry used the Third Republic law to resist certain Vichy and German encroachments. In short, the crushing of the labour movement had been carried out before 1940. It had been initiated, not by the *patronat*, but by the state. Furthermore, it had been carried out in the interests of rearmament. One of the key aspects of the crushing of the labour movement had been the outlawing of the Communist party because of its opposition to the war. In the circumstances of the liberation, when the state and the Communist party were once more allied in support of the war, the period 1938/9 was highly embarrassing to all concerned. An Orwellian rewrite of history, in which the crushing of the labour movement had been carried out under Vichy, was convenient for everyone – except the *patronat*.

One incident illustrates very neatly the way in which the business *revanche* was moved from the immediately pre-war period to the occupation. Duvernoy had been the head of the Renault personnel office. In 1944 he was eased out of his job. It was implied that he had been sacked for collaboration during the occupation. In fact, a court to which he had taken his case decided that he had been sacked because his presence was unacceptable to the new government and the unions: 'the concern [was] to give the firm a staff whose opinions would conform to the political tendencies in government circles...besides, the overt opposition of Duvernoy to trade unions would hardly have allowed him to be kept on without risking conflicts'.[80] Furthermore, the court found that Duvernoy had been effectively suspended from his job at the beginning of the occupation because his presence was not felt to be conducive to the social peace demanded by the new regime (this was yet another example of the way in which the sanctions taken against managers in 1944 resembled those which had been taken in 1940). It was therefore clear that Duvernoy had incurred the enmity of the unions and the left before the war. In fact, it seems reasonable to assume that this enmity was due to the very active part

[80] AN, undated report in 39 AS 964. There were other examples of managers being punished at the liberation for things that they had done before 1940. One resistance leader reported in December 1944 that two managers at the Gooderich factory in Colombes had been punished for giving information about Communists in the factory to the police in 1938: Lecompte Boinet, unpublished diary, entry for 26 December 1944.

which he played in the employers' reaction against the Popular Front between 1936 and 1939. It is misguided to say that the employers used Vichy to overturn the workers' victory of 1936. It might be more accurate to say that the labour movement used the liberation as an opportunity to reverse the *patronat*'s victory of 1938/9.

Chapter 10

Who controlled the Vichy industrial organization?

Introduction

At first glance the Vichy industrial system looks beautifully simple. Each sector was controlled by a Comité d'Organisation (CO) the president of which was appointed by the government. Supply was controlled by a different body also appointed by the state. The system of Comités d'Organisation was unified at a national level by the Centre d'Information Interprofessionnelle. All this contrasts sharply with the undisciplined industry of the pre-war years. It seems to anticipate a well-organized statist economy that might be seen to underlie French post-war prosperity. But the real situation was more complicated. The powers of the bodies set up by Vichy were not clear-cut. Authority on paper did not necessarily coincide with real influence. Furthermore, the committees of the wartime French economy were far from being tranquil cloisters in which industrialists learnt the benefits of co-operation with each other and with the state. Rather they were often battlefields on which the conflicts of the pre-war French economy, which had been intensified by the conditions of the war economy, were fought out.

The Comités d'Organisation

Historians studying Vichy industry have tended to concentrate on the COs. This is easy to understand. On paper, the committees had a very wide range of powers; in particular, they had planist and dirigist functions which fitted in well with the perspectives that post-war developments imposed on the Vichy economy. Generally it has been suggested that the COs served the industrialists whom they were supposed to control better than the state that they were supposed to obey: 'the president in charge...was almost always...the head of the largest firm in the sector'.[1] Such contentions are sustained by statistical studies of the membership of the COs. Rousso concludes that 80 per cent of presidents of COs had been businessmen or the leaders of business associations. Various specific weaknesses can be identified with these statistical studies.[2] But more generally it can be asked whether statistical studies of office-holding really illustrate the balance of power in the committee. The fact that the heads of the COs shared the social and professional origins of the industrialists in their sector does not necessarily mean that they shared the same outlook. Presidents who came from the industry over which they presided did not always promote the interests of that industry. Many heads of COs belonged to the *avant-garde du patronat* (whose divergence from the preoccupations of ordinary industrialists was discussed in chapter 5). It was relatively rare for these men to distance themselves explicitly from their former roles (as Deteouf did by resigning from his directorship of Alsthom when assuming the presidency of the CO for the electrical industry). But it seems likely that many, such as Painvin (see chapter 8), had ceased to play an active part in the life of their own firm.

François Lehideux, president of the CO of the automobile industry (COA), provides a good example of the possible ambiguities in the exercise of this power. Lehideux was the nephew-in-law of Louis Renault, the largest manufacturer of the sector. He had effectively run the Renault business in the years immediately preceding the war. This has led some historians to imply that he was the prime example of the way in which large-scale industry controlled the COs.[3] However, in the pre-war period it had been widely recognized that Lehideux's priorities differed vastly from those of his fellow motor industrialists, and especially from those of Louis Renault. He had battled to promote *ententes* and to construct a kind of corporatism in an industry that was notable for fierce economic liberalism. His efforts had

---

[1] Henri Rousso, 'L'organisation industrielle de Vichy', *Revue d'histoire de la deuxième guerre mondiale*, 116 (1979), 27–44, at p. 29.

[2] The studies of both Rousso and Jones are based upon an examination of the professional origins of presidents of COs. This fails to allow for the fact that the president was not always the key power broker in a committee. Some committees, such as that which controlled the rolling stock industry (see below), regarded the president as being their employee rather than their leader. Sometimes the interests of an industry were protected by someone other than the president of the CO; Fabre, the secretary of the COH, seems to have played such a role: see Richard Vinen, 'The French Coal Industry during the Occupation', *Historical Journal*, 33 (1990), 105–30. Rousso's study is also undermined by the fact that he puts both businessmen and leaders of business syndicates in the category of 'patrons'. In fact a few leaders of associations who became leaders of the COs had never been businessmen (Taudière, the leader of the Association de l'Industrie et de l'Agriculture Françaises who became president of the CO for the mechanical industry, was such a case).

[3] Rousso, 'L'organisation industrielle de Vichy', pp. 29 and 43.

been met with outright hostility by most of his peers.[4] Furthermore, during the period of French participation in the allied war effort Lehideux had helped to administer the Renault firm after it had been requisitioned by the government.[5] This action earned him the undying hostility of Louis Renault. In fact, far from seeing Lehideux as his representative, Renault believed during the early months of the occupation that Lehideux was part of a plot to exclude him from the northern zone of France.[6] Renault was hostile to Lehideux's appointment as head of the COA.[7]

Lehideux used his new position to enforce the kind of discipline that had been resisted before the war. This policy did not make him popular. Fernard Picard was later to describe the COA as exercising 'neo-Nazi' powers and Lehideux as an industrial 'Führer'.[8]

Lehideux clearly had a loyalty to Vichy that extended beyond the limits of industrial self-interest. He became Vichy's minister of industrial production (from July 1941 to April 1942), and he is still the leader of the Association pour Défendre la Mémoire du Maréchal Pétain. Lehideux's relations with industry were not unique; Pierre Pucheu, who headed the CO for the mechanical industry, was in a similar position. But Lehideux was unusual. When he was a minister this became clearer. His clash with the presidents of the COs about whether workers should be sent to Germany (see chapter 9) is especially revealing. It shows the separation between Lehideux's ideological commitment to the aims of the government and the commitment of most heads of COs to the interests of their sector.

Among industrialists it was widely perceived that men like Lehideux represented a threat to industrial interests. At a meeting of the Comité Directeur des Constructeurs et Reparateurs de Locomotives, Voitures et Wagons on 8 October 1940, M. Lebert was reported to have said: 'the choice of a real dictator for the automobile industry may have been necessary. But, as for himself, he had no intention of being under the authority of a director paid, in part, by himself.'[9]

The Arbel archives provide a rare inside view of the formation of a CO. They contain the transcripts of the meetings at which the pre-war rolling stock manufacturers' syndicate discussed the formation of the CO for their

---

[4] For the debate on corporatism in the motor industry, see chapter 5. For further examples of the psychological distance between Lehideux and Renault see Patrick Fridenson, *Histoire des usines Renault*, vol. I: *Naissance de la grande entreprise, 1898–1939* (Paris, 1972), p. 285.   [5] Gilbert Hatry, *Louis Renault: patron absolu* (Paris, 1982), p. 354.

[6] Ibid. p. 369. Hatry suggests that, in fact, Belin initiated a scheme to keep Renault confined to the southern zone and that Lehideux opposed this scheme.

[7] Ibid. Renault wrote to Peyrecave (one of his directors): 'It seem likely that he put himself forward for the job of Führer in the automobile industry, obviously he tried to increase his power in order to act against me.'

[8] Rousso, 'L'Organisation industrielle de Vichy', p. 33.

[9] Paris, Archives Nationales (AN), 70 AQ 430, transcript of meeting of Comité Directeur des Constructeurs et Réparateurs de Locomotives, Voitures et Wagons, 8 October 1940.

industry: MATFER. These present a situation sharply different from that of the COA. The rolling stock manufacturers regarded the president of the CO as their appointee (though formally he was appointed by the government) and as paid by them (though in law the enterprises attached to a CO had no power to withdraw their contributions). It was said that, although the powers of the president were greater than expected, 'there is no cause for alarm at this, because M. Roy will be chosen by the manufacturers themselves and paid by them'. It was suggested that under these circumstances 'an amicable collaboration with M. Roy' would be relatively easy.[10]

The Vichy supply system

The Vichy supply system was established by the law of 10 September 1940. This law set up l'Office Central de Répartition des Produits Industriels (OCRPI). In theory, this had none of the semi-private status of the COs. It was led by a Secrétariat à la Répartition (created by the law of 27 September 1940). This was presided over by Bichelonne, the Secrétaire Général au Commerce et à l'Industrie. Attached to the secretariat was a *section centrale*, and attached to this were twelve specialized setions dealing with iron, steel, non-ferrous metals, coal, petrol, fats, chemicals and textiles.

Though the OCRPI attracted less attention than the COs, certain observers regarded it as more powerful: 'Now that the supply sections have become...motors of the French economy, the Comités d'Organisation remain...with a few exceptions, in suspense. They have not been able to impose themselves like the supply sections, and as professional organizations they have still not acquired the importance that was intended for them.'[11] This is not surprising; in an economy of penury it is natural that great significance should attach to the distribution of raw materials. But this gives us a very different perspective on the Vichy economy. As has been mentioned, the COs fit into a post-war perspective of planisme and modernization. But, while the COs drew up grandiose statements about the possibilities of the future, the OCRPI was preoccupied with the narrow limitations imposed by the present. For example, the plan of the COA to

---

[10] Ibid.
[11] AN, F12 1043, translation of article from *Kölnische Zeitung* of 1 November 1942. The Germans had always taken a keen interest in the organization of French industry (Kolboom uses many German articles in his work on the *patronat* before the war). During the occupation they were especially well-placed observers since so much of the French economy depended upon them. The fact that French official archives so often contain quotations from German articles suggests that the quality of German information was respected.

construct an entirely aluminium car was hardly likely to get off the drawing board at a time when the German aircraft industry devoured every morsel of bauxite extracted from French soil.[12]

According to Belin the OCRPI's functions were relatively clear. It divided up supplies of raw materials between the various COs, which in turn divided these up among individual enterprises. In reality, the system was more complicated. A note from the COA suggested that there were no fixed rules. Some commodities were allocated by the CO for redistribution; some were allocated by the OCRPI to individual firms. Sometimes the lack of clear distinction between the powers of supply sections and COs led to conflict. The president of the OCRPI section for chemicals complained in May 1941 that 'in marking out their sphere of action, which was not properly defined, the officials stretch their authority, expand their staff and tread on each other's toes'.[13] But more often the division between OCRPI sections and COs was blurred by the incestuous relations that existed between the two kinds of body. The president of an important CO, such as Aimé Lepercq of the coal industry, would also be a member of several OCRPI sections.[14]

The actual techniques of distribution varied. Sometimes commodities were allocated directly; sometimes they were to be had in return for 'monnaie matière'. In the latter case the *monnaie matière* certificates were often traded illegally between firms.[15] Furthermore, some industrialists maintained illicit stocks of undeclared material; some of these stocks were still in existence at the end of the occupation.[16]

The Germans regarded the supply system as the key to the French economy.[17] In collaboration with the Vichy authorities they could ensure that the provision of raw materials favoured firms working to meet their requirements. In addition to this general control, a variety of special arrangements were made for firms working for German needs that cut across all fixed rules. Those who required metal to fulfil German contracts could obtain it with 'Zast bonds'. Coal was automatically allocated as a matter of priority to firms that were useful to the Germans. Sometimes control became even more direct. In the Nord and Pas-de-Calais the

[12] For the plan to construct an aluminium car see Henri Rousso, 'Les paradoxes de Vichy', in P. Fridenson and A. Straus (eds.), *Le capitalisme français 19ᵉ–20ᵉ siècle: blocages et dynamismes d'une croissance* (Paris, 1987), p. 82. For the German seizure of bauxite see Alan Milward, *The New Order and the French Economy* (Oxford, 1970).

[13] AN, F37 77, note dated 2 May 1941.

[14] See the list of the *comité consultatif* for petroleum in AN, 68 AJ 1001. Jones suggests that 62 per cent of members of consultative committees were also members of COs.

[15] The persistence of this practice is reflected by the attempts of the authorities to suppress it. See AN, 68 AJ 90, circular of 17 August 1942.

[16] In 1944 the GIMMCP suggested that the maintenance of illicit stocks was one of the acts of 'resistance' carried out by its members (AN, 39 AS 964, article dated 16 December 1944).

[17] Richard F. Kuisel, *Capitalism and the State in Modern France: Renovation and Economic Management in the Twentieth Century* (Cambridge, 1981), p. 140.

Germans controlled the quantities of coal which were issued day by day.[18]
In the last resort the Germans would step in and make *ad hoc* arrangements
for a particular company. Thus in 1941 the German army gave coal from its
own private supplies to a firm supplying components to the Luftwaffe.[19]

Conflicts within industry

The truth is that the powers of Vichy industrial bodies did not spring
directly from their legal attributions. Vichy industrial legislation had been
phrased in terms so broad as to be meaningless. A remit that ran as follows:
'survey companies, draw up production schemes, organize the acquisition
and distribution of raw materials' (the law of 16 August), could mean
anything or nothing. Most, though not all, bodies ignored their theoretical
subjugation to the authority of the state and acted as independent agencies
or as instruments of the industrialists in their sector.[20] The degree of control
that COs and supply sections were able to exercise over supply of raw
materials, over the protection of the labour force or over links with the *zone
interdite*, all varied enormously. Legislation simply laid down the framework
within which these bodies competed in a kind of 'institutional Darwinism'.[21]

Success in this struggle depended on several factors. Firstly, bodies
representing industries that were useful to the German war economy were
at a huge advantage. They could secure access to supplies and a protected
labour force. Secondly, bodies representing large-scale enterprises had an
advantage. It was easier to control and discipline a concentrated industry
than a fragmented one. Furthermore, since large-scale enterprises were not
constantly threatened by imminent closure, they were more likely to hold
firm in a conflict with the Vichy or German authorities. Thirdly, it was
easier for industrial committees to handle sectors which already had a
tradition of organization and discipline. The supreme example of a CO
which had all these advantages was the one which controlled the coal
industry (the COH). It has already been shown how the COH was able to
use the value of its production to the German war economy to negotiate
protection for its labour force (see chapter 9). In addition to this, the COH
represented a highly concentrated sector – the average mine employed 8,000
men. Furthermore, ownership and management of the mines were separated.

---

[18] AN, F 37 31, *note de service* on events in December 1940.
[19] AN, F 37 31, secretary of state for industrial production to Barnaud, dated 22 July 1942,
saying that 900 tonnes of coal to the steel works at Saint-Michel et Maurienne which was
supplying steel to Renault to fulfil Luftwaffe contracts would be supplied directly from the
Germans.   [20] See below.
[21] This phrase was coined by Schoenbaum to describe the economic system of Nazi Germany.

This meant that the COH did not have to contend with the fierce independence of the traditional French *patron* which afflicted many industries. Indeed the mining schools and the tradition of co-operation with the inspectorate of mines had created a strong managerial culture in the mining industry. The head of the COH, Aimé Lepercq, was aware of his fortunate position:

The mining industry is made up of a small number of enterprises with a small number of simple products. Companies have been subjected to the control of the mining administration for over a century; they are, therefore, used to a certain corporate discipline. Finally, they put together a professional organization, by means of freely entered *ententes*, years ago. It was easy for the Comité to complete this independent organization by adapting it to the principles of the controlled economy that are imposed by circumstances.[22]

By contrast the shopkeepers' CO (COGC) represented a sector that was, for the purposes of the war economy, marginal. It was also fragmented, dispersed and disorganized. The result of this was not merely that the COGC did not have enough authority with the Germans to protect its labour force; it did not even have authority over its own members. At the end of the war, 200,000 shopkeepers had never filled in their forms and 80,000 had never paid their dues to the committee.[23]

The struggles in the Vichy economy did not just take place between different bodies. There were also struggles within each sector and industry. These struggles had existed before the war when organizations like the Comité des Forges had been severely divided. But before the war two factors had encouraged industrialists to seek some kind of unity. The first of these factors was the need for political mobilization in a democracy to confront an organized working class. The second was the need to form cartels to restrain production and divide up markets. The first of these pressures was ended by the suspension of democracy and the suppression of the formal powers of the organized working class. The second pressure was ended by the conditions of a war economy. Limited markets were now a thing of the past. Instead of collaborating with each other in order to restrain production, industrialists were now brought into conflict by the scramble for labour and raw materials.[24]

The prefect of the Rhône described the war of all against all which was

---

[22] AN, 68 AJ 131, written by Lepercq in December 1941 and published by the COH in 1944.

[23] Henry Ehrmann, *Organized Business in France* (Princeton, N.J., 1957), p. 87.

[24] This situation is very close to the 'war of all against all' described by Mason in the Nazi war economy. Of course in theory it is quite possible that collaboration might ultimately have developed among industrialists in order to confront problems of shortage of supply just as it had once developed to confront limited markets. In practice, however, there was not enough time for such collaboration to develop.

being waged in the Marseille shipbuilding industry at this time.[25] Far from restraining this competition, the industrial committees of Vichy France were instruments by which it was carried on. A company that could get control of a particular committee could then use it to secure supplies of materials and labour for itself, and to cut these off from its competitors. One proprietor of a small metallurgy firm in Paris complained that managers who were appointed to COs often favoured their former employers.[26] The archives of Etablissements Arbel give a more clear idea of how COs could be exploited. The Arbel management at Douai expressed outright terror at the suggestion that the section for *emboutissage à chaud* of Mecanor (the committee controlling the mechanical industry in the *zone interdite*) should be led by one of their competitors: 'It is unacceptable that hot metal stamping should be run by the manager of a forge...the decision puts us at the mercy of Cail, and of Fives Lille, who have both forges and stamping works; no doubt it will all culminate in our elimination.'[27] Arbel's competitors also seem to have feared that the economic committees of Vichy France would be used as the instrument of one company. These fears surfaced when a former manager of Arbel (Jacquier) was appointed as president of Mecanor.[28] In fact the struggle within the *gros emboutissage* industry was still going on after the liberation.[29] Far from teaching industrialists the virtues of co-operation, the occupation seems to have enhanced the conflicts which already existed within certain industries.

The industrial organizations and the state

Generally it has been argued that though the state set up the Comités d'Organisation and the OCRPI sections it was able to exercise little control over them. Jones suggests that the government commissioners appointed to the Comités d'Organisation were able to exercise little control over them because they were simply too overburdened by the weight of their administrative responsibilities. In fact it seems dubious whether questions about the balance of power in the committees can really be expressed in such simple terms. It has already been pointed out that there were divisions among industrialists so that presidents of COs like Lehideux or Pucheu were

[25] Cited by Robert Mencherin, unpublished talk given to conference on *Les entreprises françaises pendant la seconde guerre mondiale*, Centre d'Etudes Pédagogiques, Sèvres, 25/26 November 1986.

[26] AN, 39 AS 209, letter dated 26 February 1941 from Giraudin et fils to GIMMCP.

[27] AN, 70 AQ 430, note from Douai, 5 October 1941.

[28] AN, 70 AQ 436, note dated 12 February 1941.

[29] AN, 70 AQ 428, letter from Arbel to the secretary-general of the mechanical industry, dated 29 January 1945.

actually closer to the mentality of the leaders of the Vichy government than to that of their own colleagues. But there were also divisions within the Vichy state. These divisions were especially significant within the Vichy administration; for example, the conflict between the ministry of finances and that of production dogged all Vichy's attempts at rational policy-making.[30]

The backgrounds of high-ranking civil servants were often similar to those of industrialists. Like industrialists, certain civil servants made efforts to distance themselves from Vichy when it became obvious that the regime could not last. These efforts were especially vigorous in the finance ministry. The defection of Couve de Murville seems to have acted as a catalyst in this respect. The Germans believed that the policy of the minister of finances was being undermined by his own civil servants. In 1943 they arrested no less than forty-three civil servants in the finance ministry.[31] Vichy loyalists railed against the efforts of 'les inspecteurs de finance' to subvert government policy. Industrialists who worked against 'the state' as represented by a Vichy minister were sometimes working in collaboration with 'the state' as represented by civil servants. This was especially marked in the coal-mines. Here the management of mines and the mining administration had a tradition of close collaboration. It is clear that attempts by the mines to obstruct the government's efforts to send labour to Germany were supported by civil servants in the inspectorate of mines.[32]

Industrial organization in the *zone interdite*

In the Nord and the Pas-de-Calais, or *zone interdite*, relations between industry and 'the state' were even more complicated. In the rest of France the state at least had nominal control of all industrial organizations, but this area was ruled directly by the German command in Brussels (OFK 670). The German authorities assumed certain powers that had formerly belonged to the French state. Thus the authority to decide whether new enterprises should be allowed to open, which had been vested in the French state by the mobilization laws, was now exercised by OFK 670.[33] A separate system of economic organization was also established in the area. At first this took the form of *Warenstellen*, closely modelled on the Germans' own industrial

---

[30] AN, F 37 77, Bardet, 'Reflexions sur 6 mois d'activité du CII': 'One of the basic factors underlying the present confusion is the deep hostility between finances and production.'
[31] AN, 72 AJ 1927, de Brinon to Laval, 11 August 1943.
[32] Vinen, 'The French Coal Industry during the Occupation'.
[33] This power had been established by the law of September 1938 and the decree of September 1939.

committees. In March 1941 the system became more formal when Bureaux Régionaux d'Organisation and Bureaux Régionaux de Répartition were established. These bodies were quite separate from the economic institutions that existed in the rest of France. They were appointed directly by the German authorities, and there was no French government commissioner on them.

Not surprisingly the Vichy government was hostile to this separate system. There were numerous attempts to bring it into closer contact with that of the rest of France. Pucheu negotiated for such a change in June 1941. The archives of the Délégation Générale aux Relations Franco-Allemandes are full of references to the status of the Nord and Pas-de-Calais. Industrialists of the area were not merely passive spectators to the debate that was being conducted about the future of their region. They felt that they were treated more harshly than their colleagues under French administration. There is evidence that the coal industry's leaders sought to exploit the miners' strike of 1941 to provide Pucheu's initiative with diplomatic ammunition (see chapter 9). But, even within the organizations that existed, industrialists could do much to mitigate the isolation of the area; for many of the companies that had their main plants in the Nord and Pas-de-Calais had head offices in Paris and clearly these head offices wished to know what was happening in the *zone interdite*. Thus on 8 February 1941 the Paris office of Etablissements Arbel asked to be given full accounts of the meetings of Mécanor (the body which oversaw the mechanical industry in the north).[34] This transmission of information also operated in the opposite direction. On 18 November 1942 the Paris office of Etablissements Arbel sent the Douai office an account of a meeting of MATFER (a Comité d'Organisation).[35]

However, this activity should not be presented as simple subversion of German authority. The Germans themselves were sharply divided. There was great rivalry between the high command in Paris and that in Brussels. Industrialists were aware of this rivalry and may have attempted to exploit it.[36] Certainly the German headquarters in Paris seems to have sanctioned the informal links between individual bodies in the *zone interdite* and those of the rest of France. A note from the Paris office of Etablissements Arbel of 29 May 1941 said that, although unwilling to give official approval for such links, Dr Michel (a German official in Paris) recognized that contact between the institutions of the *zone interdite* and the rest of France would exist:

[34] AN, 70 AQ 300, Paris to Douai, 8 February 1941.   [35] Ibid., 18 November 1942.
[36] AN, 39 AS 960, note of 17 June 1941, composed from contacts with GIMMCP members: 'links between the CECs [headquarters] in France and in Belgium are difficult; for example two weeks ago it was decided that all French departments, with the exception of Alsace and Lorraine, would depend on the CEC in France but the CEC in Belgium got the order revoked. Since then the differences between the two CECs have got worse.'

'contact with MATFER being maintained by the head office'.[37] In this case French industrialists were working with one German faction to acquire a power that was independent of the Vichy state and that was actively opposed by another faction among the Germans. The situation was rendered even more complicated by the fact that the German high command in Brussels did not pursue a consistent policy with regard to links between the *zone interdite* and the rest of France. On some occasions they attempted to suppress such links; for example, on 24 March 1942 the Douai office of Etablissements Arbel spoke of a note circulated by the Germans stating that all contact with the rest of France should be made via the German authorities themselves.[38] But in a meeting with Bucher (the head of the mining *comptoir* in the Nord and Pas-de-Calais) OFK 670 seems to have approved of such contacts.[39]

The Centre d'Information Interprofessionnelle

The bodies established by the legislation of August and September 1940 were all intraprofessional, that is to say they concerned themselves with only one industry. On 30 April 1941 the government created an interprofessional body, the Centre d'Information Interprofessionnelle (CII). The CII was designed to provide information for the Comités d'Organisation and supply sections, and to liaise between these bodies. Attached to the CII was a consultative committee headed by Gerard Bardet. The other officers of the CII were de Tavernost (its delegate general) and Weinman (its secretary until his resignation in December 1941).

This institution epitomized many of the ambiguities and contradictions in the relationship between industry and Vichy economic organization. Firstly, the status of the CII was not clearly defined. In some respects it was an institution designed to represent the *patronat*. It inherited the funds of the CGPF, and many in the *patronat* regarded it as the successor to this body.[40] But the CII was also designed to help to devise Vichy's new economic order; the *conseil consultatif* produced reports on planisme and on the taxing of

[37] AN, 70 AQ 430, Paris to Douai, 29 May 1941.
[38] AN 70 AQ 430. Judging from the reply of the Paris office of 7 April this instruction was simply ignored.
[39] AN, F 37 39, undated note of secretary of state for industrial production concerning meeting between Bucher, Schmidt and Sponeman. The Vichy authorities were told of this meeting. The Brussels high command seems to have seen this initative as part of their struggle with the Paris high command. Schmidt concluded: 'his colleagues in Paris [the Germans] did not look on this link between the Vichy government and the military authorities in Brussels and Lille in a very favourable light'.
[40] AN 70 AQ 420, Aymé Bernard speaking to the northern section of FAR meeting, 20 June 1941.

profits. To proselytize the new order, the CII established a school of professional organization and arranged conferences.

The uncertain role of the CII was reflectd in its membership. It contained some convinced Vichy supporters such as Jules Verger, but its delegate general, de Tavernost, was to become an active opponent of Vichy. Within the *conseil consultatif* of the CII there were some sharp divisions. Bardet himself accepted that alongside the supporters of Vichy corporatism there were some 'more or less unrepentant liberals'.[41] This ambiguity was reflected even in the personality of the president of the CII. His background and his willingness to present certain demands in the name of industry suggest that he was a representative of industry.[42] But the interest which he took in projects for profound economic reform and his willingness to serve on numerous Vichy committees suggest a commitment to the regime which marked him out from most industrialists. On certain issues, notably the *Charte du Travail*, he steered a middle course between the position of industry and that of the government.

The CII also reflected certain conflicts within industry. Bardet mounted a campaign against the UIMM. He wrote to the president of the UIMM on 15 November 1941 to deny rumours that the CII represented metallurgy interests. He suggested that the UIMM should be dissolved,[43] while the delegate of the CII on the economic commission of the Conseil National tried to have the UIMM split into two or three sections. Bardet even suggested that the troubles of the CII might be inspired by big business: 'one might ask if the attacks on the Centre d'Information themselves are not part of a political manoeuvre in which your ministry, is, unwittingly, serving the purposes of former economic powers'.[44] Bardet's campaign sprang from the traditional hostility of industries which consumed metal to the organization of founders. This hostility was probably compounded by the poor opinion which those loyal to Vichy had of the powerful heavy industrial federations. However, this feud reveals some of the contradictions in Bardet's position, since his opponents often bracketed him with Lente, the head of the UIMM, as a representative of 'grosse industrie', and since on occasions, notably that of their resignation from official functions in March 1944, Bardet and Lente did indeed seem to be acting together.

Relations between the CII and the government soon became tense. Rumours reached Bardet that the *conseil consultatif* of the CII was to be dissolved. He complained vigorously: 'the outside pressure against the CII has been increased again. But the minister in charge, while having direct contact with heads of service placed under the CII office, has seen fit to call

[41] AN, F 37 77, letter Bardet to Pucheu dated 31 March 1941.
[42] For example, Bardet requested higher rations for workers in 1943 (see chapter 9).
[43] F 37 77, letter Bardet to Pucheu dated 31 March 1941.   [44] Ibid.

neither TAVERNOST nor WEINMAN, whose intellectual honesty led him to resign at the end of January, nor myself.'[45] It was clear that in the eyes of the government the CII was proving too good at representing the *patronat* and not good enough at representing the government. Bardet recognized that the minister of industrial production saw 'the shadow of a revived CGPF'.[46]

Eventually the *conseil consultatif* of the CII was dissolved. Superficially, the dissolution made little difference. A new body, the Conseil Supérieur de l'Economie Industrielle et Commerciale (CSEIC), was set up; it inherited the studies which the CII had prepared, it inherited most of the personnel of the *conseil*, and Bardet remained in effective control as vice-president. However, a key change had taken place. The CII had combined the representation of the *patronat* and the planning of a new economic order. It had been based upon the assumption that industrialists would be favourable to these plans. This assumption had proved to be false. From now on there was a separation between the CSEIC, which participated in the planning of Vichy's economic new order, and the CII, which represented the *patronat*, often in opposition to Vichy policy.

[45] F 37 77, Bardet to Barnaud dated 7 April 1942.
[46] F 37 77, Bardet to Pucheu dated 31 March 1941.

Chapter 11

An industrial new order?

Introduction

How much did Vichy change the mentality of French industry? At first glance the dynamism of post-war France looks very different from the malthusianism, individualism and isolation seen to have characterized industry in the Third Republic. In particular, it could be argued that Vichy anticipated the foundations of French post-war prosperity in three respects. Firstly, Vichy was founded on a search for a new role in Europe for France; it might be suggested that this was the first step on the road which was to lead to the European Coal and Steel Community and eventually to the EEC. Secondly, the idea of a national economic plan was first seriously discussed by the Vichy government; this was an idea that was to become central to the French economy with the advent of the Monnet plan in 1946. Thirdly, it can be argued that the pressure of the war economy drove the French industry to rationalization and modernization. This chapter will examine the attitude of industrialists to these changes. It will be suggested that the rhetoric of Vichy politicians did indeed anticipate certain post-war developments, but that the peculiar circumstances of war and occupation meant that industrialists were very sceptical about these grand projects presented to them by the government.

A new Europe?

The idea of Franco-German co-operation was the justification for the very existence of Vichy. More generally, Vichy politicians wished to search for a new role in a Europe free from Anglo-Saxon influence. All this had considerable implications for the Vichy economy. Before the war there had been concern about the threat that America presented to the French economy. Now some hoped to construct a united Europe that would be strong enough to fight off the American challenge. It should not be suggested that everyone connected with the Vichy government ever subscribed to this tendency. Before the war there had been a great deal of talk about the instability of German autarky and the natural economic superiority of the allies. This thinking persisted, and it made many sceptical about a new order under German domination. When the Comité de Coordination was asked to write a report on 'le Bloc Européen et le Bloc Américain', it was singularly lukewarm about the possibilities opened up by Franco-German collaboration. The whiggish perspective of many historians has led them to overestimate the role that Europe played in Vichy thinking; correspondingly the role ascribed to the French Empire has been underestimated. But it is true that certain key economic ministers, notably Lehideux, did have high hopes for European collaboration.[1]

Vichy officials expected the search for an economic new Europe to arouse the enthusiasm of industrialists. At the beginning of the regime a government delegate assured an assembly of businessmen that the 'ridiculous' European system, in which there had been six customs frontiers between Berlin and Constantinople, would now be ended.[2]

The response to the New Europe varied considerably from one industry to another. It was notably enthusiastic in industries connected with transport. Almost by definition such industries were international in their operation, and this tended to make their leaders sympathetic towards international collaboration at a political level.[3] For example, the manufacturers of rolling stock already had a tradition of international co-operation, and this made industrialists in this sector sympathetic towards projects for similar international collaboration at a political level. They had been organized into an international cartel, the Association Internationale de la Construction du Matériel Roulant (the AICMR), since 1930.[4] This body survived the war surprisingly well. It moved its headquarters to Belgium, and it was later noted: 'official discussion that we undertook with the French and British governments dealing with relations between AICMR and its German members developed favourably, although they did not produce a definite conclusion, so that, under the cover of the discussions, the regular operation of AICMR went on even though its management committee could

[1] Lehideux discussed his ideas for a united Europe to confront American competition at a conference at the Ecole Libre des Sciences Politiques in February 1941. See Robert Paxon, *Vichy France: Old Guard and New Order, 1940–1944* (New York, 1972), p. 354.

[2] Paris, Archives Nationales (AN), 70 AQ 442, M. Motigny to the meeting of the Fédération des Associations Régionales on 22 November 1940.

[3] De Tarde, of the Compagnie des Chemins de Fer de l'Est, had suggested, as early as 1922, that international cartels might aid rapprochement between France and Germany: see Henry Ehrmann, *Organized Business in France* (Princeton, N.J., 1957), p. 48.

[4] AN, 70 AQ 431. An account of the history of the AICMR was given to its meeting of 25 April 1941.

never be convened'.[5] The AICMR was given a new dimension by the occupation, and it seems to have encouraged its members to co-operate with the Germans. One of the industry's syndicates stressed the importance of an organization 'which has already facilitated relations with the occupying authorities, who are bound to play the dominant role for the time being'.[6] The international liaison that had developed before the war carried on under the occupation. Indeed it reached extravagant lengths. In 1941 the AICMR met in Nuremberg, and its members were lectured on the benefits of the European new order: 'already in Europe under German direction, a new economic regime is being installed'.[7]

There was also some enthusiasm for European co-operation among manufacturers of cars and aeroplanes (the two industries were closely linked). Lehideux had begun his Vichy career as president of the Comité d'Organisation for the automobile industry. He had attempted to launch a policy of co-operation with the German and Italian industries.[8] Though Lehideux's views on the internal organization of the motor industry differed sharply from those of his former colleagues (see chapter 11), his views on international co-operation do seem to have struck a chord. The chief threat to this industry before the war had come from America, so it was not surprising that plans for a more independent Europe should excite interest.[9] In the 1930s the French motor manufacturers had looked enviously at the support provided by the German government for their colleagues across the Rhine.[10] Great excitement had been aroused by the German *autobahns*, and it is worth noting that the construction of a French *autoroute* system to link up with German roads was one of the most ambitious of Lehideux's pan-European projects.[11] Another factor behind the attitude of this sector was the relative flexibility of its production. This meant that industrialists could obtain work in the short term in the war economy, but also that they could hope to convert to peacetime production in the long term.[12]

However, the attitude of French heavy industries like coal and steel production was very different. For these industries the pre-war industrial

[5] Ibid., speech of the president to meeting of the AICMR on 17 June 1941.
[6] AN, 70 AQ 430, Réunion des Constructeurs et Réperateurs de Locomotives et Voitures of 8 October 1940.
[7] AN, 70 AQ 431, speech of secretary-general to meeting of 17 June 1941.
[8] Paxton, *Vichy France*, p. 219.
[9] Louis Renault – for example – displayed interest in Franco-German collaboration in the industry in the late 1930s. See Gilbert Hatry, *Louis Renault: patron absolu* (Paris, 1982), p. 349.
[10] AN 91 AQ 4, report of meeting of *comité pour la défense de l'industrie automobile* of 2 January 1939.
[11] It is interesting to note that many of France's post-war modernization projects also concerned international transport. Perhaps this suggests that such projects were linked to a search for international prestige as much as economic efficiency (see chapter 15).
[12] AN F 37 16, note of 2 April 1941. When the Germans proposed to link the aircraft industries of the two nations they claimed that it would be relatively easy to switch plants to civilian production.

competitor had been not America but Germany. Far from having a tradition of international co-operation, these industries had a tradition of hostility to Germany. The occupation exacerbated the suspicion felt in these industries towards Germany. For, though the Germans might require these industries to increase production as long as the war lasted, it was clear that if peace came there would be surplus production. In a German-dominated Europe German industrialists would be able to dispose of much of this surplus by obtaining cuts in French production. A leader of the German coal industry, meeting one of his French counterparts, made his expectation of cuts in French production after the war tactlessly clear. He said that he was opposed to the desire of de Peyerimhoff to keep the subsidy given to French national production. He believed that a harsher regime for the French mines would make post-war adjustment to a more limited demand easier, and added threateningly: 'In Germany itself measures of working flexibility (short time) have been anticipated. It is inconceivable...that French miners should be treated differently from those in Germany.'[13]

The attitude of French heavy industrialists to collaboration with the Germans was greatly influenced by the trepidation that they felt about the role that would be assigned to them in a German-dominated Europe. This trepidation was illustrated by a note, which found its way to the Délégation Générale aux Relations Franco-Allemandes, written by an industrialist signing himself 'MD'. He complained that the French administration was encouraging industrialists to collaborate, and that, for industry, such collaboration would be 'your own suicide'. He was quite specific about the dangers of a German-dominated Europe:

It may well be feared that England and the USA, if victorious, will make us pay dearly for their coal and oil, but we can protect ourselves against this danger by developing our own sources of raw materials to the full. On the other hand, in the European economy, prepared by Germany, we need have no illusion...we will return to being an agricultural people, and we will till the soil for the Germans, who will send us in exchange – when they want to encourage our agricultural effort – the products of their industry at a fixed price, without any possibility of competition.[14]

'MD' went on to suggest that industrialists should impede production in order to lower the chances of German victory. However, from the tone of his note it is clear that he believed that the majority of French industrialists were not taking such measures. In fact it is important to make a distinction between collaboration and collaborationism; that is to say, between willingness to collaborate with the Germans on a business level and a desire

---

[13] AN, F 37 31, account of meeting on 13 June 1941 between Russel of RW Kohlen Syndicate and Lafitte Laplace of the *comptoir des mines* of the Nord and Pas-de-Calais.

[14] 'Note sur les rapports économiques franco allemandes depuis l'armistice' dated August 1941 by an industrialist signing himself 'MD', in AN, F 37 77.

to see the French state collaborate on a political level in a European new order. This distinction is important because many of the heavy industries that were most useful in the short term to the German war economy had most to fear from a German peace economy. For example, the coal industry 'collaborated' with the Germans by maximizing production, yet most of the leaders of the industry, especially in the north, were deeply hostile to the German occupation.

The hostility of French industrialists to the idea of a European new order was further exacerbated by the industrial geography of France. Heavy industry was concentrated in the north and especially the Nord and Pas-de-Calais. Industry in this area was very vulnerable to the exactions of the occupying forces. This made industrialists sceptical about Vichy's plans for co-operation with the Germans. This scepticism was especially acute in the Nord and Pas-de-Calais because industrialists here felt that their special position under direct German administration would deprive them of any benefits which might be extracted from Franco-German collaboration. Thus the textile manufacturers of the *zone interdite* wrote to the ministry of industrial production complaining that, though recent agreements had given the rest of France greater economic liberty, their region remained under strict control. They suggested that they were being used as hostages to balance concessions to others.[15]

In the occupied zone there was also hostility to Franco-German collaboration, though this hostility was less acute than that displayed in the *zone interdite*. A letter from northern industrialists in 1941 stressed their loyalty to Marshal Pétain, but added that they had certain doubts about whether the armistice was proving an equal exchange.[16] In fact there was a notable distinction between the enthusiasm with which north and south greeted Vichy's projects for collaboration. This contrast was especially visible in the coal industry, which had branches in both zones. Olivier Kourchid has shown how the leaders of the industry in the Saint-Etienne basin were keener to increase production and co-operate with government plans than their colleagues in the Nord and Pas-de-Calais.[17] The policy of resisting Vichy's encouragement of the STO programme seems to have been initiated in the northern zone.[18]

With time the idea of a new European economy became less relevant, even to the Vichy government. It became painfully apparent that the Germans

---

[15] AN, F 37 39, note dated 20 May 1941.

[16] AN, F 37 48, declaration by 'northern industrialists' dated 13 October 1941.

[17] Olivier Kourchid, *Production industrielle et travail sous l'occupation: les mines de Lens et les mineurs 1940–1944* (Paris, 1986), p. 203.

[18] In particular pressure was applied to Perrin Pelletier of the Roche-la-Molière mines to take more workers threatened by STO. See Richard Vinen, 'The French Coal Industry during the Occupation', *Historical Journal*, 33 (1990), 105–30.

were not really interested in long-term collaboration with France. Furthermore, American entry into the war made it increasingly unlikely that Germany would have the chance to found a new Europe; this had a great impact on those who had supported Franco-German collaboration precisely because they feared American power. Lehideux lost interest in Franco-German collaboration in 1942. Norguet passed into the Resistance and was eventually arrested by the Germans. But, even when the idea of a European new order had been popular in government circles, it had attracted little interest among businessmen. They realized that the conditions of the time would provide a poor basis for drawing up a new order because those conditions were necessarily temporary. Industrialists recognized that, whichever side won, peace would bring these conditions to an end. Norguet described the thinking that underlay the hostility of industrialists to his plans: 'Either Germany wins, and whatever private *ententes* we have drawn up will be annulled, or Germany loses and the situation will be automatically favourable to us without us having to make special efforts.'[19]

Planisme

A planned economy had been a subject for discussion on the political fringes of the Third Republic. Vichy offered the chance to put such ideas into practice; indeed the Vichy government gave its approval to two plans. The first of these was that drawn up by the Délégation Générale à l'Equipement National in 1941, a plan designed to provide for the next four years. The second was drawn up in 1944 to cover the following ten years.[20] The circumstances of Vichy were especially propitious for such initiatives in three ways. Firstly, the idea of planisme that Vichy inherited from the 1930s had been conceived primarily as a response to unemployment. At first it seemed that unemployment would be the main economic problem confronting Vichy. Lehideux's first post under the new government was as head of the Commissariat pour la Lutte contre le Chômage. He went on to head the Délégation Générale à l'Equipement National which was designed to absorb surplus manpower with a programme of national re-equipment. It was this body that drew up both of Vichy's plans. The first of these plans was still presented as part of a struggle against unemployment. The second factor that underlay Vichy's planisme was an awareness that the switch to a peacetime economy would cause as much chaos as the defeat of 1940. It was believed that a plan might help to mitigate the dislocation of the

---

[19] AN, F37 27, note dated 2 December 1941.
[20] Philippe Mioche, 'Aux origines du plan Monnet: les discours et les contenus dans les premiers plans français (1941–1947)', *Revue historique*, 265 (1981), 407–36.

economy; this was a major motive for the plan of 1944. The third factor was a kind of resistance. This resistance was not based upon a desire to see Germany defeated but upon a wish to spare France the worst excesses of German exploitation. It was felt that if materials and labour were focused into the long-term future of the French economy they would be protected from being pillaged in the short-term interests of the German war economy.[21]

It is tempting to present planisme as existing in a kind of political ghetto at Vichy. It seems strange that something which was apparently linked with France's post-war industrial expansion should have any place in a regime which was so archaic and anti-industrial. The view that there was an isolated clique of modernizing ministers at Vichy will be challenged in general terms in the following chapter. However, in a more limited context it is important to stress that Vichy planisme was by no means as separate from the rest of Vichy policy as it might at first appear. As has been stressed, Vichy planisme originated with an effort to combat unemployment. This struggle lay at the root of much of Vichy thinking. This was partly because unemployment persisted in the southern zone under direct Vichy control long after it had evaporated in the northern zone. It was also because 'making work for idle hands' was a doctrine that appealed to the boy scout mentality of many at Vichy. Another sign of the unity between the first plans and the general thrust of Vichy policy was the emphasis that the former placed upon rural values. The first plan emphasized the need to maintain a large peasant population at the base of the French economy and was suffused with rhetoric about the moral superiority of rural life.

Both these elements in Vichy planisme made it rather remote from the preoccupations of most industrialists. Ruralism was not calculated to appeal to industrialists: nor was the struggle against unemployment of great interest to industrialists who were obsessed with the need to obtain labour. Indeed when the Commissariat pour la Lutte contre le Chômage sent a pamphlet to the Comité d'Organisation for the coal industry entitled 'employers have no fear of unemployment' they received a politely ironic reply pointing out that unemployment was the last thing that the coal industry feared.[22]

Though industry did not share the concerns that lay at the origins of planning it could be argued that it took a keen interest in the finished product. The COs, which represented industrialists, might be seen as

---

[21] Henri Rousso, 'Les paradoxes de Vichy', in P. Fridenson and A. Straus (eds.), *Le capitalisme français 19e–20e siècle: blocages et dynamismes d'une croissance* (Paris, 1987), p. 81. Norguet, the director of mechanical and electrical industries, justified his action in these terms. Norguet certainly did become anti-German; he was arrested in August 1943. However, his claim to have been operating against German interests in 1941 is open to question (see above).   [22] AN, 40 AS 43, 9 June 1941.

instruments of a kind of planning. Indeed Bardet argued that the planning functions of the COs should be made much more explicit; he suggested that a 'bureau du plan' should be set up to work with each CO, and that a national bureau should centralize the work of these bodies.[23] The CSEIC, a body made up of industrialists, produced a report on planning.

However, the industrialists on the CSEIC were conspicuously isolated from the concerns of most of their colleagues. Industry as a whole was too concerned with the day-to-day business of survival to have much time for planning for the future. Obtaining supplies was a key part of this day-to-day battle. Bardet seemed to recognize that the long-term planning functions that he envisaged for the COs were being undermined by the scramble to obtain materials: 'In many committees production and supply are seen to be opposed...it seems to be forgotten that the problems of production are long-term ones, whereas the problems of supply are products of circumstances.'[24] The difficulty of obtaining supplies often meant that the kind of long-term reconstruction envisaged by the planners was pure fantasy. The steel supply agency summed up this situation in a note of 1941: 'the tonnage at our disposal is hardly enough for the upkeep of food supply, agriculture and transport...whatever desire one might have to build up our equipment...we must concentrate on the immediate existence of the country.'[25]

The focus on short-term needs was exacerbated by the fact that the Germans wished to squeeze as much as possible out of the French economy as fast as possible. They had no desire to see resources invested in projects that would not yield results until after their own battle for survival was over. They could do this either indirectly, by cutting off supplies of labour or raw materials, or by brutally direct intervention. Thus in 1942, for example, the German authorities in the Côtes-du-Nord simply forbade all building works worth over 100,000 francs that were not directly authorized by themselves.[26] The state to which the French economy was eventually reduced by this coalition of short-term pressures was summed up by one civil servant who remarked tersely, 'we are here to save the furniture'.[27]

Even if industrialists were not interested in Vichy's grand planning experiments, it could be argued that the pressure of the war economy made French industry more efficient. Resources and manpower were concentrated on those firms capable of producing most efficiently. Furthermore, those firms who were least efficient were directly closed through the industrial

---

[23] AN, F 37 77, 'Réflexions sur six mois d'activité'.   [24] Ibid.

[25] AN 68 AJ 90, note of 24 March 1942.

[26] Christian Bourgeard, unpublished talk on 'Les côtes du nord' given at conference on *Les entreprises françaises pendant la seconde guerre mondiale*, Centre d'Etudes Pédagoqiques, Sèvres, 25/26 November 1986.

[27] AN, 72 AJ 1926, note by Baudard of May 1944. Baudard was head of a committee which was assigned to alleviate France's coal shortage by institutionalized foraging.

concentration programme. Assessing the economic changes brought to France by the war is well beyond the scope of my researches, perhaps beyond the scope of anyone's researches. However, there are a number of doubts which need to be aired about the extent to which rationalization occurred during the occupation.

Firstly, the economy was not always controlled very efficiently. The aim of supply policy may have been to concentrate production in efficient plants.[28] But the continuing trade in *monnaie matière* shows that materials were often not used by the firms to which they had been granted. Even more striking is the fact that large firms often obtained German contracts, and the consequent access to raw materials, but then passed the work to smaller firms. Secondly, productivity in almost all sectors declined as ageing plant was not replaced. Thirdly, those industrialists who were provided with most business by the war economy were well aware that this economy was temporary; they were therefore reluctant to change their production in any way that might prove inconvenient when the war ended and demand dropped. Fourthly, the penury of wartime produced an economy of improvisation. In this 'make do and mend' world small-scale enterprises sometimes did well. Thus the return to horse-powered transport induced by the shortage of petrol meant a boom for wheelwrights and blacksmiths;[29] the artisanal trades of the third arrondissement of Paris were set to work repairing objects that would have been thrown away in normal times;[30] radio repairmen did a flourishing business converting sets to receive the BBC.[31]

The reality of Vichy industry's attitude to modernization can be illustrated with a brief look at one sector: coal-mining. Modernization was an essential part of the industry's post-war apologia. Fabre, the secretary of the COH, claimed that one of the aims of the COH during the occupation had been to 'keep our production intact for the post-war period'.[32] This effort to pump resources into investment, which would yield long-term benefits for France, rather than into short-term exploitation, which would help Germany, was presented as a kind of resistance. Fabre suggested that it had been necessary to struggle with the Germans in order to maintain and renew equipment and carry out preparatory work: 'The mine managers had either

---

[28] In fact there is some interesting evidence that the German authorities envisaged the policy of concentrating industrial production in large enterprises not as a means of obtaining efficiency but as a means of keeping closer control over production. Kehrl remarked during the Speer Bichelonne meeting of 1943: 'it is better to concentrate on a small number of large enterprises... in order to be able to watch the execution of orders more easily'. AN, 72 AJ 1926, transcript of meeting in Berlin, 27 September 1943.

[29] Steven Zdateny, 'The Artisanat in France: An Economic Portrait, 1900–1956', *French Historical Studies*, 13 (1984), 415–40, at p. 428.

[30] S. Berger and M. J. Piore, *Dualism and Discontinuity in Industrial Societies* (Cambridge, 1980), p. 101.   [31] Ibid.

[32] AN, 40 AS 43, 16 October 1944, 'Note sur l'activité du COH depuis sa création'.

to conceal their operations from the occupation authorities, or to argue vigorously with them in order to safeguard the future of the pits, by carrying out new work or executing programmes designed to provide for future needs.'[33] It is true that a special part of the price subsidy given by the government to the collieries was earmarked for investment. Fabre claimed that by 1944 obligatory investment was running at 1,250,000 francs per year, and that the real figure exceeded even this.[34] However, this figure is deceptive; much of the new work consisted of opening new but temporary pits (see below).

Several factors restrained real long-term investment. Firstly, the scarcity of materials made new work of any kind difficult. This scarcity was reflected in the coal industry in a shortage of pit props. Secondly, the kind of protection that the labour force was given in the mines afforded little scope for new work. Young men were only immune from labour service in Germany if they were *travailleurs du fond*: in other words, coal-face workers. Much preparation and maintenance work involved using workers in workshops above ground. The effect of this was that merely keeping up production took all the resources available: 'Our maintenance workshops are overworked. The whole pace of enterprise is tied to their operation. Any interruption of the activities of these workshops would cause an immediate reduction in production.'[35]

Thirdly, and most importantly, it seems most unlikely that the mines had any interest in long-term investment. Odette Hardy-Hémery has shown that the mines had been reluctant to invest in machinery even before the war, and that they had sought rather to achieve increased production by more efficient exploitation of their workforce.[36] Now there was all the more reason for caution. The circumstances of the war were clearly temporary; eventually it was inevitable that there would be a fall in demand and a rise in supply. New investment would have left the mines with a lot of expensive machinery lying idle at the end of the war. The reluctance of the mines to take measures to increase production in the long term was illustrated in 1941 when a mining engineer, Loustau, proposed a scheme to reorganize working practices. Pucheu, the minister of industrial production, supported the scheme vigorously and hoped that it would achieve a 20 per cent increase in production. But the mining industry was hostile. The head of the industry in the Nord and Pas-de-Calais was reluctant even to let Loustau into the area.[37] Pucheu noted sadly in his memoirs that the head of the coal industry,

[33] Hoover Institute, *La vie de la France sous l'occupation* (3 vols., Paris, 1959), vol. I, p. 363.
[34] Ibid.
[35] AN, 40 AS 44, letter, dated 26 September 1942, from the Loire Chamber of Mines to the COH.
[36] Odette Hardy-Hémery, 'Rationalisation technique et rationalisation du travail à la Compagnie des Mines d'Anzin, 1927–1938', *Le mouvement social*, 72 (July–Sept. 1970), 3–48.   [37] Kourchid, *Production industrielle et travail sous l'occupation*, p. 171.

Lepercq, was unwilling to enforce the scheme on an unreceptive *patronat*: 'Lepercq was a liberal and wanted to act only by persuasion.'[38] The plan was shelved.

The effect of the drive for short-term increases in production without investment was described by Bichelonne during his meeting with Speer of 1943: 'yielding to necessity we have sacrificed too many preparatory works in favour of immediate production'.[39]

It is illuminating to study the techniques that the coal industry did use to increase production. The first technique lay in the use of labour. Odette Hardy-Hémery suggests that before the war the malthusianism of the mines had encouraged them to rely on labour rather than mechanization to increase production. Now they were provided with a huge reservoir of labour in the form of young men who wished to escape from Service du Travail Obligatoire. Furthermore, it was possible to drive these workers hard through the restoration of payment by results. Of course this labour was inexperienced and therefore not very efficient. It was also temporary; the workers would clearly leave the mines at the end of the occupation. However, the mines could afford to sustain inefficient labour because of the premium on scarce coal. They could also contemplate the departure of their workforce with equanimity since demand for coal would drop with the end of the war.

The second technique that the mines used to raise production was the opening up of new works. Increased production was extracted from the mines of the south where higher production costs normally impeded production. Within individual mines, narrower and less productive seams were opened up: 'the mines generally took advantage of circumstances to exploit low-quality and impure veins and to keep the best deposits for after the war'.[40] Firms that needed coal were even permitted to open up certain mines where production costs were exceptionally high and to run them for their own private use. This exploitation of low quality seams suited the circumstances. Demand was so high that coal of almost any quality could be sold,[41] and a system of subsidies had been established with the precise aim of subsidizing high-cost extraction. One of the COH's post-war apologias admitted that the use of low-quality seams suited the industry very well under these circumstances: 'anyway it was obviously in the material interests of the managers, in the absence of commercial competition and when faced with a policy of strict price control and taxation of profits, to conserve the best reserves for after the war'.[42]

---

[38] Pierre Pucheu, *Ma vie* (Paris, 1948).
[39] Transcript of Speer Bichelonne meeting in AN, 72 AJ 1932.
[40] Hoover Institute, *La vie de la France sous l'occupation*, vol. I, p. 365.
[41] AN, 68 AJ 130, note of 27 March 1942: 'the mines are less than usually interested in the maintenance of the quality of coal produced'.
[42] AN, 40 AS 44, 'La politique des houillères', p. 10.

It was always clear that this policy was only designed to provide temporary increases in production. Very few high-cost seams would remain viable in peacetime. The note of 16 November 1944 more or less admitted this with its half-hearted statement: 'several of these enterprises, among the most developed, seem capable of surviving in normal economic conditions'. In short, both of the techniques by which coal production was increased were short term and inefficient, in that they entailed a fall in productivity. It is hard to imagine a less 'modernizing' policy.

Chapter 12

Pro-Vichy business leaders

Introduction

The picture drawn so far has tended to stress the divergence between business and Vichy. This cannot disguise the fact that many businessmen, or men who had been active in the business movement, were pillars of Vichy support. Crudely speaking, the supporters of Vichy among businessmen came from two distinct groups. One of these groups consisted of the men who had arisen in the employers' movement after the Matignon accords purporting to represent small business. The other was the *avant-garde du patronat*. This chapter will examine the role of these groups under Vichy. Special attention will be paid to their relationship with the rest of industry, in order to determine to what extent their presence among Vichy supporters can be taken as symptomatic of business attitudes. But the relationship of the two groups to each other also deserves to be examined. Historians have generally assumed that the post-1936 leadership of the employers' movement was associated with an 'archaic corporatist' strand at Vichy that contrasted sharply with the 'technocratic' ethic of the business *avant-garde*. The hostility, which was sometimes expressed in very violent terms, between the two groups would seem to confirm this interpretation. However, examination of the ideologies of the two groups suggests that, beneath this hostility, they were often working towards similar goals.

The leadership of 1936 under Vichy

The generation of leaders who had risen in the employers' movement after the Matignon accords provided Vichy with some of its staunchest supporters. A number of these men (Gignoux, Nicolle, Verger, Gingembre,

Bernard, Duhem) occupied some kind of official position in the regime.[1] Before the war this group had been linked by both common ideologies and by personal association. The post-1936 leaders of the *patronat* remained an identifiable group at Vichy. The diary of Pierre Nicolle records the personal links between these individuals. On a more formal level, Gignoux, Bernard and Nicolle were all associated with the FAR, while Nicolle, Verger and Gingembre were all members of the Comité d'Etudes pour la Petite et Moyenne Entreprise. The involvement of these men in the Vichy regime is not very surprising. Socially, they had claimed to represent small business and the *classes moyennes*; Vichy directed much of its rhetoric at these classes, Geographically, the reform of the employers' movement after 1936 had been associated with the rise of leaders from the southern provinces: Vichy was based in the south. Ideologically, the new leaders had been corporatist, anti-étatist and anti-democratic; these were the ideologies that surfaced at Vichy. However, if Vichy was a victory for the ideas of this group, it was a hollow one. For it soon became obvious that implementation of the ideologies which the post-1936 leadership of the employers' movement had espoused undermined their own power. I intend to illustrate this process with a general survey of the whole group, and then to make more detailed studies of two of its members (Bernard and Gingembre).

The post-1936 leadership and the Vichy political system

As has been stressed, perhaps rather laboriously, the context in which these men operated between 1940 and 1944 was very different from that which had existed in the aftermath of 1936. In 1936 they had been closely allied with heavy industry, although they had also been associated with rhetoric hostile to it. But this alliance had been rooted in particular circumstances. First of all it had been the product of the electoral system of the Third Republic and especially the pivotal importance of the Radical party.

---

[1] Gignoux was a member of Vichy's Conseil National; Nicolle was a member of the Comité d'Etudes pour le Petite et Moyenne Entreprise (CEPME); Verger was a member of the Comité d'Organisation Professionnelle and the CEPME; Gingembre was secretary of the CEPME and a member of the cabinet of the minister of industrial production; Bernard was a member of the Conseil Supérieur de la Production Industrielle; Duhem was a member of the Comité d'Information des Employeurs – the role of Duhem seems to have been very minor (as it had been between 1936 and 1939). In this chapter I intend to concentrate on the first five of these leaders. It should also be stressed that there were some leaders of the *patronat* who rose after 1936 and did not have links with the Vichy regime. Germain Martin does not appear in official Vichy circles. The only explicitly anti-Vichy figure among this group was George Mauss who, as a Jew, would hardly have been welcome among Vichy supporters. At the liberation Mauss became a member of the National Council for the re-establishment of 'liberté syndicale' (UIMM circular dated 26 November 1944 in AN, 70 AQ 300). The most inexplicable absentee is Prax: his southern origins, small business credentials and violent anti-marxism would all normally be associated with a vigorously pro-Vichy stance, but he seems to have occupied no official position.

Ironically Vichy's suspension of democracy, so vigorously supported by men like Nicolle, helped to make them redundant. Secondly, the alliance had been based on the need to confront a mobilized working class. Under Vichy this working class threat no longer existed, or at least it existed only in a very different form. Heavy industry, which had sought to appear allied with the *classes moyennes* against the proletariat, was now seeking to ally with the proletariat. Under these circumstances the men of 1936 were counter-revolutionaries without a revolution.

The alliance with heavy industry was now broken. In fact the post-1936 leaders of the employers' movement often provided the most vigorous support for measures that the government took against big business. For example, it has been suggested that Gignoux inspired Pétain's attack on the trusts of 11 November 1941.[2] It might be argued that many of the men of 1936 were no longer business leaders at all, but purely political figures. They were interested in the whole thrust of Vichy policy, not merely in its economic aspects. Gignoux was the most striking example of this transition. With the dissolution of the CGPF he lost all formal association with organized business. Instead he became mayor of a small town in the Loire, as far removed as possible from the concerns of the industrial north.[3] He also became a member of the inner circle of Vichy advisers both formally, as a member of the Conseil National, and informally, as an intimate of the Marshal's.[4] It was even rumoured that Gignoux was offered the ministry of industrial production.[5]

Corporatism

The 1936 leadership of the *patronat* was hostile to the industrial system established by the law of 16 August 1940. They were mostly men who had founded their careers upon interprofessional associations; they had only shallow roots, or no roots at all, in any one profession. They had purported to be the representatives of small business. The Comités d'Organisation were founded upon single industries. Furthermore, they were dominated by big business.

But the Comités d'Organisation did not, at first, give great cause for concern. They were only meant to be provisional. The true hopes of the Vichy loyalists lay in the permanent arrangements that were to be established by the *Charte du Travail*. They took great interest in this *Charte*

---

[2] Jean Paillard, *La révolution corporative spontanée* (Paris, 1979).

[3] For accounts of Gignoux's activities in this capacity see Monique Luirard, *La région stéphanoise dans la guerre et dans la paix 1936–1951* (Saint-Etienne, 1980).

[4] Pierre Nicolle, *Cinquante mois d'armistice, Vichy, 2 juillet 1940–26 août 1944: journal d'un témoin* (2 vols., Paris, 1947), vol. II, p. 20, entry for 24 August 1942: 'He is undoubtedly among the closest advisors of the Marshal.'

[5] Ibid., vol. II, p. 360, entry for November 1941.

and especially in its corporatist aspects; after all corporatism had been the doctrine of this group during the 1930s.[6] In fact the dichotomy that was presented between the Comité d'Organisation system and the corporatism of the *Charte* was false. Corporatism would also exclude interprofessional leaders. This was not immediately evident; the very vagueness of corporatist doctrine helped to conceal its potential effects.

However, as the *Charte* was implemented the impact which corporatism would have on interprofessional leaders became clearer. Nicolle reported that in August 1943 Laval was confronted with 'the express wish of numerous delegates to see interprofessional organizations re-established'.[7]

The Chambers of Commerce provided a further illustration of the ironies of Vichy corporatism. The Chambers had been heavily involved in the reaction against the Popular Front. They claimed to represent the *classes moyennes* which were so important to Vichy. Much of the ideology of Vichy had been discussed before the war in the Chambers of Commerce.[8] Many of Vichy's keenest supporters came from the Paris Chamber of Commerce.[9] But, as interprofessional institutions, the Chambers of Commerce were cut out of the picture by the Vichy industrial system. Indeed the Association of Presidents of Chambers of Commerce was dissolved by Vichy.[10] This exclusion aroused considerable resentment; the Paris Chamber of Commerce commented upon the law of 16 August 1940 as follows: 'For the state to act with proper information, it needs to be officially advised by interprofessional organizations that are well suited to take a broad and complete view of the matter under discussion.'[11]

Relations with the state

The relations between the state and the group of business leaders who had risen after 1936 were awkward. Anti-étatisme had always played a large part in their rhetoric. Yet now they were closely connected to the Vichy

---

[6] Nicolle, Verger and Bernard all submitted projects for the *Charte* (see chapter 8). Gignoux and Gingembre were both prisoners of war for much of the period during which the *Charte* was being prepared.

[7] Nicolle, *Cinquante mois d'armistice*, vol. II, p. 13, entry for 9 August 1942.

[8] Bagnaud (who was admittedly an extreme example) had displayed anti-democratic (Paris Chamber of Commerce archives (C de C), p-v for meeting of 7 July 1937) and anti-semitic (transcript, C de C meeting of 23 November 1938) sentiments.

[9] For example Painvin, de Canisy, Laguionie.

[10] There is an important distinction to be made between the position of the Chambers of Commerce and that of the post-1936 leadership of the CGPF. The latter were not businessmen themselves and therefore could have no role in the COs or the corporations as individuals. But the members of the Chambers of Commerce were all businessmen. Therefore even though as *institutions* the chambers lost out their members could enjoy considerable power as *individuals*. Thus Painvin, Laguionie and Bagnaud all presided over COs.   [11] C de C, Paris, p-v, 28 December 1940.

government; far from really wishing for a professional economy run by businessmen, they were relying on the government to protect them from the power that big business was exercising via the Comités d'Organisation. The myth of synarchic conspiracy, to which some of these men subscribed, was, at least in part, a product of this ambiguous relationship with the state (see below).

Eventually the Vichy government recognized that some of its closest supporters were being excluded from its industrial system. In 1943 the corporatism of the *Charte du Travail* was moderated by the creation of a number of interprofessional bodies. One of these bodies was the Comité d'Etudes de la Petite et Moyenne Entreprise; another was the Centre d'Information des Employeurs. The president of this latter body specifically linked its foundation to a revival of the interprofessional level: 'In creating these centres of information...you have perfectly understood the need to revive the notion of the interprofessional level, to which the *Charte du Travail* gave only secondary importance.'[12]

The Chambers of Commerce also experienced something of a revival at this time. They were closely connected with both the CIE and the CEPME,[13] and in 1944 the Assembly of Chambers of Presidents of Commerce, which had been dissolved by early Vichy legislation, was reinstated.[14]

The appointment, in March 1944, of Déat to the ministry of labour seemed to consolidate the revival of the fortunes of the post-1936 leadership of the employers' movement. Déat had been close to this group and shared their hostility to big business and to the syndicalism of the previous ministers of labour. Those who were seen as representatives of big business, such as Bardet[15] and Lente,[16] resigned from their official posts. Nicolle clearly saw Déat's appointment as the final victory of his group over the representatives of big business: 'for them this marks the failure of the Bardet plan much to the disappointment of the anti-social and synarchic *polytechniciens*'.[17]

However, victory within the Vichy government in 1943 and 1944 was a mixed blessing. For it was at precisely this point that industrialists were seeking to distance themselves from the regime. The president of the CIE recognized the difficulties of the position: 'a task that circumstances render

---

[12] AN, F 22 1839, 9 February 1944.
[13] André Roussillière, the president of the CIE, was also president of the Chamber of Commerce of Bordeaux. In a note dated 24 March 1944 (F 22 1839) Roussillière called for the Chambers of Commerce to be given a greater role. For links between the CEPME and the Chambers of Commerce see below. [14] JO, 16 June 1944.
[15] Bardet's resignation letter (dated 24 March 1944) can be found in AN F 22 1839. It sheds little light on the reasons for his departure which he explains in terms of 'raisons techniques'.
[16] Nicolle, *Cinquante mois, d'armistice*, vol. II, p. 383, entry for 15/16/17 March 1944.
[17] Ibid., entry for 1/2 March 1944.

especially thankless'.[18] Indeed it seems likely that the arrival of Déat rather suited the purposes of men like Lente and Bardet by giving them an opportunity to escape from the government. Nicolle recognized as much: 'the representatives of big business...were on the point of resignation...taking advantage of the chance to clear their names'.[19] Under these circumstances having the support of political circles at Vichy was like owning stock in a bankrupt company.

The representation of *petite et moyenne entreprise*

The formal organization of *petite et moyenne entreprise* (PME) had been one of the products of the employers' defeat in 1936. The fate of such organizations between 1940 and 1944 illustrates some of the ironies in relations between business and Vichy. The regime had close links with those who claimed to represent the PME. The Petite et Moyenne Industrie et Commerce (PMIC) section of the CGPF had nurtured the corporatist doctrines in the employers' movement in 1938 and 1939. Two of the most vocal supporters of the new government, Nicolle and Verger, had been members of the PMIC. It was hoped that Vichy would open a golden age for small business and those who claimed to represent it; such hopes were dashed.

The Petite et Moyenne Industrie section of the Parisian Metallurgy Association

Because of the dissolution of the CGPF in November 1940, the PMIC ceased to exist. However, the organization that had given birth to it, the small business section of the Parisian Metallurgy Association (GIMMCP), remained in existence. Through the archives of this body it is possible to trace the fate of small business during the first three years of the Vichy government.

This fate was conditioned by the economy of war. The economic consequences of French participation in the allied war effort had done much to alienate small business from the Republic in 1938 and 1939 (see chapter 7). But the advent of the Vichy government changed little. Soon French industry was participating, with similar effects, in the German war effort. The complaints of the PMI section in this period echo those that they had made in 1939 and 1940. In such a period much of the economy depended on contracts with the state. The large-scale enterprises of the *secteur abrité* had

[18] AN, F 22 1839, 12 July 44.
[19] Nicolle, *Cinquante d'armistice*, vol. II, p. 283, entry for 15/16/17 March 1944.

the contacts and experience to negotiate for such contracts and the privileges that accompanied them. Once it had acquired such advantages it was in a position to exploit smaller enterprises by subcontracting. Thus one correspondent complained that larger firms were acquiring *Zast* bonds, which gave them the right to raw materials to fulfil German contracts, but were then passing on the contracts to smaller firms and hoarding the bonds.[20] Small businesses with few administrative staff were hard hit by the paper work involved in an increasingly étatist economy. Since such concerns were likely to be working on tight margins they were also vulnerable to late paying by the administration.[21]

Under these circumstances it was not surprising to find that small business began to express a certain disillusion with the new government. Pinet (the leader of the PMI) wrote to Bichelonne:

Many small and medium-sized industrialists had hoped, after the events of June 1940, that a real transformation of government methods would be mapped out that would allow the French economy to prepare a total renewal after the present war...they will conclude that, for all the promises so often repeated by the new government, there has been no change and the national revolution has yet to take place.[22]

Small business had grown used to expressing its grievances in anti-étatist language during the Third Republic. The fact that the state was now highly sympathetic to small business, and indeed was often trying to shield it from the power of heavy industry or the demands of the German authorities, did not change this language. The PMI repeatedly stressed the suspicion that they felt for the intention which lay behind government policy. On 20 June 1941 the PMI complained: 'policies that push...small and medium-sized businessmen towards a state of exasperation that will bring grave dangers of social disorder in the future. Everything still seems to revolve around very large enterprises and it is forgotten that 80 per cent of industrialists and shopkeepers are small businessmen.'[23] In April 1941 Pinet complained to Bichelonne of 'an excessive application of new economic theories seeking to develop numerous activities in big businesses that exceed French capacities'.[24] The Vichy government was often carrying out economic policies that had been initiated by the Germans. Because of this, measures were not always explicable in terms of the stated aims of the government. This exacerbated suspicions that the economy might be guided by a hidden agenda. Pinet expressed such suspicion:

[20] AN, 39 AS 209, letter of February 1941 from Giraudin et fils.
[21] Ibid. Pinet (the leader of the PMI) complained about late payment by the army in a letter to Bichelonne dated 29 June 1941. A letter to Pinet (dated 1 February 1944) from the Usines de Montage made a similar complaint about the navy.
[22] Ibid., Pinet to Bichelonne, 25 April 1941.
[23] Ibid., Pinet to Bichelonne, 20 June 1941.   [24] Ibid., 25 April 1941.

I have the honour of drawing to your attention the uncertainty that has been created among industrialists of small and medium importance by the comments of the government on the evolution that you anticipate for the economy, in view of the uncertainty of the future and the ignorance of the conditions in which industrial concentration may occur, no indication having been given on this matter.[25]

However, it should be stressed that in some ways the small business section of the GIMMCP was not typical of French small business. Firstly, the metallurgy sector benefited considerably from the general buoyancy of the war economy. Some of this benefit filtered down even to small businesses. The PMI admitted that very few firms in its constituency had been forcibly closed.[26] What concerned small enterprises in this sector was not the outright extinction that faced much small business in France, but exploitation by larger firms.

Secondly, the nature of the GIMMCP placed sharp limits upon the activity of the PMI section. Parisian metallurgy was at the core of the industrial establishment in France. It contained much of France's large-scale business. The PMI section was therefore in no position to launch the kind of really violent attacks upon big business that were common currency in other organizations during this period. The dilemma was illustrated by a note of July 1943 in which reference was made to the 'unfair competition' posed by vertical integration by 'motor manufacturers who want to make everything themselves' and to 'the social dangers of concentrating 30,000 workers in a single plant'.[27] It is clear that this was an implicit attack upon the Renault firm. Since Renault was the largest and most influential member of the GIMMCP it is not surprising that the attack never became explicit. Generally the PMI's rhetoric took the form of requests addressed to big business, not attacks on it. Sometimes these requests were addressed in an almost obsequious tone; firms that had not payed their subcontractors were implored to pay merely a fraction of what was owed.[28]

The distinction between the attitude of the PMI and other representatives of small business was particularly marked with reference to the events of 1936. In retrospect men like Nicolle and Verger did not hesitate to describe the Matignon settlement as a conspiracy between big business and the government that had betrayed small business. The GIMMCP, which had itself been a signatory of Matignon, could hardly permit such talk. Indeed the PMI went out of its way to deny this interpretation of Matignon: 'it is quite false to allege that in the negotiations of 1936 the interests of one category of business were sacrificed to those of another ... the whole dossier

[25] Ibid., Pinet to Bichelonne, 14 August 1942.
[26] AN, 39 AS 209, note on recent activity of PMI, 15 February 1944.
[27] AN, 39 AS 213, note of July 1943 headed 'Recherche sur les moyens propres à créer un climat favorable au développement de la Petite et Moyenne Industrie'.
[28] Ibid., circular dated 30 January 1942.

of the discussions shows that the employers' delegates were mainly concerned with the fate of small enterprises'.[29]

Finally, the metallurgists were part of a body that was always rather hostile to the occupying authorities. This attitude is clearly evident in PMI notes at a surprisingly early date; Pinet suggested to Pucheu in April 1941 that 'the considerable number of enterprises and their dispersal over the whole country keeps them especially safe from requisition and destruction'. In a note of 15 May that year it was also stressed that giving work to small business would 'avoid requisition of the factories by the occupying forces'.[30]

The Comité d'Etudes de la Petite et Moyenne Entreprise

In response to the complaints of small business, the minister of industrial production decided to create a body specifically to represent this group. The Comité d'Etudes de la Petite et Moyenne Entreprise was set up by decree on 27 May 1943. Twenty-six men with some claim to represent various sections of small business were appointed. To these were added seven *ex officio* leaders. Later in the year the number on this committee was expanded to forty-two. The secretary-general of the committee was Léon Gingembre, a veteran of the PMIC section of the CGPF. Though, formally, Bichelonne was president of the committee, Gingembre was recognized as its effective leader; indeed it was often known as the 'Comité Gingembre'.

The Comité d'Etudes was designed to examine problems, not to initiate new policies. It directed its attention via a series of special commissions. The committee examined the problems presented by the system of supply of raw materials, the representation of small business interests on Comités d'Organisation and on the Commission du Plan Compatible. Finally, the committee suggested that a Centre Interprofessionnel de Coopération Technique des Petites et Moyennes Entreprises be set up.[31]

The Vichy government spawned numerous study groups of this kind. Normally it is hard to gauge how much such bodies achieved. But there was no doubt about the Comité d'Etudes. It was a resounding failure. It was bombarded with complaints. One enraged correspondent remarked: 'it provides support of the kind that a rope gives to a hanged man'.[32] Even the committee's secretary-general noted wearily that 'the committee has lived, and above all, it has suffered'.[33] Why was the committee so unsuccessful?

[29] Ibid., 20 April 1943, summary of action of the GIMMCP relating to *petite et moyenne entreprise*.

[30] AN, 39 AS 209, Pinet to Pucheu dated 25 April 1941 and note of 15 May.

[31] Ce de C, 1862, 'Huit mois d'activité'.

[32] Ibid., letter of Jousset of Société Parisienne de Cimentation to Bichelonne, dated 1 February 1944.   [33] Ibid., account of activity, 1 February to 19 April 1943.

To understand the committee's plight it is necessary to remember that it was, in many ways, a reincarnation of the leadership of the employers' movement that had arisen after 1936. Nine members of the original CGPF committee formed in 1937 went on to be members of the Comité d'Etudes. Perhaps more importantly three of the most prominent figures in the post-1936 leadership of the *patronat*, Verger, Nicolle and Gingembre himself, were members of the committee. The committee's fate illustrates once again some of the contradictions in the position of this group during the Vichy regime.

Interprofessionalism versus corporatism

The small business movement had been associated with the rise of corporatism immediately before the war. Representatives of this group pressed for a corporatist settlement in the *Charte du Travail*. They continued to stress that they wanted a 'professional' economy, not one organized by the state. In fact of course many of these leaders had founded their power on broad political movements and had very shallow roots in any one profession; a truly corporatist economy would leave them without a role. To some extent the Vichy government seems to have recognized that some of its keenest supporters were being deprived of a role by the very economic system which they claimed to support. In 1943 the government revived a number of bodies operating at the interprofessional level. The Comité d'Etudes was part of this revival. It worked closely with the Chambers of Commerce which were also enjoying something of a renaissance after having been left out of the picture by early Vichy legislation. But the problem was that a corporatist regime could only allow such bodies a certain latitude. Bichelonne stressed to the introductory meeting of the CEPME that study was the only possibility at the interprofessional level; action would have to remain within the framework of individual professions.[34]

The Comité d'Etudes and the state

The Vichy government was a vigorous supporter of the committee. That support was manifested on 27 August 1943 at a full session of the committee. This meeting was attended by both the head of state and the prime minister. The latter even went so far as to express his own disquiet with the Comité

---

[34] Ibid., Bichelonne to inaugural session of 14 May 1943.

d'Organisation system: 'I do not accept functions of the Comités d'Organisation as they work now.'[35]

As has been stressed, all those who claimed to represent small business had some trouble reconciling their close relations with the government with a traditionally anti-étatist rhetoric. For Gingembre the problem was especially acute. Others could play the loyal opposition. They could support the broad policy of the government, while opposing certain aspects of its industrial policy by suggesting that the wishes of the Marshal were being undermined by treacherous administrators. No such option was available to Gingembre. His committee was closely connected to the administration and the ministry of industrial production as well as to the cabinet of Marshal Pétain. The minister of industrial production, Bichelonne, was not merely the founder of the committee but also its president. Four civil servants were *ex officio* members of the committee. Indeed, as a secretary to the cabinet of Bichelonne, Gingembre himself was officially a civil servant.

Under these circumstances the committee was in no position to attack the industrial organization of the government. The administration was reluctant to admit that small business problems came from real conflicts of interest. Instead it stressed 'misunderstandings'. Bichelonne expounded this philosophy to the opening session of the committee: 'problems of the PME are essentially psychological'.[36] Starting from such assumptions meant that the committee acted more as an emitter of propaganda directed at small business than as a transmitter of its demands: 'From the first session it was clear that above all it was important...to show to the PME that...the equity of the measures applied to them was above suspicion.'[37] The committee almost invariably reached the optimistic but implausible conclusion that problems would disappear with better communication.

The committee's subservience to official policy alienated it from many potential supporters. Gingembre recognized that it was widely believed that the difficulties of small business did spring from government policy: 'They [small businessmen] are all the more worried because it seems that this situation is due to the application of a doctrine which anticipates new forms of the economy marked by ever greater concentration...where they will have no place.'[38] Some members of the committee baulked at its dependence on the state. Nicolle grumbled: 'the civil servants intend, even in organizations where they were invited as observers, to direct the debates and impose the policies that they have determined in advance'.[39] At the meeting of 27 July 1943 Nicolle complained about the refusal of the government to

---

[35] Ibid., 27 July 1943.　　　　　　[36] Ibid., 14 May 1943.
[37] Gingembre addressing the meeting of 17 June 1943.
[38] C de C, 1862, Gingembre speaking to session of 27 August.
[39] Nicolle, *Cinquante mois d'armistice*, entry for 16–18 June 1943.

accept the committee's report about the supply system: 'a system of control over supplies had been promised to solve the problem. He is astonished that after so many weeks a counter project is now proposed.'[40] The committee's official links meant that it was in danger of being outflanked by more independent bodies. Gingembre was especially aware of the threat posed by the Groupement Interprofessionnel des Petites et Moyennes Entreprises. He complained of its more strident and agressive tone: 'the Groupement Interprofessionnel des PME...is of purely political origin and seeks to direct the action of the PME outside the professional framework towards simple demands'.[41] This tone was exemplified by the programme of the Groupement. It talked of 'the incomprehension of the liberal regime of yesterday, just like the "Revolution National" today'; it added that 'the state continues its present policy of depending on the trusts, and faceless capital, and continues to move towards a large-scale economy and the impoverishment or disappearance of the social and professional world of the small and medium-scale businesses'.[42]

Links with the Vichy government were especially awkward at the time that the committee was formed. For at this time the room for manoeuvre of the state was severely limited by the pressure of the occupying authorities. This meant that there was little that the government could give the committee except kind words. Gingembre discreetly alluded to this impotence, remarking that 'political circumstances' imposed limits even on 'leaders'. But, since the committee could hardly admit to the impotence of the government to which it was tied, it could never confront the problems of the economy realistically. This meant that the most serious problem of all which faced business in Vichy France, the labour shortage, which was a direct product of the German *relève*, was never mentioned by the committee.

It was also increasingly obvious at this time that the Vichy government could not last. Businessmen were beginning to distance themselves ostentatiously from a doomed regime. These efforts were particularly strenuous in the GIMMCP. A number of GIMMCP members did serve on the committee. But the most important of the GIMMCP leaders who had been involved with the small business movement, Clément, was conspicuous by his absence. This absence was surely due, at least in part, to the fact that

---

[40] C de C, 1862, transcript of meeting of 27 August 1943.

[41] Ibid., note of 1 May 1943 on other bodies representing the PME. This note also mentions the Association Corporative des Entreprises à Capital Personnel. But this latter body was clearly seen as less of a threat although it was compromised by links with 'certain private interests'; 'their suggestions deserve to be taken into account because of the technical ability of some of their leaders'.

[42] AN, F 10 5098. The programme is to be found with a covering letter to René Gousset in archives which are concerned with the formation of the peasant corporation. The Groupement had been formed in September 1940. The president of the Groupement was Paul Clément (not to be confused with Roger Clément) who had been the representative of road transport in the PMIC set up by the CGPF.

Clément was a member of the group of Parisian metallurgists preparing for the liberation (see chapter 9). It seems likely that the problems of the doomed regime also underlay the decision of the Paris Chamber of Commerce not to set up a permanent Bureau to liaise with the CEPME at a time when allied troops were almost in the suburbs of Paris.[43] Businessmen were quite explicit about the uselessness of a committee which was tied to a doomed government:

One question alone preoccupies us now: if the war finishes suddenly tomorrow what measures are envisaged by the committee to guarantee the continuation and finance of our enterprises during the time between the transition from the war economy to the peace economy...If the committee is only interested in the present, it will disappear at the same time as the circumstances that created it.[44]

Big business and the committee

The committee enjoyed ambiguous relations with big business. Many on the committee were violently hostile to 'the trusts'. Gingembre himself had resigned from the CGPF in 1939 in protest at the influence of big business. But a number of members of the committee, including Gingembre, were linked to big business via the Parisian metallurgy association. Furthermore it may well have been felt that given its semi-official nature the committee could not rock the boat. Certainly the committee stressed that the Centre d'Etudes, which it planned to set up, 'in no sense aims to spread hostility between small and medium-sized business and large business, nor to bring about a division between professions'.[45] The extent to which this position isolated the Comité d'Etudes is once again highlighted by the proposals of the Groupement Interprofessionnel de la Petite et Moyenne Entreprise. This body had no hesitation in expressing violent hostility to 'the conspiracy of high finance and the trusts arrayed against small business with tenacious determination'. In the classic style of those who claimed to represent small business at Vichy the group looked back on the Matignon negotation as a conspiracy hatched by big business and a left-wing government:

As a result of the economic and social experiment of June 1936, small and medium-sized business were both puppets and victims. They saw social regulations applied that in nine cases out of ten had been designed for large businesses; this handicapped them greatly. They were not represented at the 'Matignon' accords, the starting-point for policies that affected the whole nation. This alliance of big business and Bolsheviks confronted small and medium-sized business with a problem of life and death.

[43] C de C, 1862, note dated 3 July 1944.
[44] C de C, Jousset letter to Bichelonne, 1 February 1944.
[45] Ibid., transcript of committee meeting, 17 April 1944.

In fact the representatives of small business had enjoyed their heyday in the aftermath of the Popular Front precisely because of an alliance with heavy industry. The irony of this alliance was that heavy industry needed to present its demands under a cover of small business support because of the political system of the Third Republic (and particularly the pivotal position of the Radical party). Yet the small business representatives had campaigned against that political system and supported the Vichy government's destruction of the Republic. Now that democracy was suspended big business did not require small business allies. It could afford to regard the rhetoric of the PME with far more scepticism. The clichés, which small business leaders like Gingembre had been churning out for years, were suddenly questioned. Practically every speech by a leader of small business during the previous seven years had started with a 'tour d'horizon' in which the general importance of small business to French society was demonstrated with a barrage of statistics. But in 1943 Barbier, the president of the Chamber of Commerce of Versailles, dared to challenge Gingembre's statistics. Extrapolating from a study in Versailles he concluded that small businesses were far less significant in the French economy than was generally assumed.[46] Most significantly of all, businessmen began to question whether small business had any unitary interest and indeed whether the term petite et moyenne entreprise really meant anything at all. A note for the president asked whether it was really possible to imagine that the Baron de Neuflize (a prominent merchant banker) and a chef had the same interests.[47]

The Confédération Générale des Petites et Moyennes Entreprises

It would be easy to fit Gingembre into the whiggish Hoffmannite interpretation of the Vichy economy. Gingembre's weakness seems to spring so obviously from the fact that big business freed itself from the chains of the republican synthesis which had attached it to small business.[48]

But there is a weakness in this argument. Gingembre's eclipse did not last after the liberation. In October 1944 the CGPME was formed. Gingembre was initially confined to being the delegate-general of this body, apparently because of his Vichy record. But there was little doubt that he was the real force behind the CGPME and in 1953 he became its president. It would

---

[46] C de C, 1862, transcript of meeting of 13 March 1944. Barbier expressed doubt about the Gingembre's claim that there were 250,000 businesses in the small business category in France. He suggested that the true figure was 90,000.

[47] Ibid., 'Note pour le Président 10 September 1943'.

[48] See chapter 15 for a more extended exposition of the Hoffmannite interpretation of the Vichy and the French economy.

probably be fair to say that of all those who had played a role in the economic life of Vichy, Gingembre achieved the greatest success in post-war France. He did not resign until 1975.

In fact on close examination it becomes obvious that Gingembre did not succeed in spite of his wartime experience but because of it. The GIMMCP stressed that the success of the CGPME was not unconnected to the previous organization of small business. How did Gingembre's wartime experience lead to his post-war success? Firstly, the increased scepticism with which small business leaders were regarded by other business representatives led Gingembre to a new definition of petite et moyenne entreprise. No longer was it acceptable simply to put all businesses employing less than 500 men in this category. Now the definition was a more flexible and sophisticated one that revolved around the nature of the business.[49] There was also an increased sophistication evident in the tactics of the post-war small business movement. During the Vichy period the small business movement had suffered from the capacity of heavy industry to abandon its social allies when they ceased to be useful. After the war it was Gingembre who proved adept at changing alliances to suit himself.

Another aspect of Gingembre's platform which seems to have developed during the war was the emphasis on the possibility of combining advanced technology and small business.[50] Again it is possible to argue that this was a lesson which had been learnt at Vichy. For the traditional view that Vichy could be divided into technocratic 'jeunes cyclistes' and 'vieux romains' who were intent on protecting small business is false. In fact the same men were often seeking to promote economic modernization and to protect small business. Gingembre's *patron*, Bichelonne, was perhaps the arch example of such a figure, and it would not be surprising if the idea that modernity and the traditional social structure of France were not antithetical first developed in Bichelonne's cabinet. Of course in the context of the Nazi war economy the efforts both to protect small business and to modernize industry were unrealistic. But in the economy of post-war France things were very different.

[49] On 10 September 1943 a 'note pour le président' remarked that the definition of a small business 'is not something that can be quantified; it is above all a subjective matter'.

[50] C de C, 1862. Gingembre declared to the constitutive meeting of the CGPME that the PME were not the cause of the 'vieillissement de l'économie française'.

Aymé Bernard during the Vichy regime

Bernard's faith in Marshal Pétain was never in any doubt. The association that he led in Lyon had called for Pétain to lead France as early as March 1940. On the first occasion that Bernard was able to address the northern section of the FAR on 22 November 1940 he opened the meeting with 'an expression of confidence and faith in Marshal Pétain',[51] and went on to expound Pétain's vision for France. Before the war, business leaders like Bernard had been obliged to pose as outsiders in a corrupt and hostile political system (such a pose did not necessarily rule out the establishment of good political contacts). Now Bernard seemed to take an almost schoolboyish delight in being an insider: 'M. Bernard relayed in confidence some information that he had been able to glean in government circles.'[52] Bernard solemnly recounted to the FAR meeting various platitudes relayed to him by Pétain during a recent visit to Lyon. In the journal of the Lyon business association (AICA) his eulogy of Pétain was even more enthusiastic. He stressed the difference between Pétain's words and the usual clichés of politicians: 'this was wisdom itself'.[53] Bernard's attitude to Pétain is thrown into relief by another account of the same visit by another business leader. George Villiers reports that Pétain was so senile that at one point he forgot that the First World War had ended.[54]

Bernard had close links with the Vichy regime as a whole. He himself made his first visit to Vichy immediately after the defeat on 2 July 1940.[55] Three of his lieutenants sought office at Vichy. Bernard's colleague Nicolle spent the war at Vichy (he describes his position as that of economic councillor and delegate of the FAR). Fougère, the president of the FAR, hoped to enter the cabinet of the new minister of industrial production.[56] Bernard's lieutenant in Lyon, Dupraz, did acquire a position as *chef du cabinet* to the secretary of state for supply in 1941.

The articles that Bernard wrote were often devoted to defending the Vichy regime. He argued that much of its policy was inevitable: 'the unavaoidable consequences of defeat'.[57] He argued that Vichy had saved France from the breakdown in order which had occurred during the 'démobilization à l'allemande'.[58] But he did not merely regard the Vichy government as the product of external circumstances; it was a desirable institution in itself. He stressed the bankruptcy of the Third Republic: 'France defeated, wiped out in six weeks, following a century of mistakes

---

[51] AN, 70 AQ 420, transcript of meeting of FAR, 22 November 1940.   [52] Ibid.
[53] *Documentation*, 22 November 1940.
[54] Georges Villiers, *Témoignages* (Paris, 1978), p. 32. Villiers was mayor of Lyon at this time. Though a *résistant* he was by no means systematically hostile to Pétain.
[55] Nicolle, *Cinquante mois d'armistice*, vol. I, p. 23, entry for 2 July 1940.
[56] Ibid., vol. I, p. 33, entry for 17 July.   [57] *Documentation*, 4 September 1942.
[58] *Documentation*, 2 August 1940.

capped by twenty years of politicking';[59] and the need for a new order: 'The first task of the new government is for the time being a matter of policing, policing with regard to men and above all with regard to the ideas that drive men.'[60]

It is clear that during the Vichy period Bernard was not merely acting as a spokesman for business interests. Many of his associates moved out of the world of business organization altogether and became politicians. Bernard himself dabbled with a variety of initiatives that had broad political, rather than merely business, overtones. Thus he offered a scheme for rationing to the appropriate ministry,[61] and proposed to discuss solutions for unemployment with prefects and the government.[62] His articles during this period show similarly broad preoccupations. He justified his support for the regime with references to the broad interests of the nation. Indeed, he urged his readers to look beyond mere material concerns.

Perhaps the most conspicuous of the broad concerns that underlay Bernard's thinking was anti-marxism. It may seem strange to suggest that anti-marxism reflects the distance between Bernard and conventional business spokesmen. After all, anti-marxism had been one of the major strands of the pre-war business mobilization. However, this changed during the occupation. The Communist party became increasingly identified with opposition to the Germans rather than opposition to the capitalist system. Many in the business movement did recognize this evolution.[63] But Bernard denied that the party had changed. He argued that the dissolution of the comintern was irrelevant,[64] and he attacked the idea that the Resistance cause could lead to a realignment of loyalties (see below). Furthermore, Bernard's anti-marxism was phrased in terms that resembled the social conservatism of Vichy more closely than the simple defence of capitalism that had been current in the business movement. Thus he wrote on 18 July 1941: 'Everyone knows what loyalties teachers have to Moscow.'[65] Most remarkable of all is the history of AICA's anti-Communist activity given by Bernard. In this he describes the year 1936 as the time of AICA's opposition to the prospect of Russian alliance, he does not mention AICA's resistance to the Communist-led strikes or to the internal policy of the Popular Front (issues which would normally attract some attention from an employers' leader). His articles also touch on numerous other subjects with no immediate relation to the business movement: educational reform, the

---

[59] Ibid., 20 March 1942.   [60] Ibid., 2 August 1940.

[61] Nicolle, *Cinquante mois d'armistice*, vol. I, p. 120, 13 October 1940.

[62] Ibid. p. 104, entry for 3 October 1940.

[63] GIMMCP report of 23 June 1943: 'By a somewhat extraordinary set of circumstances, the communists ... now appear as the most fierce (and to some extent the only) defenders of the patriotic ideal' (see chapter 9).   [64] *Documentation*, 11–18 June 1943.

[65] W. D. Halls, *The Youth of Vichy France* (Oxford, 1981) discusses the role which 'gauchistes' teachers' leaders played in Vichy mythology.

preservation of the family, and the 'décrépitude juvénile' induced by listening to jazz music.[66]

The debate over economic organization

Bernard's staunch support for the Vichy regime in general was combined with growing dissatisfaction with that aspect of the regime which affected him most: the organization of the economy. The corner-stone of Vichy industrial organization was the Comité d'Organisation established by the decree of 16 August 1940. In retrospect it seems obvious that these bodies would threaten Bernard's position. His power was founded on interprofessional voluntary associations whose power was limited to 'social matters' (that is, to labour relations). The Comités d'Organisation were based on particular industries, membership was obligatory, and they had powers over a whole range of economic matters, such as labour and the supply of raw materials, that dwarfed the powers of the voluntary syndicates. Most significantly, the COs were usually led by industrialists or at least by men whose reputation had been built in the leadership of the relevant industrial syndicate. Bernard was not an industrialist and had no connections with any one particular industry. In spite of these things Bernard's hostility was not immediately apparent. He wrote that the legislation was a recognition of the fundamental integrity of French business: 'the law of 16 August implicitly pays homage to this level balance'.[67]

Two things kept Bernard's hostility in check. First was the fact that the legislation was designed to be provisional. He regarded it as a necessary and limited response to circumstances that would eventually be replaced by a wholly new industrial regime: 'the measures of control are only provisional and will only apply where necessary'.[68] Secondly, his confidence in Pétain reassured him about the character which this new regime would possess: 'It can be hoped that the final definitive measures... will aim to safeguard the autonomy of enterprises, and the responsibility of employers, both of which are indispensable foundations of the spirit of initiative wanted by the Marshal in his struggle against étatisme.'[69] Even as Bernard moved towards opposing the COs his hostility was always moderated by the belief that Pétain's dislike of étatisme and centralization would make reform of the COs imminent: 'Such a regionalism needs an especially flexible professional structure... that is to say a transformation of the current professional committees, which, by all accounts, will have to follow the Marshal's

---

[66] *Documentation*, 29 May 1942, 16 April 1942 and 13 September 1940.
[67] *Documentation*, 27 March, 1940.   [68] Ibid.   [69] Ibid.

directives and decentralize themselves and become more responsive to needs.'[70] As late as July 1941 Bernard was still hoping for a political initiative to reform the COs.[71]

Bernard's opposition to the law of 16 August became explicit in May 1941. The FAR in the northern zone was told: 'After a period of waiting, he has taken an openly hostile view of the CO, which he blames for certain abuses... an excessive verticalism which he hopes to see corrected by a reorganization on a regional basis.'[72] Bernard never translated discontent with the industrial regime into an attack on Vichy itself, and he never lost all hope of reform of the COs. But his opposition to the COs did become very vigorous. In July 1941 it was reported, of Bernard, that 'He wants, in place of the present dirigisme, modelled too closely on our neighbours, and even pushed to a degree that astonishes them, a more specifically French arrangement, built not by doctrinaires who try to treat life in the abstract but by the legitimate representative of the profession.'[73]

Bernard's isolation from industry

Bernard's opposition to the COs was phrased largely in the anti-étatist terms which he had developed before the war. In fact this line of attack was rather inappropriate. The COs were only nominally subject to state control. In practice they were generally controlled by the major industrialists of the sector. This of course led to an increase of big business power, an increase that was especially marked in heavy industry which occupied a vital position in the war economy and hence exercised a good deal of negotiating strength. Consequently powerful industrialists did not share Bernard's hostility to the COs at all. The difference of opinion between Bernard and his former allies became apparent even within the FAR. While he was attacking the COs, industrialists were using the same forum to defend them. Arnaud (a Parisian metallurgist) suggested that the provinces should keep up better with the central industrial organization: 'They seem out of touch with Paris's instructions relating to the controlled economy.'[74] Even Bernard's associate, Fougère, appealed for help to be given to the COs in their 'exhausting task'.[75]

[70] *Documentation*, 22 November 1940.
[71] AN, 70 AQ 442, p-v of FAR, 18 July 1941.
[72] Ibid., 16 May 1941. This is probably a reference to the statement which finishes up in the Belin archives marked 'note d'origine patronale'. *Documentation* refers to a vote of a patronal organism at this time. Presumably the note was submitted in the name of the southern zone FAR.   [73] AN, 70 AQ 442, p-v of FAR, July 18 1941.
[74] AN, 70 AQ 442, p-v of FAR, 31 January 1941.
[75] AN, AQ 442, p-v of FAR, 21 March 1941.

Bernard seems to have been aware of the clash with heavy industry. He alleged that the professional organizations were 'led by certain big business elements hostile to regional interprofessionalism'.[76] He had always been associated with a certain amount of rhetoric against the business establishment. But in the past this rhetorical stance had been restrained and had been combined with close relations with the very groups being attacked. Now that Bernard was genuinely excluded from power in the industrial establishment his case was stated with far more vigour. He attacked the notion that size and technological sophistication were automatically desirable assets for a business.[77] He also attacked the belief that all problems could be solved by technology again in March 1942.[78] Agitation against big business frequently involved emphasis on the particular suitability of small business to French society. Bernard began talking this kind of language: 'It is absolutely necessary to respect the French social structure.'[79]

Bernard's isolation from heavy industry was part of a much wider realignment of social alliances that was occurring during the occupation. Before the war the key ally of industry had been the *classes moyennes*. This alliance had been of use to industry in its fight against the power of the left and the organized working class. But with the war and especially with the advent of the Vichy regime this conflict with the working class was largely at an end. Strikes and overt labour mobilization were rarely possible in the circumstances of the war. Industry did not therefore need the kind of combative leaders that it had used in the period following 1936. Bernard himself seems to have recognized that the new circumstances might leave him without a role. He expressed a desire to resign as leader of the FAR at the beginning of the occupation, saying 'having been a man of conflict he did not think that he could be one of reconstruction'. Now industry was so hungry for labour to feed the war economy that its efforts at appeasement were focused on the proletariat. Employers even lobbied the government for permission to award pay rises during the occupation.

It is especially interesting to note that Bernard's new isolation led him to rewrite the history of his former relations with the business establishment. As has been shown above, his entry into the CGPF had been smoothly accomplished in 1936, and his relations with the heavy industrialists had been rather good. But now he described Matignon as the result of 'serious mistakes' imposed by the Parisian leadership upon the provincial *patronat* and wrote: 'the provinces were then obliged to reconquer, the term is not too strong, the position that was their right in the decision making bodies of the *patronat*'.[80]

---

[76] AN, 70 AQ 442, p-v of FAR, 18 July 1941.
[77] *Documentation*, 22 August 1941.   [78] *Documentation*, 20 March 1942.
[79] *Documentation* 7 January 1944.   [80] *Documentation*, 13 February 1942.

Bernard and the *Charte du Travail*

Of course the 16 August law was only one aspect of Vichy industrial legislation. Furthermore, it was not meant to be definitive. Heavy industry took little interest in the steps to draw up a more permanent industrial order. It had no interest in such a new order; it was already doing well out of the CO system. The fact that pay was controlled and unions effectively suppressed meant that industrialists had little to gain by new labour relations legislation. The fact that the Comité d'Organisation system was only provisional was of little importance since very quickly industrialists came to regard the whole Vichy regime as provisional (see chapter 8 for a fuller explanation of heavy industry's attitude to the *Charte du Travail*). On the other hand those who believed in Vichy's talk of a new order might be expected to watch the construction of the *Charte du Travail* with some enthusiasm. Bernard's position was slightly ambiguous. On the one hand he was a keen supporter of Vichy, but on the other he was not a corporatist, and, as it turned out, corporatism was going to play a large part in Vichy's schemes. Bernard's views on corporatism do not seem to have changed with the advent of the Vichy government. Indeed in July 1942[81] he wrote an article about *ententes* that echoed his 1939 defence of cartels and opposition to corporatism (this was all the more remarkable since Bernard was now estranged from the heavy industrialists who benefited from such cartels). Furthermore, obligatory and intraprofessional corporations could be as inimical to Bernard's position as the COs. He recognized this potential conflict as early as December 1940. After the formation of the corporation of the peasantry he wrote: 'an essential condition of future legislation...should be the respect of existing unions'. However, since corporatism was the official ideology of the regime, Bernard's anti-corporatism had to be even more muted than it had been during the business *revanche*. Furthermore, the battle-lines were not clearly drawn. It was not simply a question of corporatism versus defenders of the old union system. The minister of industrial production himself was in favour of leaving some role for the old unions of both *patrons* and workers. Bernard could therefore see cause for hope in the *Charte du Travail*. He was all the more favourably disposed towards the *Charte* because it offered the prospect of reducing the powers of the COs.

In fact, reading the correspondence from business associations in the Belin archives,[82] one is sometimes left with the impression that all of it is from Bernard or his associates. Dupraz submitted a proposal; Bernard submitted

---

[81] *Documentation*, 3 July 1942.
[82] Two large files of documents relating to Belin (mostly correspondence about the *Charte du Travail*) is to be found at the Institut de l'Histoire Sociale.

one; and Nicolle submitted the same project three times purportedly from different bodies. When the meaning is distilled from Bernard's twenty-eight pages of turgid prose, it is clear that the main aim of his project was to avoid rigid corporatism and to maintain some role for independent unions, 'Realistically speaking unions have…their bad sides and their abuses, but also certain obvious achievements and much potential.'[83] The need to defend the foundations of his own power led Bernard to use arguments which seem incongruous in view of his previous stance. Firstly, Bernard had always been violently hostile to the trade unions. Indeed this hostility was carried over into the Vichy period. Bernard continued to attack union leaders such as Jouhaux. More generally, Bernard continued to express fears about working-class power. Thus on 5 November 1943 he suggested that workers' leaders saw the role which they had been given by the regime as a 'stage' that would ultimately lead to worker control of industry. But the defence of employer' syndicates necessarily involved the defence of workers' unions. In spite of having spent most of his career fighting trade unions Bernard found himself effectively supporting the same syndicalist line as the former trade unionists in Belin's cabinet. He was even obliged to recognize that industrial conflict was inevitable: 'It cannot be denied that there are employers' interests and workers' interests and that they are not always the same', and that workers' unions were a good thing: 'workers' unions have been, in spite of some of their dubious methods, a force for progress'.[84] Secondly, Bernard always argued that he wanted industry to choose its leadership and not to have it imposed by government. Such an argument fitted into a broad anti-étatist line of right-wing pre-war politics. Once again Bernard maintained this line under Vichy. He wrote: 'The real question is to know whether we will try to build an étatist economy or one founded on the professions.'[85]

Even in his projected *Charte* Bernard repeated his desire to see professional leaders chosen by their peers. But in fact of course if such a system were applied it would have left Bernard, who represented no industry, without a role. His exclusion from the Comité d'Organisation system showed what he could expect. Consequently Bernard did not want the power of those chosen by the professions to extend all the way to the top. He preferred that the state retain control of the commanding heights of the economy (a preference that was no doubt reinforced by the fact that he was on good terms with the Vichy state and on bad terms with powerful sections of industry). In his desperation to avoid describing this retention of

---

[83] Belin archives, file B. The project is marked 'projet d'origine patronal'. However, the wording of the document, and especially its similarity to Bernard's later intervention in the Conseil Supérieur de l'Economie, makes it clear that Bernard is the author (p. 7).

[84] Belin archives, 'projet d'origine patronale', p. 8.

[85] *Documentation*, 22 August 1941.

state control as étatist (his own favourite term of abuse) Bernard was reduced to inventing the word 'regalian': 'economic matters are initially under the control of the employers...social affairs are initially under the joint control of workers and employers, but, on reaching national level both lose their specific character and become regalian'.[86] In fact Bernard's pronouncements on étatisme and union power illuminate the contradictions of his position under Vichy. For his power in business circles was founded on opposition to the power of the state and the working class. But when industry effectively triumphed over both these powers, as it did during the occupation, Bernard was redundant. He was like a mercenary in the Thirty Years' War: always wanting war but never victory.

The *Charte* that did finally emerge was reasonably satisfactory from Bernard's point of view. He was able to welcome it with an article that stressed yet again the need to preserve elements of the old unions: 'the social committees will not do everything. It is even to be hoped that they will not do everything...in existing social institutions there is a great wealth of experience; they have been useful and will remain useful in their current form.'[87] However, Bernard's dissatisfaction with the new order seems to have increased as time went on. In June 1943 he submitted an angry note to the Conseil Supérieur de l'Economie Industrielle et Commerciale. In this note he complained again about the powers of the COs.[88] He repeated his statements made during the preparation of the *Charte*, urging the preservation of existing unions and a 'regalian control' of the economy.

Bernard continued to be regarded as an important figure by those occupying official positions at Vichy. For example, when the Centre d'Information des Employeurs made plans for an enquiry about the economy in early 1944, it proposed to consult a number of regional figures. For every other region the Centre consulted the president of the appropriate Chamber of Commerce, but for Lyon it simply proposed 'M. Aymé Bernard', a name that apparently needed no further justification.[89] Of course others involved in Vichy industrial policy grumbled. But Bernard was the only one who began to express this discontent by withdrawing from participation in official bodies. To understand this contrast it is necessary to remember that many who had exercised some function at Vichy were really jumped up nobodies like Jules Verger or Pierre Nicolle. Whatever discontent these men may have felt was always kept in check by delight at their apparent importance in the Vichy elite. Bernard had been born in the purple of the *haute bourgeoisie,* and he had normally exercised power which had exceeded his official functions. Vichy reversed this position, leaving Bernard

---

[86] Belin archives, 'projet d'origine patronale', p. 4.

[87] *Documentation*, 7 November 1941. [88] AN, F 12 9953, 1 June 1943.

[89] AN, F 22 1836, note of 24 February 1944.

with great official status but little real influence. He was not a man to be fobbed off with high-sounding titles.

Resistance and attentisme

Bernard was unequivocal in his opposition to the Resistance movement. In an article of 25 July 1941 headed 'Dissidences', Bernard compared Gaullism to the Dreyfus affair.[90] He suggested that the movement was dividing France. He condemned it in these terms: 'real Gaullistes, that is is to say those who seek to serve France by the intervention of England, are fewer and fewer, because the criminal attacks...have, in the end, had an impact on people of good faith'.[91] He condemned 'terrorism' again on 13 August 1943 and attacked resistance sabotage on 2 December 1943.[92] He condemned the fact that many were allying themselves with the Communist party in the Resistance: 'because they think that they are helping the liberation of the country'.[93] Bernard's attacks on the Resistance were another sign of the distance between him and the industrial community. For heavy industry was often concerned to distance itself from the regime and to develop some resistance credentials as it was realized that the allies were going to win the war.[94]

Bernard himself seems to have been aware of the probable outcome of the war. Obviously it was not possible openly to discuss the subject in print. However, as Sauvy points out,[95] calculations about the outcome of the war could easily be made from certain economic statistics, particularly those concerning American shipping. Bernard's articles are full of references to such statistics.[96] Indeed at one point Bernard quotes a correspondent who has analysed his articles and drawn from them the conclusion that 'you are saying, in short, that European production cannot make up for imports of raw materials in the long run'.[97] Bernard's apparent awareness that allied victory was likely makes his continued opposition to the Resistance all the more surprising. But he specifically condemned those who based their actions on prudent calculations about how the war would end: 'Many people discuss the date and the nature of this event and subordinate their

[90] *Documentation*, 25 July 1941.   [91] Ibid.
[92] *Documentation*, 13 August 1943 and 2 December 1943.
[93] *Documentation*, 13 August 1943.
[94] Richard Vinen, 'The French Coal Industry during the Occupation', *Historical Journal*, (1990), 105–30.
[95] Alfred Sauvy, *La vie économique des Francais de 1939 à 1945* (Paris, 1978), p. 92.
[96] *Documentation*, 13 August and 20 August 1943. Bernard discusses the effect of lend lease in these articles.   [97] *Documentation*, 10 January 1942.

personal and business life to it.'[98] He seems to have gone on nailing his colours to the mast of a ship that he knew to be sinking.[99]

The *avant-garde du patronat*

The second group of businessmen who supported Vichy came from the *avant-garde du patronat*. These were men like Loustau, Painvin, Detoeuf, Barnaud, Pucheu and Lehideux. They were, or had been, businessmen. But they were separated from most of their colleagues by the interest that they took in social and political matters. Whereas the rest of the *patronat* regarded politics as a means to an end, the *avant-garde* regarded the organization of society as a matter of interest in itself. Before the war they had congregated in organizations like *Nouveaux Cahiers*, X crise and Redressement Français and in political parties like the Parti Social Français. But the projects discussed by these groups had never come close to being implemented under the Republic. Not all of these men became Vichy supporters. In the later part of the war many of them turned against the regime, and certain resistance organizations, notably the Organisation Civile et Militaire, provided forums in which the *avant-garde* could discuss their projects. But in the immediate aftermath of the armistice the members of the *avant-garde*, with a few exceptions,[100] welcomed Vichy as offering a chance to implement their ideas. Pre-war plans for reform were dug out of desks and dusted down. For example, Pucheu sent the scheme that he and Robert Loustau had drawn up in 1936 for a reform of business organization to Barnaud, the secretary of the Délégation Générale aux Relations Franco-Allemandes.[101] A group of men who had been connected with the various pre-war study groups and political parties soon gathered in Paris. Benoist Méchin was introduced into the group by Claude Popelin. He described it thus: 'a group of young men who met from time to time to study the political situation and propose solutions to current problems'.[102] Vichy established a huge number of commissions dedicated to precisely the kind of general reform of society that the *avant-garde* relished. The first of these

---

[98] *Documentation*, 12 November 1943.

[99] Indeed Bernard did not attempt to distance himself from Vichy even after its fall; as late as 1955 he referred to Pétain's government as one of 'Sauvetage National'. See Aymé Bernard, *L'entreprise et ses hommes* (Paris, 1962), p. 100.

[100] The most notable of these was Ernest Mercier. His long-standing opposition to Nazism and his Jewish wife made him an almost inevitable opponent of Vichy.

[101] AN, F 37 77, Pucheu to Barnaud dated 6 September 1940. Barnaud was the first of this group to attain office and he seems to have become a clearing house for the schemes which his associates wished to present to the government.

[102] Benoist Méchin, *De la défaite au désastre* (2 vols., Paris 1984), vol. I, p. 53.

bodies to be set up was the Comité d'Etudes pour La France. This informal body concerned itself with everything from industrial experimentation to the supply of potatoes.[103] Later the enthusiastic reformer could air his ideas in the Commission d'Organisation Professionnelle, the Comité Consultatif of the Centre d'Information Interprofessionnelle, the Conseil Supérieur de l'Economie Industrielle et Commerciale, the Commission Economique of the Conseil National, the Commission Consultative de la Délégation d'Equipement National, the Conseil d'Information des Employeurs.

The extent to which the *avant-garde du patronat* formed a coherent group at Vichy and the extent to which this group was linked to certain elements in the government was reflected by the widespread belief in a 'synarchic conspiracy'. Synarchy was portrayed as a semi-masonic conspiracy among Vichy officials and businessmen to undermine Vichy government policy. Few historians have taken the idea of an organized conspiracy seriously. However, there is little doubt that the myth of synarchy had some roots in reality; there really was a group who were linked by personal association and by a common view of the world. Benoist Méchin accepted that such a group existed, and that he himself, Lehideux, Pucheu, Barnaud and the Leroy Ladurie brothers were members of it. Outsiders tended to define the synarchic group in broader terms; Pierre Nicolle regarded it as including a large number of the French elite formed by common training in the *grandes écoles* and the *corps d'état*. Nicolle included certain ministers not mentioned by Benoist Méchin such as Baudouin, Bouthillier[104] and Bichelonne.[105] He also included a large number of businessmen such as Bardet.[106]

However, the existence of such groups has given rise to two misconceptions. The first of these misconceptions is the belief that the business *avant-garde* represented an enclave of business interests at Vichy. One commentator even suggested that there was a faction of 'affairistes' within the *synarchs*, dedicated to the maintenance of business interests. In fact, as has been stressed, there had always been a division between the *avant-garde* and the rest of industry. Under Vichy this division was exacerbated. On the one hand the members of the *avant-garde* became even more preoccupied with grand schemes for social and economic reform, while on the other hand ordinary businessmen were preoccupied with day-to-day survival in a war economy. Indeed even the opponents of the *synarchs* recognized that the driving force for the group was an idealistic desire to reform society rather than simply the pursuit of class interest.[107]

---

[103] Some of these reports can be found in AN, F 37 77.
[104] Nicolle, *Cinquante mois d'armistice*, vol. I, p. 14, suggested that Baudouin and Bouthillier were 'well supported by the bank of Worms'.
[105] Ibid. p. 351, entry for 4 November 1941: 'The anti trust policy...is completely at odds with the policy followed by Lehideux, Barnaud, Belin and Bichelonne.'
[106] Ibid., 1/2 March 1944.
[107] Du Moulin de Labarthète, *Le temps des illusions* (Geneva, 1946).

This did not mean that the separation between the *avant-garde du patronat* and ordinary businessmen was entirely sharp. The frontiers of the group were always blurred. For example, Aimé Lepercq of the coal industry was ambiguous in his attitudes to the projects of the *avant-garde*. His interest in planning and the *Charte du Travail* appear to be classic symptoms of the general support for an industrial new order that was expressed by members of the *avant-garde*. But when an attempt was made to apply an industrial new order to the coal industry, in the form of Loustau's plans for rationalization, Lepercq resisted them vigorously.

However, at the core of the group were men whose separation from industrial interests was clear. Sometimes this separation was marked formally. Thus Detoeuf resigned from Alsthom (the electrical company) when he became head of the Comité d'Organisation for the electrical industry; Lehideux and Pucheu became ministers; Loustau and Romier attended meetings of the Comité d'Organisation Professionnelle as representatives of the government, not as representatives of business. Other members of the group retained their directorships but were so committed to their official functions that they had little time to participate in ordinary commercial life. Painvin was the supreme example of this latter category. A post-war investigation discovered that though he had retained his post at Ugine his official functions as a member of the Comité d'Organisation Professionnelle, the Conseil Supérieur de la Charte, and the Comité d'Organisation for the chemical industry, had not left him enough time to play much of a role in his own company.[108]

In fact the *synarchs* were often fiercely opposed to heavy industrial interests. Thus Bardet attempted to have the UIMM dissolved. Bouthillier also voiced concern about the survival of heavy industrial power. Lehideux and Pucheu both found that their attempts to implement reforms, in the automobile and coal industry respectively, brought them into sharp conflict with industrialists.

The second misconception about the synarchic group is that they were ideologically distinct from the rest of the Vichy regime. Historians have argued that there was a sharp contrast between the traditionalists and the modernizers at Vichy.[109] The archaic vision was subscribed to by the men associated with the Marshal's cabinet and by small business representatives at Vichy, such as Verger and Nicolle. It is argued that this ideology was characterized by corporatism, ruralism and the desire to protect small business. The *Charte du Travail* can be presented as the product of such an

---

[108] Henri Rousso, 'Les élites économiques dans les années quarante', *Mélanges de l'Ecole Français de Rome*, 95 (1982–3), 29–49, at p. 35.

[109] See Richard F. Kuisel, *Capitalism and the State in Modern France: Renovation and Economic Management in the Twentieth Century* (Cambridge, 1981), p. 149. 'The impulse towards economic and technological rattrapage struggled against the conservatism of Vichy official ideology.'

ideology. On the other hand it can be argued that there was a modernistic current at Vichy which was subscribed to by the *synarchs* and which was expressed in the plans drawn up by the Délégation Générale à l'Equipement National.

There is some truth in such a distinction. Men like Lehideux and Bichelonne clearly had an awareness of the possibilities of industrial modernization that set them apart from many of the rest of the Vichy government. However, two things blunted the separation between traditionalists and modernizers. Firstly, in the context of business life, the two visions were united by their unrealism. Neither the archaic vision nor the modernistic one could possibly be applied in the conditions of wartime. As far as most businessmen were concerned there was not much to choose between Lehideux's vision of modernizing France with a great system of *autoroutes* and Claude Paillard's vision of a restored *artisanat*. Both visions were rooted in fantasy. Secondly, the modern and traditional visions were not mutually exclusive alternatives. The *synarchs* were often keen supporters of the supposedly archaic corporatism. Indeed those who took most interest in modernization, represented by the plans, also took most interest in corporatism, represented by the *Charte du Travail*. The modernizers did not reject the traditionalist vision but attempted to incorporate it into their own projects; hence the ruralism of the first plan (see chapter 11). This attempt to achieve modernity without rejecting the traditionalist vision was illustrated by the Speer–Bichelonne meeting of 1943. Normally this encounter is presented as a meeting of like-minded technocrats. But, in fact, there was a very notable contrast between the attitude adopted by the German negotiators and Bichelonne. The former equated economic efficiency with large-scale enterprises. But Bichelonne wished to resist industrial concentration in order to protect the social structure of France. He insisted that industrial efficiency could be attained within an economy dominated by small business.[110]

Relations between the *avant-garde du patronat* and the post-1936 leadership of the employers' movement

All this poses interesting questions about the relations between the *avant-garde du patronat* and the group of small business leaders who had risen in the employers' movement in 1936. Some of the men of 1936, notably Nicolle, were fiercely hostile to the *synarchs*. Normally it is assumed that this was

[110] AN, 72 AJ 1927. 'It is a typically French form of production of which account must be taken when programmes are drawn up.'

because the *synarchs* represented big business interests, to which Nicolle was now hostile, and because they opposed the traditional and corporatist ideology that Nicolle espoused. But in fact the *synarchs* were sharply distinct from ordinary business. Furthermore, the ideological distance between the *synarchs* and the traditionalists has been greatly overestimated. Indeed the *synarchs* and the post-1936 leadership were probably closer to each other than they had been before the war. Previously the post-1936 leadership had been allied with heavy industry in opposition to the organized working class while the *avant-garde* had sought to arrive at a better relation with the working class. Now both groups were separate from heavy industry, and the Vichy suppression of the working-class organizations had made this potential cause of disagreement less evident. In some respects the *synarchs* were startlingly close to those who were most hostile to them. This is especially evident in Benoist Méchin's account of synarchy. He suggested that the France envisaged by the *synarchs* would be 'imperialist, anti-English and anti-Jewish'.[111] The same words could have served to describe the programme of those who were most opposed to synarchy.[112]

Why then were post-1936 leaders of the *patronat* like Nicolle so hostile to the *synarchs*? There are some relatively simple answers to this question. Firstly, the antipathy was, in part, the product of faction struggles at Vichy. The *synarchs* were sponsored by Darlan; the men of 1936 had close links with Laval, who was ejected from the premiership by Darlan in December 1940. Secondly, the hostility simply sprang from the differences in background. It is notable that one of the many terms of abuse which Nicolle applied to the synarchic group was 'polytechnicien', and indeed there certainly were conspiracies at Vichy to protect students of the Ecole Polytechnique.[113]

But hostility to the synarchic group was also the product of a third factor that illustrates something very interesting about the dilemma of many Vichy loyalists. For the post-1936 leadership of the *patronat* were among Vichy's most vigorous supporters. Yet, as has been shown, both they and the class that they claimed to represent did singularly badly under the regime. Small business suffered in the war economy, while its leaders were no longer needed in the new political situation. To explain this apparent paradox the men of 1936 adopted a policy similar to that which a historian of the *ancien régime* would recognize as 'loyal opposition'. They argued that they were loyal to the 'real Vichy' of Marshal Pétain. But then they argued that Pétain's policies were being subverted by 'disloyal courtiers': 'a man eighty-

---

[111] Benoist Méchin, *De la défaite au désastre*, vol. I, p. 54.

[112] This is especially true of Nicolle. The anti-English and anti-Jewish elements in the synarchic myth are self-evident. The bank of Worms was Jewish-owned. Nicolle was to end his career agitating for Algérie Française.

[113] Vinen, 'The French Coal Industry during the Occupation'.

five years old, alone or almost alone, surrounded by young wolves with sharp teeth'.[114] The *synarchs* whose background and range of personal contacts marked them out so clearly were custom made to play this part.

Conclusion

This chapter has discussed those sections of the business movement that did support Vichy. It has been suggested that these groups were isolated from the rest of business, and that their presence among Vichy supporters did not reflect general business support for the regime. Kedward portrays Vichy as a regime divided by ideology but held together by class interest.[115] The picture which emerges from this chapter is exactly the opposite of that drawn by Kedward. The *avant-garde du patronat* came from big business, and they had the same class interests as their colleagues. Yet the Vichy period saw the *avant-garde* in fierce conflict with the rest of big business. The *avant-garde du patronat* and the leadership of the *patronat* which had emerged after 1936 were sharply divided by background; what tied them both to Vichy was ideology.

The relationship between the *synarchs* and the post-1936 leadership of the *patronat* also sheds some light on the modernization of the French economy. Normally Vichy is presented as a clash of modernizing and traditional tendencies.[116] In this chapter it has been suggested that these tendencies were not really so distinct. Traditionalists and modernizers were sometimes very hostile to each other. But there were some cases where they can be seen operating in co-operation. The Gingembre Committee, which was established by a 'modernist', Bichelonne, and led by a small business 'traditionalist', Gingembre, is an example of such co-operation. Gingembre's subsequent career suggests that it was indeed possible to achieve a fusion between the ideas of the two groups. Both elements were marginal in the context of the war, but in the changed economic circumstances of the post-war period they acquired a new importance.

---

[114] Paillard, *La révolution corporative spontanée*, p. 113.

[115] H. R. Kedward, 'Patriots and patriotism in Vichy France', *Transactions of the Royal Historical Society*, 32 (1982), 175–92. 'I believe…that Pétainism at this level is better defined in the socio-economic terms of class than in the cultural and intellectual terms of the old nationalist tradition.'

[116] Ibid. Kedward talks of 'the complexity of Vichy, with its echelons of technocratic defenders of capital oddly arrayed alongside proponents of the Ancien Regime'.

Chapter 13

Business at the liberation

Introduction

All the efforts that French business had made to distance itself from the Vichy regime were disastrously unsuccessful. The *patronat* achieved new peaks of political unpopularity at the liberation. This general unpopularity, which was reflected in political attacks and in the exclusion of businessmen from official posts, should be distinguished from the specific allegations about collaboration during the war, which were reflected in trials or in appearance before a *comité professionnel d'épuration*. In fact the unpopularity of the *patronat* was often not linked to wartime behaviour at all. In part this was because the liberation was used by the working-class movement to settle scores that dated back to the period between 1936 and 1939 (see chapter 9). More generally the wave of indignation against certain sections of business illustrated a kind of reflex action of the French political system. Indeed sometimes the attacks on business conducted under the provisional government mirrored those conducted under Vichy. Thus de Gaulle's famously chilly encounter with the delegation of industrialists led by Pinet in 1944[1] echoed that between Laval and the delegation of industrialists led by Lambert Ribot in 1940 (see chapter 8). The same groups were subjected to abuse during both periods. Thus the Comité des Forges, which had been dissolved by Vichy, hardly had time to reform before becoming a prime target for political attacks. However, under the provisional government, as under Vichy, the political hostility to big business was not converted into concrete assaults on business interests. In particular, there were remarkably few punitive nationalizations at the liberation. In this chapter the reasons for this light escape will be explored.

[1] De Gaulle is said to have greeted this delegation with the words, 'Well, I did not see any of you gentlemen in London.'

Background: purges and nationalizations

There were a variety of mechanisms by which the government and Resistance organizations hoped to purge French business of those who had collaborated with the Germans and Vichy. The most explicit of these was the *comité professionnel d'épuration*. These were established at both local and national level by an ordinance of 16 October 1944. They contained representatives from both management and workers; they were empowered to forbid an individual to hold a position of authority or to be a member of a company board or to be a partner in a business. Generally speaking the *comités d'épuration* were not very successful. In April 1945 the CGT representatives on the national committee complained of the 'desperate slowness of its work' and in July 1947 they resigned in protest at its failure to take more vigorous action.[2]

Nationalization seemed to provide another means by which businessmen could be punished. In November 1944 a public opinion poll showed that 65 per cent of the French population were in favour of taking some industries into state control.[3] It seems reasonable to assume that this feeling was induced, at least in part, by the belief that business had behaved badly during the previous four years. A number of industries were affected by nationalization during this period: notably the coal-mines, in December 1944; the deposit banks, in December 1945; the gas and electrical industries, in April 1946; and insurance companies, in April 1946. However, these nationalizations were justified in terms of economics not politics; the government did not accuse the owners of these firms of collaboration and it paid compensation. In fact nationalization was used very rarely as an instrument of punishment. Renault was the only major company whose nationalization, in January 1945, was carried out for solely punitive reasons. Furthermore, a number of firms that had been heavily and conspicuously involved in collaboration, such as Paribas the merchant bank and Berliet the truck manufacturer, were left in private hands.

Outside these official structures a good many informal, and usually temporary, sanctions were inflicted on the *patronat* in the immediate aftermath of the liberation. Some local commissioners of the republic allowed *ad hoc* seizures of factories, such as that which affected Berliet;

---

[2] For an account of the work of the *comités d'épuration* see Annie Lacroix-Riz, 'Les grandes banques françaises de la collaboration à l'épuration, 1940–1950: I. La collaboration bancaire', *Revue de l'histoire de la deuxième guere mondiale*, 141 (1986), 3–44, and 'Les grandes banques françaises de la collaboration à l'épuration, II: La non épuration bancaire 1944–1950', *Revue de l'histoire de la deuxième guerre mondiale*, 142 (1986), 81–101.

[3] Antoine Prost, 'Une piece en trois actes', in C. Andrieu, L. le Van and A. Prost (eds.), *Les nationalisations de la libération: de l'utopie au compromis* (Paris, 1987), pp. 236–46, at p. 237.

some took businessmen into protective or preventive custody. Often lists were circulated of men who should be suspended from their managerial functions.[4] Sometimes companies themselves took the lead in dismissing managers who were seen to be compromised (see chapter 9).

The survival of business

The very obscurity and complexity of business made it relatively easy for its leaders to escape retribution. Such penalties as did affect business tended to fall disproportionately on small enterprises, the operations of which were visible to all their clients, while large merchant banks, whose workings remained obscure even to their own junior employees, were hard to prosecute.[5] Furthermore, businessmen, unlike, for example, journalists, were not obliged to take any clear stance for or against the Vichy government or the occupation. Almost every business had undertaken certain actions, for example fulfilling German contracts, that could be defined as collaboration, and some actions, such as obstruction of STO, that could be defined as resistance.

Trying to make charges against a businessman stick could be a hopelessly complicated business. For example Laederich, a northern textile indus-trialist, was one of the rare businessmen who had expressed open and vigorous support for the Vichy regime; he had organized a 'Groupe des Amis du Maréchal'. Yet at his trial he was able to point out that in terms of business activity he had been hostile to the Germans, who had refused to endorse his appointment as president of the textile union.[6] The economist Charles Rist, on the other hand, was accused of having collaborated with the Germans on a business level; he was a director of Paribas. Yet he was able to point out that on the political level he had always been a vigorous opponent of Vichy.[7] To make matters more complicated still both Rist and Laederich had maintained resistance contacts during the occupation and both of them had sons who were resistance heros.[8] After the liberation most industrialists were able to dig out examples of some resistance activity. Lecompte Boinet, a leader of Ceux de la Résistance, greeted the apologias

---

[4] Lacroix-Riz, 'Les grandes banques françaises de la collaboration à l'épuration, II.

[5] Lacroix-Riz, 'Les grandes banques françaises de la collaboration à l'épuration, I.

[6] Paris, Archives Nationales (AN), 57 AS 3, note by Laederich, 'Mon activité pendant l'occupation'.

[7] Rist was interrogated by the *comité d'épuration* for the banking industry. For his activity during the occupation and his anti-Vichy views see his diary *Une saison gâtée: journal de la guerre et de l'occupation, 1939–1945*, ed. Jean-Noel Jeanneney (Paris, 1983).

[8] Laederich's son was sent to Buchenwald for his resistance activities: AN, 57 AS 3, letter of Henri Hutton to Laederich, dated 22 September 1946. Rist's son was killed fighting in 1944.

of businessmen accused of collaboration with a mixture of sarcasm and despair: 'naturally he performed services for the Resistance like all the others'.[9] The presentation of resistance credentials on behalf of industrialists became a minor industry in itself. A special association, La Fédération Française du Devoir, was set up to represent 'industrialists, artisans and professional men who did not work for the enemy'.[10]

The archives of the GIMMCP show how almost every aspect of business life was presented as resistance. Almost immediately after the liberation the GIMMCP advised its members to prepare dossiers on their resistance activity. It circulated a questionnaire to its members that touched on eight separate areas of business life. The response to this questionnaire fills up two cartons of archives. Most metallurgists concentrated on two points. Firstly, the obstruction of deportation of their workers was stressed. Secondly, the metallurgists maintained that they had kept the largest possible proportion of their production for the needs of the French civilian economy, and that they had deliberately impeded production for German needs. One member of the GIMMCP even suggested that his attempts to corner the Belgian market for stamping machines, in the face of German competition, was a form of resistance.[11] The GIMMCP's defence was by no means unique. The ministry of industrial production received apologias, couched in similar terms, from the steel and the textile industries.[12]

The cohesiveness of the French elite was another factor that helped industrialists to escape retribution in 1944. Industrialists were often sharply divided by their business interests but they were united by ties of education, personal friendship, marriage and, in the last resort, a common interest in the defence of capitalism itself. In moments of real crisis this unity came to the fore. When businessmen were arrested or excluded from their companies, they could rely on their colleagues to rally round and plead their case to the authorities. Thus, for example, when Laederich, the head of the Comité d'Organisation for the textile industry and a vigorous 'maréchalist', was arrested his fellow industrialists Henri Hutin and Jacques Warnier drew up defences of his wartime activity. Individuals who had close contacts with both the *patronat* and the new government, such as Dautry, Lepercq and Couve de Murville,[13] were used as unofficial defence counsels for industrialists who had been accused of collaboration. Businessmen also

---

[9] Lecompte Boinet, unpublished diaries, kindly lent to the author by Madame Lecompte Boinet, entry for 24 June 1945.

[10] AN, F 12 10179, contains a number of submissions by Devoir Français. The Fédération sought to prove the resistance credentials of industrialists who were seeking special privileges such as extra rations of petrol.

[11] AN, 39 AS 964, letter from SAARS company.

[12] AN, F 12 10102. The note relating to the textile industry is dated 19 March 1945. That relating to the steel industry is dated 13 March 1945.

[13] Bankers often appealed to Couve de Murville: see Lacroix-Riz 'Les grands banques françaises'. On the role of Dautry and Lepercq see below.

benefited from their links with certain elements of the administration. Civil servants ensured that favourable compensation terms softened the blow of most nationalizations.[14]

Throughout the Vichy period channels of communication had remained open between businessmen connected with the Resistance and those involved in collaboration or pro-Vichy activities (see chapter 8). During the occupation these contacts had often saved businessmen arrested by the Germans.[15] Now men who had acquired resistance credentials used them to help their colleagues accused of collaboration. For example, when Boutemy, the Vichy prefect who had saved the life of George Villiers, was arrested at the liberation he received help from Ernest Mercier, who had been an opponent of Vichy.[16] The business community displayed ostentatious solidarity during the period that followed the liberation. George Villiers, who had returned from Dachau, shared a platform with Aymé Bernard, who had been an enthusiastic supporter of Vichy.[17] Business leaders even applied pressure on politicians such as Louis Marin to display a similar degree of indulgence to former Vichy supporters.[18]

Most importantly of all, the explanation for industry's survival in 1944 lies in the economic constraints that were imposed on de Gaulle's provisional government. For France was still fighting a war until the middle of 1945, and even after the peace she was struggling to rebuild her economy during the so-called 'battle for production'. Under these circumstances it was vital to maintain production in the heavy industries that were important for war, and these were precisely the industries that had been most active during the occupation.[19] Assaults on the *patronat* might impede this production. Soon central government was doing its best to prevent such assaults. Thus in 1944 the ministry of industrial production wrote to the commissioner of the republic in the north urging him to release, or at least to give a quick trial to, the head of the Aciéries du Nord.[20] Christian Bourgeard has shown how

---

[14] Annie Lacroix-Riz, 'Les resistances dans l'administration', in Andrieu, le Van and Prost (eds.), *Les nationalisations de la libération*.

[15] For example, George Villiers had been sentenced to death by the Germans in 1944 but had had his sentence commuted after appeals from influential friends. Charles Rist, a director of Paribas, was one of the links between the Resistance and the Vichy government; his diaries detail a number of attempts to save resistance figures: Rist, *Une saison gâtée*.

[16] Jean-Noel Jeanneney, *L'argent caché: milieux d'affaires et pouvoirs politiques dans la France du XXème siècle* (Paris, 1981), p. 255.

[17] *Documentation Hebdomadaire*, Anniversary issue of November 1947.

[18] Jean-Noel Jeanneney, 'Hommes d'affaires au piquet, le difficile intérim d'une représentation patronale, Septembre 1944–Janvier 1946', *Revue historique* (1980), 81–100, gives an account of a meeting which was arranged by de Peyerimhoff between Marin and two representatives of the Centre d'Etudes Administratives et Economiques, Boutemy and Brulfer. The latter threatened to withdraw funds from Marin if he failed to support the unification of the right.

[19] Richard Vinen, 'The French Coal Industry during the Occupation', *Historical Journal*, 33 (1990), 105–30.

[20] AN, F 12 10156, ministry to *commissaire de la république* at Lille, dated 30 October 1945.

many industrialists in the Côtes-du-Nord who were accused of collaboration by the resistance organizations and the left escaped further investigation because of their continued usefulness to the war economy.[21]

A case study of the coal industry

The coal industry provides a good case study of survival at the liberation. On the one hand the industry had played a vital part in the French economy during the occupation. Coal had been the key to the maintenance of heavy industrial production and of transport. The Germans had recognized that the industry was one of supreme usefulness. But the industry survived notably well in 1944. Few managers from the industry were punished. It is true that the mines were nationalized but the kind of punitive nationalization that was inflicted upon Renault was avoided. Compensation was paid to all shareholders and the preamble to the act of nationalization stressed economic strategy not business misbehaviour. Furthermore, the impact of nationalization was mitigated by the fact that there was already a separation between ownership and management in the mines; most managers simply remained in place. The new men brought in from the inspectorate of mines and the mining schools were hardly hostile outsiders. They had already worked closely with the mining managers, especially during the occupation, and their arrival was matched by the appointment of some mine managers to important positions in the administration.[22]

The coal industry escaped censure to such an extent that one recent historian suggests that 'the mine owners in general were above reproach'.[23] In fact, as Monique Luirard and Etienne Dejonghe have shown, the mine owners were the object of extensive reproaches at local level.[24]

The mines provided an extreme example of activity that could be interpreted as either resistance or collaboration. On the one hand the mines had been useful to the German economy. But on the other they had

[21] A particularly striking example of this was the hand-grenade factory in the Côtes-du-Nord which escaped from CGT and resistance accusations of collaboration by obtaining a contract to produce weapons for the provisional government (Christian Bourgeard, 'Les Côtes-du-Nord', unpublished paper delivered at conference on *Les entreprises françaises pendant la seconde guerre mondiale*, Centre d'Etudes Pédagogiques, Sèvres, 25/26 November 1986).

[22] Henri Rousso, 'Les élites économiques dans les années quarante', *Mélanges de l'Ecole Française de Rome*, 95 (1982–3), 29–49.

[23] Herbert Lottmann, *The People's Anger: Justice and Revenge in Post Liberation France* (London, 1986), p. 226.

[24] Etienne Dejonghe, 'Les houillères à l'épreuve 1944–1947', *Revue du Nord*, 227 (1975), 643–67; Monique Luirard, *La région stéphanoise dans la guerre et dans la paix 1936–1951* (Saint-Etienne, 1980).

provided a haven for thousands of young men from Service du Travail Obligatoire. The apologias produced by the industry after the liberation made a great deal of the mines' function as a shelter from STO. In short there were two entirely different interpretations of the war record of the French coal industry.

An interesting example of the manner in which these two interpretations clashed is provided by the case of Perrin Pelletier, the head of the coal industry in the Loire. Pelletier was arrested at the liberation and sent before the local *comité régional d'épuration*. He was accused of 'having increased coal production during the occupation, and of having used techniques of flooding to do so, without taking account of the damages that this involved for the population'.[25] Pelletier was subsequently released – though forbidden to live in the area. In fact this release was the product of an appeal by the central government. Lepercq wrote a note on 3 September 1944 saying that he had persuaded de Gaulle to have Perrin Pelletier released;[26] this order was eventually passed on by the ministry of industrial production on 30 November.[27]

But the most interesting aspect of the whole affair is the fact that the ministry of industrial production urged the release of Perrin Pelletier on account of his 'patriotic attitude' during the occupation.[28] Unfortunately the document that details the manifestations of this attitude is no longer in the appropriate carton, but it seems reasonable to assume that this is a reference to the obstruction of STO in the Loire (a whole file in the COH's archives is devoted to correspondence with the Loire on this issue). Thus there were two interpretations of the activity of one man. One interpretation was believed at local level and was founded on his attempts to increase production and the supposed suffering of the working classes. The other interpretation was that put forward by the COH itself, and accepted at national level. This interpretation was founded upon Pelletier's alleged resistance to STO.

In fact there were not merely two interpretations of what Perrin Pelletier had done during the war. The local and national levels even had different beliefs about the outcome of his trial. Locally it was assumed that he had been convicted, and that his exclusion from the department was a punishment.[29] Nationally it was assumed that he had been acquitted, and

---

[25] Ibid. p. 704. It is interesting to see that the note sent to the COH entitled 'motifs uniques pour l'arrestation de Perrin Pelletier' (AN, 40 AS 78) gave a slightly different account of the charges against him – the first accusation listed in this note was that Perrin Pelletier had headed the Vichy ski association.

[26] Darryl Holter, 'Miners against the State: French Miners and the Nationalization of Coalmining 1944–1949' (unpublished PhD. thesis, University of Wisconsin, Madison, 1980), p. 60.

[27] AN, F 12 10156, letter of 30 November to Commissioner of the Republic in Lyon.

[28] Ibid.   [29] Luirard, p. 704.

that his exclusion from the department was merely designed to preserve public order: 'In order to prevent further agitation he might be excluded from the department.'[30] Those at local level also believed that as part of his punishment had had been bound over not to work in the industry. For this reason there was fury when he was appointed as the French administrator of the Saar mining basin. This provoked a CGT protest in March 1945.[31] In fact Perrin Pelletier's appointment indicated the extent to which the COH had succeeded in getting their view accepted at central government level. For a COH note of 26 October 1944 envisaged the use in the Saar of 'mining engineers, whose abilities are beyond doubt, who are excluded from the mines because of current conditions and especially because of social circumstances (labour relations)'.[32] This is clearly a reference precisely to those who were unable to work normally because they had been accused of collaboration.

There were a variety of reasons why the COH was so successful in promoting its interpretation of its activity during the war. Firstly, it benefited greatly from the personality of its former president, Aimé Lepercq. Lepercq appears to have been a genuine *résistant*. He had joined the Organisation Civile et Militaire at the end of 1942. He was used as a touchstone of good behaviour by businessmen who wished to explain their war records; when Perrin, of the chemical firm Ugine, wrote to Dautry justifying his war record he associated his activity with that of 'my dear and lamented friend Aimé Lepercq'.[33] In fact it is dubious whether Lepercq's resistance record had much to do with the 'resistance' of the COH. Lepercq left the COH in August 1943, whereas most of the activity which the COH claimed as resistance (that is, the obstruction of STO) occurred after this date. In his post-war testimony Fabre, the secretary of the COH, said that Lepercq left the COH 'a little before his arrest by the Germans',[34] implying that his leadership of the COH led to his arrest. In fact Lepercq's arrest occurred nine months after his departure from the COH. The COH's list of its employees who had been arrested during the occupation does not include Lepercq.[35] Furthermore, none of the apologias drawn up by the mines immediately after the liberation refer to Lepercq. However, in specific cases, such as that of Perrin Pelletier, Lepercq was able to use his influence with the government. More generally the COH benefited from its association with such a distinguished *résistant*; as Fabre put it: 'Aimé Lepercq is not a man to be doubted...by those who govern in the national interest.'[36]

[30] AN, F 12 10156, letter of 30 November 1944.
[31] Luirard, *La région stéphanoise dans la guerre et dans la paix*, p. 702.
[32] AN, 40 AS 46, note of 26 October 1944.
[33] AN, 307 AP 140, letter Perrin to Dautry, dated 27 September 1944.
[34] Hoover Institute, *La vie de la France sous l'occupation* (3 vols., Paris, 1959), vol. I, p. 363.
[35] AN 40 AS 47, undated.
[36] Hoover Institute, *La vie de la France sous l'occupation*, vol. I, p. 363.

The second advantage that the mines had in fending off retribution in 1944 was their share structure. Since management and ownership were separated, and since ownership was so dispersed (shareholders were four times as numerous in the industry as workers), it was hard to punish specific individuals. In the battle over compensation for shareholders the Chambre Syndicale des Houillères made great play of the dispersed ownership of the industry: 'it is essentially small investors who made possible the exploitation of these natural riches'.[37] The large number of shareholders also meant that considerable public pressure could be applied to ministers.[38]

The confused circumstances of the liberation made it easier for the mines to avoid retribution. For most people simply did not realize how lightly the industry was escaping. Alongside the very small purge of managers, which really happened, was a very large 'phantom purge' which was believed to be happening.[39] The fact that managers were often detained for their own protection added to this belief. Furthermore, as Dejonghe suggests, many in the mining basins did not understand the nature of the nationalization of the mines and assumed that it was punitive. Indeed even some very well-placed people believed that the mines were being penalized for their wartime activity. The belief of the administration in the Loire that Perrin Pelletier had been punished when central government was actually protecting him has already been mentioned. Similarly, the prefect of the Haute Loire wrote to the minister of industrial production in consternation because his brother-in-law had been suspended from his post as mining engineer during the nationalization of the mines. He had to be assured that 'it is not a question of a personal sanction'.[40]

The most important trump card of all that the mines held at the liberation was their strategic position in the economy. They were vital for both war production and for the subsequent 'battle for production'. Under these circumstances the very last thing that the government wanted was a campaign against management that would damage production. Central government therefore made every effort to restrain the purge in the mines. Thus the ministry of industrial production wrote to the *commissaire régional de la république* in the north stressing the undesirable effect on production of widespread arrests of managers, 'among them many technicians whose inactivity is damaging to the French coal-mines and national interest'. The *commissaire* replied tersely: 'I am only too well aware of the regrettable consequences that the eviction of numerous engineers and pit deputies may have.'[41]

[37] AN 40 AS 2, pamphlet of Chambre Syndicale des Houillères.
[38] Holter, 'Miners against the State', p. 125.   [39] Ibid.
[40] AN, F 12 1056, letter dated 13 February 1945 from ministry to prefect in answer to his letter of 30 November 1944.
[41] AN, F 12 10156, letter dated 11 December 1944.

Postscript: liberation and Americanization

The fact that the *patronat* escaped relatively lightly from the post-war purges does not mean those purges left no scars. A brief spell of preventive detention or an exclusion order from a particular industry might seem trivial punishments when compared to those that were meted out to collaborators in other walks of life, but to wealthy and well-connected men, who had not been punished by anyone since leaving the *terminale* at Louis le Grand, this kind of treatment could seem humiliating and frightening. In the bulletins of the Centre des Jeunes Patrons and in the pages of the right-wing journal *Ecrits de Paris* many businessmen continued to express resentment against the left and de Gaulle for years to come.[42]

The archives of one businessman, Jacques Warnier, suggest that the sense of isolation and encirclement felt by much of business during and after the liberation may have had a more concrete legacy. The *patronat* may have been encouraged to look for friends abroad in order to help against their enemies at home. For it was well known that the Western allies were not noted for their admiration of de Gaulle; it was also hoped that they would take steps to resist the spread of Communism. Special hopes were placed in the Americans; they were expected to be more sympathetic to those accused of supporting Vichy: they had, after all, had diplomatic relations with Vichy until the end of 1942, and they were known as vigorous defenders of capitalism. In November 1944 a confidential journal circulated among businessmen expressed hopes that the Anglo-Saxons might intervene in French domestic politics: 'the secret intentions of the English [are] to organize a union of Mediterranean countries against Russian domination. They would have means at their disposal in the form of a Radical group going from Queille and Bastid to the American tendency (Chautemps).'[43] In February 1945 it was suggested that businessmen should enter into contact with the English and the American authorities to show them that 'some able Frenchmen want a solution to professional problems outside political clans'.[44]

America and England never did intervene in French internal politics to the extent that Warnier and his friends hoped. But the generally favourable attitude that developed among some French businessmen may have had more long-term consequences. For America was soon playing a large role in the French economy, a role underlined by the Marshall plan and the increasing tendency of French industrialists to visit America on 'Missions de

[42] For examples see AN, 57 AS 12.
[43] AN, 57 AS 12, *information sociales et politiques* dated 13 November 1944.
[44] Ibid., 28 February 1944.

productivité et plein emploi'. Warnier himself was an enthusiastic participant in one of these missions in 1951, and returned preaching the virtues of all things American. It was clear that in part his enthusiasm was inspired by memories of the American role during the liberation; one of the first men that he tried to contact on arrival in the USA was the colonel who had been billeted in his area in 1944.[45] The enthusiasm of Warnier and his friends was also partly due to the continued belief that America would be more sympathetic to the interests of French capitalism than a French government. They were keen to ensure that American aid should remain in the private sector and not come under the control of the government: 'It is indispensable that the financial operations take place in an entirely separate sphere from those of the state, especially as the Americans do want these new sums to increase the state budget'[46] and 'it seems most important to convince the Americans of the need to ... arrange things so that this aid really does go to private enterprise without the unfortunate intervention of the state'.[47] It was even suggested that French industrialists might persuade the Americans to pressure the French government to be more helpful to business.[48]

Of course the Warnier archives only give us a restricted picture of the French *patronat*'s relations with America. A proper study of the issue would require more detailed work, more attention to economic and social changes in France and more study of changes in the nature of French industrial leadership. However, the possibility that French business's enthusiasm for America may in part have been due to political factors does open up an interesting perspective. For, as Kuisel has pointed out, French interest in the *missions de productivité et plein emploi* began to tail off during the 1950s.[49] As will be suggested below, this may largely have been due to the fact that the French economy had begun to modernize within a traditionally French social structure, but it may also have been partly due to the fact that, as the tensions engendered by Vichy and the liberation died away, the French *patronat* felt less in need of outside protection.

Conclusion

The fate of business at the liberation was full of irony. All the strenuous efforts which business had made to acquire political credit with the Resistance and the working-class movement during the last years of the

---

[45] Documents concerning these missions can be found in AN, 57 AS 4.
[46] AN, 57 AS 4, Warnier note on mission (undated).   [47] Ibid.
[48] AN, 57 AS 4, President of CJP to Warnier dated 25 October 1951.
[49] R. F. Kuisel, 'L'American Way of Life et les missions françaises de productivité', *Vingtième siècle. Revue d'histoire*, 17 (1988), 21–38.

occupation came to nothing. Certain sections of business, especially large-scale heavy industry, were faced with the same kind of political attacks as they had suffered under Vichy. These sections of business had leverage with the provisional government for the same reasons that they had leverage with the Vichy government and the Germans; that is to say because of their usefulness to the war economy.

After the war French organized business was reformed into the CNPF under George Villiers. This organization was always reluctant to enter into political debates. Historians have assumed that this reticence was a product of the humiliation which the *patronat* had suffered in 1944 and 1945. But perhaps the real lesson that the *patronat* had learnt from the Vichy period and the liberation was that political popularity was not a necessary condition of commercial prosperity.

Chapter 14

Comparative and theoretical perspectives

In the final part of this book I intend to put my conclusions into perspective by comparing them with those reached by historians doing similar work on other countries and with more abstract theories devised by political scientists studying relations between capitalism and the state.

The Belgian example

It might be expected that the experience of French business would be most closely mirrored in Belgium. Belgium bordered on one of the most industrialized area of France, the Nord and Pas-de-Calais, and the economies of the two areas, dominated by coal-mining and iron production, were similar. Furthermore, Belgian industrialists, like their French counterparts, had to deal with democratic government, until 1940, and thereafter with defeat, invasion and occupation. Indeed, after 1940, Belgium and the Nord and Pas-de-Calais were subject to the same German authority based in Brussels.

Yet the political reactions of industrialists in France and Belgium could not have been more different. Industrialists in Belgium worked closely with the country's political elites in order to negotiate with the occupying authorities. This co-operation was illustrated by the Galopin committee that brought together businessmen and administrators during the occupation.[1] French industrialists, on the other hand, felt sharply alienated from the Vichy government (see chapter 8).

There are three reasons for the different reaction of French and Belgian industrialists to defeat and occupation. Firstly, the invasion of Belgium, unlike that of France, was not a 'strange defeat'. This had given the ruling

[1] R. Gillingham, *Belgian Business in the Nazi New Order* (Brussels, 1977), p. 31.

elite time to prepare and co-ordinate their strategy. Indeed the Belgian finance minister had begun planning for occupation from the moment that Germany reoccupied the Rhineland.[2]

Secondly, the banking systems in France and Belgium were very different. Belgian banks were highly developed. Not only were they rich but they also had substantial investments in industry. Numerous bankers acted as directors of industrial companies and bankers were recognized as leaders of Belgian capitalism. Indeed banks were so powerful that during the First World War the Société Générale had effectively issued its own currency to keep the economy going. Their role after 1940 in knitting together businessmen with each other and with the political elite was crucial; the Galopin committee was dominated by bankers. French banks were not able to play the same kind of role; they were less rich and less involved in industry than their Belgian counterparts. Companies raised capital through auto-investment; few directors of industrial companies were bankers and finance played only a limited role in the peak industrial association.

Thirdly, heavy industry was more politically vulnerable in France than in Belgium. Heavy industry dominated the whole of the Belgian economy; it provided most of the nation's wealth and employment for many of its citizens. The Belgian ruling classes were indissolubly linked to finance and heavy industry; as Gillingham puts it, 'The kingdom of Belgium is the creation of an elite class which owes its predominance to its control of the nation's economy and through it of fundamental institutions... Money-making was the bond that united the ruling classes.'[3] For this reason protecting Belgium inevitably meant protecting its industry.

Certain French industrial areas did resemble Belgium in economic terms but the political situation of these areas was rendered entirely different by the fact that they were merely enclaves in a wider economy that remained dominated by agriculture and small business. It was therefore all too possible for a government, based in the south and drawing its support from non-industrial areas, to seek to protect France without protecting its heavy industry. Indeed in many respects the Vichy government sought to buy concessions from the Germans at the expense of French industry. Thus under the Service Travail Obligatoire scheme prisoners of war, from primarily agricultural regions, were sent home in exchange for industrial workers. French industrialists in the North and Pas-de-Calais, the area that most resembled Belgium in economic and administrative terms, were most alienated from the Vichy government since they feared that it might give their whole area to the Germans in return for concessions in the rest of France (see chapter 8).

[2] Ibid. p. 25.   [3] Ibid. p. 16.

The German example

German business and the collapse of the Weimar Republic

The role of business during the final stages of the Weimar Republic seems to offer many parallels with the role of business during the final stages of the Third Republic. German industry reacted against the wage regulation and expensive social policy of Weimar just as French industry reacted against the Matignon accords. In both cases business acquired certain links with leaders who were subsequently to be instrumental in the establishment of an authoritarian regime. However, it would be unwise to push the comparison of German business relations with the Nazi party and French business relations with proto-Vichy groups too far. Recent research has tended to play down the intimacy of links between big business and the Nazis.[4] Even after it had abandoned its extreme social radicalism of 1923 the NDSAP remained, at least ostensibly, socialist. Industrialists could never be entirely sure that it did not threaten the rights of property and they could never feel comfortable with a party that, as late as 1932, co-operated with Communists in the organizing of a Berlin transport strike. By contrast the small business leaders who were supported by French industry used anti-big business rhetoric but they never flirted with outright opposition to capitalism.

Furthermore, the NSDAP was an independent movement with a solid basis of mass support that provided it with both money and votes. It was the leading partner in its relations with big business, attracting interest from big business only after it had proved its potential power in the elections of 1930; thereafter much business funding for the party was stimulated by fear and the desire to buy protection in the face of rising Nazi power. The decline in the closeness of links between business and Nazism after 1932 was the product of a change in tactics by the Nazis, who were playing the card of parliamentarianism against the von Papen cabinet, rather than of a shift in position by business. Finally, business was threatened into providing funds for the Nazis between Hitler's victory in the Reichstag elections of January 1933 and his final consolidation of power in 1934.[5]

The leaders who became allied with French business after 1936 had a far weaker basis of independent support. They operated through existing business organizations rather than through political parties. Furthermore, though these men claimed to represent small business and the lower middle

---

[4] H. A. Turner, *German Big Business and the Rise of Hitler* (Oxford, 1985).

[5] Ibid. For details of the threats applied to extract money from business after the Reichstag elections of January 1933 see Peter Hayes, *Industry and Ideology: IG Farben in the Nazi Era* (Cambridge, 1987), p. 83.

classes, their links to these groups seem to have been insubstantial (see chapter 4). For these reasons the new leaders were dependent upon the goodwill of big business that provided them with positions in business organizations and with funds. It was big business that had called the new leadership into prominence in 1936 and the new leaders began to lose influence after November 1938 when big business no longer needed them (see chapter 6).

The aims of French and German big business were not very different. Neither wished to see the kind of radical change of regime that ultimately took place in both countries. Rather they hoped that conservative forces would be able to take power within the existing system. German business conspicuously failed to achieve this objective; they had no power to restrain the Nazi party from attacking the von Papen government which incarnated their own hopes. By contrast French business was able to quell the campaign against the Republic once the Daladier government had overturned the Matignon agreement and restored the authority of employers. The period between the suppression of the general strike in November 1938 and the fall of France saw exactly the kind of socially conservative, economically liberal government that industry wanted established.

The social effect of the war economy in France and Germany

The implementation of a war economy had similar effects on labour relations in the two countries. Scarce labour meant that, in spite of the formal abolition of trade unions and the right to strike, workers maintained certain informal powers at shop-floor level. Furthermore, in both countries employers who no longer faced an organized left or the need to cartelize in order to carve up limited markets were less interested in industrial organization. Indeed competition for labour, raw materials and access to state contracts often brought industrialists into conflict with each other in what Mason, referring to Germany, describes as a 'war of all against all'.[6]

However, in one crucial respect the implementation of the war economy had a different effect in France and Germany. For in Germany the beginning of economic mobilization in 1936 was bad news for industrialists. Aspects of the Four-Year Plan, such as the project to use low-grade iron ore, were implemented against the will of industrialists, and Schacht, the conservative finance minister who had been a protector of business interests, was dismissed. By contrast economic mobilization in France took place in a context that was highly favourable to industrialists. It brought the

---

[6]   T. Mason, 'The Primacy of Politics', in S. J. Woolf (ed.), *The Nature of Fascism* (London, 1968), pp. 165–95.

revocation of the Matignon accords and the suppression of much labour discontent. In part this difference can be explained in terms of internal politics in France and Germany. The fact that the German rearmament took place three years after Hitler's seizure of power meant that labour organization had already been suppressed. Consequently German industrialists, unlike their French colleagues, did not associate rearmament with gains in the sphere of labour relations. Furthermore, the Nazi party was much more socially radical and contemptuous of economic orthodoxy than the leadership of the Third Republic.

In part the different pattern of rearmament in France and Germany must be explained in terms of international relations. For Germany was rearming to fight against powers that were economically stronger than herself. It was inevitable that such a policy would mean a high degree of isolation from the world economy. It could only succeed by abandoning conventional economics and trusting to rapid military success. Such a policy was bound to bring the Nazi leadership into conflict with cautious and profit-minded industrialists who wished to maintain economic freedom and existing trading relationships. The French, on the other hand, were rearming to fight in alliance with the major industrial powers: Britain and, it was hoped, America. French politicians and industrialists shared the belief that the maintenance of trading relations and economic liberalism was essential to such an alliance.

Vichy and the Third Reich

Both the Vichy and Nazi governments had aims for the economy which amounted to more than the simple accumulation of profits. The Nazis wished to turn Germany into an autarkic machine for waging war; Vichy wished to subordinate economic growth to the preservation of a certain social system. These aims were viewed with considerable distaste by industrialists. In both countries businessmen who shared the regime's ideological objectives were exceptional and were liable to be shunned by their colleagues. Volker Berghahn has shown how German industrialists, like Hans Kehrl, who demonstrated ideological sympathy for the Nazi economic programme by collaborating too closely with Speer's ministry, felt the disapproval of their peers[7] just as pro-Vichy industrialists, like Lehideux, aroused disapproval in France (see chapter 10).

However, the capacity of industrialists in Germany and France to resist state measures that they did not like was certainly not equal. Industrialists

[7] V. R. Berghahn, *The Americanization of West German Industry, 1945–1973* (Leamington Spa, 1986), p. 54.

in France were able more or less to ignore the corporatist projects embodied in the *Charte du Travail*; German industrialists who tried to ignore the autarkical projects of the Four-Year Plan soon began to feel very uncomfortable indeed. There are several reasons for this. Most obviously the Vichy state was far weaker than the Nazi one. Vichy was in power for less than half the life of the Third Reich, it did not possess the economic administration of the German state, and most of all it was a regime that had emerged from defeat and had to share power over its most industrialized areas with the German authorities. French industrialists were always able to counterbalance the political power that Vichy sought over them with the economic power that they possessed over the Germans.

There was another less obvious restraint on the power of Vichy over French industrialists; class unity. The Nazi party leaders came from outside the traditional German ruling classes; they were generally men from lower-middle-class backgrounds. They had not been members of duelling clubs, student fraternities or even the officer corps of the Prussian army: the loyalties forged in such institutions meant nothing to them. All this did not necessarily mean that Hitler brought about a 'social revolution'; as long as the ruling elites did as the Nazis wished they were left in place. However, when they tried to resist, the Nazis did not flinch from the severest possible measures. Industrialists began to feel the effects of this ruthlessness as early as 1934. Heinrich Gattineau, an executive of IG Farben, who had joined the SA, was arrested in the aftermath to the Night of the Long Knives and was lucky to escape alive.[8] Again in 1936 the Ruhr industrialists had their telephones tapped and were threatened with severe retribution after trying to derail Goering's plans for the exploitation of low-grade iron ore.[9] These events shed an interesting light on Hitler's remark that 'We have no need to socialize the banks and industrial companies – we socialize human beings.' The Nazis did not need to set up new institutions to direct the economy when they could threaten even the most powerful industrialists in the country with the concentration camp.

By contrast the Vichy government was almost never willing to apply really severe coercion to the French upper classes. The regime that was willing to select working-class hostages to be shot by the Germans was unwilling to take any action at all against well-connected individuals like Dautry or Charles Rist even when they maintained half-open contact with the Resistance. Indeed Vichy even sought to protect the business leader George Villiers when he was arrested by the Germans for direct participation in Resistance activity. The reasons for this are not hard to discern. Unlike the Third Reich Vichy was founded upon the existing French elites. The

---

[8] Hayes, *Industry and Ideology*, p. 122.
[9] Richard Overy, 'Heavy Industry and the State in Nazi Germany: The Reichwerke Crisis', *European History Quarterly*, 3 (1985), 1312–40.

corridors of the Hôtel Majestic were full of high-ranking army officers and civil servants. The background of these men was often very close to that of French industrialists; they had been brought together by attendance at the smart Parisian *lycées* and *grandes écoles*, and by service in the army and the *corps d'état*.

Even when the *patronat* and the Vichy leaders disagreed most sharply about broad political issues they could unite on matters of class defence. This was shown in 1943 when Aimé Lepercq (the leader of the French coal industry and a Resistance hero) worked with Bichelonne (a Vichy minister and arch collaborator) in order to protect students at the Ecole Polytechnique from deportation for compulsory labour service in Germany.[10] This common background did not mean that Vichy administrators and industrialists agreed about how the state and the economy should be run, but it did mean that Vichy administrators ruled out violence as a means of imposing their view on industrialists.

As the war progressed industrialists in both countries began to base their calculations on the assumption that the Axis powers would be defeated. Both sought to cushion themselves from the effects of such a defeat by distancing themselves from their own governments.[11] However, the French were in a far better position in this respect than their German counterparts. Firstly, France had a highly developed internal resistance movement with which industrialists could make contact; secondly, France had close links to America even after she signed the armistice with Germany. The Americans remained relatively sympathetic in their attitude to French society, and they were willing to give even those who were seen as 'Vichyite' by their own compatriots the benefit of the doubt. German industrialists found it far more difficult to dive clear when it became clear that the Nazi bandwagon was heading over the precipice. The Americans were less willing to distinguish Germans from their government than Frenchmen from theirs and indeed they often assumed that industrialists had been an especially important pillar of Nazi support.

Liberation, de-Nazification and Americanization

The post-war period offers many parallels between French and German experience. In both countries business survived the attacks to which it was subjected after the war with remarkable success. In France the networks of mutual protection that had operated within the ruling class during the Vichy period continued to work – indeed those with Resistance credentials who had been protected by Vichy officials now protected those officials (see

---

[10] Richard Vinen, 'The French Coal Industry during the Occupation', *Historical Journal*, 33 (1990), 105–30.

[11] Berghahn, *The Americanization of West German Industry*, p. 54.

chapter 13). In Germany contacts within the ruling groups became important again now that the Nazi intrusion was removed; once again survival and prosperity might depend on membership of duelling clubs.[12] In both countries industrialists established their own informal mechanism for judging the records of their colleagues. A key role was played by men that Volker Berghahn has labelled 'doorkeepers' – men like Dautry or Poensgen[13] – who were regarded as sufficiently authoritative to decide which industrialists should be readmitted to the fold.

America played a central role in the business life of France and Germany after the war. America was seen as the most powerful of the victor nations, and American economic hegemony was soon underlined by the Marshall plan. Under these circumstances it is hardly surprising that there was much talk in business circles about the desirability of imitating American models of management. The enthusiasm felt for such ideas in both countries was reflected by the numerous projects to establish European versions of the Harvard Business School. However, there were key differences in the response of French and German businessmen. For the Americans came to Germany as invaders seeking to impose alien ideas, such as decartelization, on German business. Berghahn suggests that the political hostility which such attempts aroused was only appeased as economic change brought to the fore new industrial sectors that were more sympathetic to liberalism. In France, on the other hand, the Americans came as liberators. Far from regarding them with hostility, French businessmen actually looked to the Americans for protection against their own domestic enemies (see chapter 13). However, in due course this politically motivated enthusiasm was eroded by economic progress that made it clear that the French economy was not necessarily destined to develop on American lines (see chapter 15).

The Italian example

Fascist Italy presents an interesting comparison with both Vichy France and Nazi Germany. At first it seemed that relations between fascism and business would be closer to the German than the French model. Though industrialists funded fascism it remained an independent movement and one that they had cause to regard with some trepidation. Mussolini never entirely renounced his socialist past, and radicals within his movement, like Rossini, discussed measures that might have done business considerable harm.[14]

[12] Ibid. p. 53.   [13] Ibid. p. 60.
[14] R. Sarti, *Fascism and Industrial Leadership in Italy 1919–1940* (Berkeley, Calif., 1971), p. 5.

As it turned out such fears proved to be ungrounded; the fascist regime inflicted remarkably little damage upon business. In many ways the situation in fascist Italy was similar to that in Vichy France. Italian corporatism proved, like the *Charte du Travail*, to be an ineffective measure that produced 'more smoke than fire'.[15] More significantly the Italian Istituto per la Ricostruzione Industriale operated in a manner that was remarkably similar to the French Comité d'Organisation system. In both countries institutions that were nominally under the control of the state proved in practice to be controlled by big business and run in its long-term interests.[16]

However, there is an important difference between the political context within which business operated in Vichy France and fascist Italy. The corporatist and anti-big business rhetoric of the Vichy government was quite sincere; it would have enforced its projects had it possessed the power to do so. What deprived it of such power was its own subordination to the German war economy. No such constraint existed in Italy. Mussolini ruled for eighteen years before Italy's entry into the Second World War. But Mussolini had little interest in changing the position of Italian business. Indeed business in Italy was often listened to sympathetically by the administration, and the peak association of Italian industry, the Confederazione Generale dell'Industria Italiana (CGII), remained in existence throughout the fascist period. However, Italian industry was aware of the fact that it owed its security to the regime's goodwill. Mussolini did occasionally demonstrate his authority with spectacular gestures. The dismissal of Olivetti – the head of the CGII and a personal enemy of Mussolini's – in 1934[17] was such a gesture, and Cohen suggests that even the revaluation of the lira that was carried out in 1926 owed much to the fascists' desire to assert their power over the Italian business community.

When Mussolini began to take Italy into the German alliance and towards war with the Western allies he aroused reactions from Italian business that were very similar to those that the Vichy government aroused from French business. German industrial power frightened both French and Italian industrialists. It was feared that if Germany won the war she would reconstruct Europe in a manner designed to ensure the hegemony of her own industry, and that this would damage industries in other countries that might provide competition for Germany.[18] When it became clear that Germany was not going to win the war, fear of retribution after allied victory made industrialists in France and Italy even keener to distance themselves from their respective governments. In 1944 Mussolini bitterly

---

[15] This phrase was used by Acquarone cited in Jon Cohen, 'Was Italian Fascism a Developmental Dictatorship?', *Economic History Review*, 12 (1988), 95–113.
[16] Sarti, *Fascism and Industrial Leadership*, pp. 80–8.   [17] Ibid. p. 14.
[18] Ibid. p. 130. For French fears on this score see chapter 7.

remarked to the German ambassador: 'many leaders of Italian industry are awaiting the Anglo-Saxons with open arms and in great part are responsible for the treachery of September 8'.[19]

The American model

Of all the countries where relations between business and politics have attracted the interest of scholars, America presents the sharpest contrast with France. Businessmen in America have had an easier life than those in France. While French business has had to contend with a Socialist and Communist threat, in America even the extreme left of the electable political spectrum, the liberal wing of the democratic party, accepts capitalism and indeed accepts subsidy from capitalists.[20] Furthermore, most American politicians have expressed admiration for the role of big business: Eisenhower remarked, 'What's good for General Motors is good for America.'[21] In France big business was violently unpopular even, and sometimes especially, on the right; it would have been political suicide for a French prime minister to suggest that what was good for the two hundred families was good for France.

The sympathetic political climate within which American business organizations operated militated against business organizations. Large firms tended to seek specific advantages through discreet lobbying within the political system rather than through allying with other businesses in order to defend their general interest. Business organizations in America have been underfunded, and isolated from many of their own members.[22] No organization could claim to speak for American business in the manner that the CGPF could claim to speak for French business.

In spite of these obvious differences it is possible to draw certain direct parallels between the political experiences of business in France and America. The first of these parallels relates to the New Deal period. The New Deal brought state regulation and taxation, which seemed to be inimical to business interests; indeed it was greeted with considerable hostility by much of American business. Yet theorists like Block argue that in fact the New Deal served the interests of business by reflating the economy and buying off the threat posed by working-class discontent. They suggest that the New Deal is an example of the way in which a 'relatively autonomous state' can serve the long-term interests of capitalism by rising

[19] Ibid. p. 132.
[20] Edward Handler and John Mulkern, *Business in Politics: The Campaign Strategies of Corporate Political Action Committees* (Lexington, Ky, 1982).
[21] G. K. Wilson, *Business and Politics* (London, 1985).   [22] Ibid. p. 30.

above the short-term and narrow-minded preoccupations of individual capitalists.[23] It might well be argued that the Matignon settlement served a similar purpose in France. Indeed in some respects Matignon fits into the theoretical structure devised by Block better than the New Deal. For, Matignon was a response to a social threat, the strikes of 1936, that was so immediate that the leaders of business organizations recognized that concessions would have to be made. But the leaders of business organizations recognized that it would have been impossible to persuade individual businessmen to subscribe to the Matignon accords unless the state had taken responsibility for some of its more unpopular provisions.

The second obvious parallel relates to what has been called 'military Keynesianism'. Historians like Robert Collins have suggested that this concept became current in American business circles during the late 1940s. Businessmen came to feel that a certain amount of counter-cyclical investment by the state was economically desirable and that such investment might take place without undesirable social consequences so long as it was channelled into military rather than social programmes. The magazine *Business Week* described this policy in the following way: 'There is a tremendous social and economic difference between welfare pump priming and military pump priming... Military spending doesn't really alter the structure of the economy. It goes through regular channels. As far as a businessman is concerned, a munitions order from the government is much like an order from a private customer.'[24]

There is obviously a tempting parallel here with France. Certain sections of French business had benefited considerably from armaments contracts that they had received during the French economic mobilization after 1938. Just as military Keynesianism was acceptable to American businessmen who had rejected the social spending of the New Deal, so armaments production was acceptable to French businessmen who had rejected the Matignon settlement. Indeed French military spending was not just socially conservative but socially reactionary, since it was economic mobilization that made possible the destruction of the Matignon settlement.

French military spending was not maintained after 1945 at levels comparable to those prevailing in America. However, to some extent 'military Keynesianism' in America was paralleled by 'Marshall plan Keynesianism' in France. For Marshall plan spending was acceptable to business because it was funded by the gift of a foreign government seen as sympathetic to business rather than with taxation raised by Socialists (see

---

[23] Fred Block, 'The Ruling Class Does Not Rule: Notes on the Marxist Theory of the State', *Socialist Revolution*, 33 (1977), 6–28.

[24] Robert Collins, *The Business Response to Keynes* (New York, 1982), cited in Berghahn, *The Americanization of West German Industry*, p. 266.

chapter 13). Furthermore, Marshall plan spending was seen as a temporary measure to restore economic health, and bolster Western Europe against Communism, rather than as a move towards a more planned economy.

Theoretical structure

In recent years debate about business and politics has come to centre on the role of the state. The state is seen to have a key role in the control of industrial relations. Indeed Marxist historians suggest that a certain degree of state autonomy is a necessary precondition of the state's ability to serve capitalism. An autonomous state is able to take a more long-term view than individual capitalists; it is able to impose a unity upon capitalism that would normally be precluded by business rivalry, and at times it is able to force capitalists to make concessions to labour that hit profits but guarantee the survival of the capitalist system.

Our study of business politics between 1936 and 1945 certainly suggests that the state played a central role. In 1936 business leaders recognized that, whatever their long-term aims, they needed to strike a deal with the unions in order to bring the strike wave to an end. However, business leaders would never have been able to impose such a deal on their own members. What allowed them to get the Matignon deal through was the intervention of the government and particularly the willingness of the government to take responsibility for certain elements of the settlement that were especially unpopular in business circles.

The fact that the state had underwritten much of the Matignon settlement left business leaders free to attack that settlement. However, it was not their attacks that brought it down. What did that was government legislation and the willingness of the government to suppress strikes called in protest at that legislation. As was shown in chapter 6, industrial organizations quite specifically counselled their members to let the state take the leading role in the struggle with the trade unions.

After 1940 the role of the state in organizing and protecting capitalism became less clear. The invasion and occupation reduced the autonomy of the French state. Furthermore, the new agencies created in order to run the war economy made it increasingly difficult to say where the state ended and civil society began. However, even during this period it is possible to see that in some ways an autonomous state continued to protect capitalism. For example, the Comité d'Organisation for the coal industry used power that had been vested in it by the state to impose policies in the long-term interest of the whole industry that were resisted by individual firms.[25]

[25] Vinen, 'The French Coal Industry during the Occupation'.

All this begs a simple question: why should the state seek to protect capitalism? Answering this question with regard to France would take another book. However, it is worth briefly examining some of the theoretical approaches to relations between capitalism and the state to see if they offer clues as to why French big business so often found itself helped by the state even when the political climate seemed most unfavourable to it. Broadly speaking, social theorists have given three kinds of answer to this question. 'Instrumentalists' suggest that the state itself is run by capitalists; 'functionalists' suggest that there are structural constraints that prevent the state from acting against the interests of capitalism regardless of who controls that state; and 'realists' suggest that the state's actions can only really be understood with reference to the struggle for power in the international arena.[26]

Ralph Miliband is the best-known exponent of the instrumentalist interpretation of capitalism and the state.[27] He suggests that capitalists benefit from state action because they have a high degree of influence over it, and because many politicians and administrators come from backgrounds that tie them to capitalism. The instrumentalist analysis has been criticized for overestimating the degree of consensus and calculation among capitalists. Capitalists rarely agree among themselves about the policies that they wish to see pursued; furthermore, policies that are seen in retrospect to be in the long-term interests of capital are often resisted fiercely by business at the time. This objection does not destroy Miliband's case. It is perfectly possible to argue that the state is run by men whose background and social position give them an interest in the survival of capitalism but who, being removed from the day-to-day pressures of running a business, are able to take a long-term view.

At first glance Miliband's analysis does not seem particularly plausible when applied to the Third Republic and especially to the period 1936 to 1939, when the state's actions did most to protect the interests of capitalism. It is hard to argue that class ties bound Third Republic politicians to large-scale industrialists: generally the two groups came from different areas, went to different schools and earned their money in different ways (see chapter 3). Miliband's analysis works better when it is applied to administrators. For Third Republic civil servants did have considerable links with large-scale industry[28] and their advice often defined the parameters within which the government was able to act. Civil servants

---

[26] Jonathen Zeitlin, 'Shop Floor Bargaining and the State: A contradictory relationship', in S. Tolliday and J. Zeitlin (eds.), *Shop Floor Bargaining and the State* (Cambridge, 1985), pp. 1–45.   [27] R. Miliband, *The State in Capitalist Society* (London, 1969).

[28] For the links between the civil service and the *patronat* see Maurice Lévy-Leboyer (ed.), *Le patronat de la seconde industrialisation* (Paris, 1979) and especially the chapters by André Thepot, 'Les ingénieurs du corps des mines, le patronat et la seconde industrialisation', pp.

were especially influential in the field of economic policy and their influence, particularly through the new ministry of armament, grew as the economy was mobilized for war.

After 1940 links between industrialists and the ruling class were far more obvious. For whether or not Vichy meant the triumph of 'administration over politics' it certainly brought the triumph of administrators over politicians. The new government brought a wave of technocrats from the *grandes écoles* and the *corps d'état* into power. To some extent these men did bring benefits to industry. Class loyalty made the Vichy state very reluctant to use violence against industrialists, and, on the periphery of the state, the Comités d'Organisation often did serve the interests of capitalism. But those at the top of the state, that is, government ministers, pursued policies that ran sharply counter to the interests of big business. Indeed French experience between 1940 and 1944 stands conventional Marxist assumptions about relations between capitalism and the state on their head. For Marxists expect individual capitalists to be preoccupied with immediate and short-term gains while the state looks to the long-term interests of the capitalist system. Yet at Vichy it was the government that was preoccupied by the immediate possibilities opened up by the war and the occupation while business looked to the long-term, post-war, post-Vichy, future.

Critics of Miliband argue that the governing class is not simply an appendage of the capitalist class.[29] They argue that the governing class is an independent group that continually seeks to expand its own power by extending the scope of state activity. However, those who control the state act within certain parameters. On the one hand they are obliged to respond to popular pressure, which, if ignored, might cause an electoral or even revolutionary threat to the government. On the other hand they are obliged to maintain business confidence because the state itself depends upon revenue raised from economic activity and because the government needs to be seen as economically successful by the electorate. Block suggests that 'the dynamic of business confidence helps explain why governments are constrained from pursuing anti-capitalist policies'.[30] Block's interpretation obviously has considerable relevance to French politics between 1936 and 1939. The government was obliged by popular pressure to cede to the strikes of 1936 and implement the Matignon settlement. However, French governments were also haunted by the need to appease the 'mur d'argent' which was seen to have brought down the left wing government of 1924. Furthermore, it was believed that investor confidence was critical to the

237–47, and E. Chadeau, 'Les inspecteurs des finances et les entreprises (1869–1968)', pp. 247–63.   [29] The most prominent critic of Miliband is Nicos Poulantzas.

[30] Block, 'The Ruling Class Does Not Rule'. Block's argument seems to have strangely conservative implications; it assumes that the free market is indeed the most efficient and most publicly acceptable way of running an economy.

success of France's rearmament programme.[31] The need to maintain such confidence goes a long way to explaining why the Daladier/Reynaud government revoked the labour gains of 1936.

However, there are a number of respects in which Block's analysis fails to match the circumstances of France between 1936 and 1940. Firstly, it suggests that a government that oscillates between appeasing popular demands and reassuring business will never be able to achieve stability.[32] In fact the Daladier government, which restored business confidence from 1938 onwards, appears to have done so without causing sufficient popular outrage to threaten its own existence.

Secondly, Block suggests that business confidence is inevitably governed by short-term factors and that this makes business especially vulnerable to the appeal of authoritarian regimes even when such regimes threaten business interests in the long term.[33] However, French business leaders often showed a remarkable capacity for long-term planning. Whereas Block suggests that social reforms are always inflicted against the will of business it is clear that many business leaders recognized that the concessions embodied in the Matignon settlement were necessary at least for the time being. Similarly, many business leaders seem to have appreciated the threat posed to them by the Vichy regime from the very beginning. Indeed, in many respects Vichy's economic policies were undermined by just the kind of 'crisis of investor confidence' that Block describes.[34]

Thirdly, Block suggests that in moments of crisis, such as war or depression, the state may cease to be constrained by the need to maintain business confidence. At such moments the state is able to acquire new powers to direct capital, and it may be able to portray business resistance to its policies as unpatriotic. The French state lived through just such a period of crisis from 1938 to 1940 as it confronted the threat of Nazi Germany. Yet it was precisely during this period that the state acted most clearly in the interests of French business. Indeed it is tempting to suggest that, whereas the state of the American New Deal – the example from which Block draws most of his ideas – used crisis to ally with popular opinion and labour in order to overcome the constraints imposed by business, the French state used the crisis of rearmament to ally with business and overcome the constraints imposed by popular opinion and labour.

---

[31] Block does in fact maintain that French rearmament is an example of business undermining government policy.

[32] The instability inherent in this model of relations between capitalism and the state is highlighted by C. Offe, 'Structural Problems of the Capitalist State: Class Rule and the Political System. On the Selectivity of Political Institutions', *German Political Studies*, 1 (1974), 33–57. [33] Block, 'The Ruling Class Does Not Rule', p. 16.

[34] For example, Pucheu's scheme to modernize the coal mines failed because of the refusal of those who ran the industry to invest (see chapter 11).

This brings us to the third explanation advanced for state action. Recently it has been suggested that the state's role should not be conceived primarily in terms of social relations at all but rather in terms of struggle for international power.[35] This means that the state is not necessarily on the side of either capital or labour, or indeed on the side of any one fraction of capital or labour, but rather that it manoeuvres, choosing those groups upon whom it bestows its favours in pursuit of its own international interest. International factors certainly go a long way to explaining the behaviour of the French state during this period. French politicians were concerned and often obsessed by the struggle against Nazi Germany. It was this threat that stimulated the French drive for rearmament. But as Frankenstein has shown it was also largely international factors, such as the desire to preserve international links and prepare for a long war, that determined that rearmament in France would take place within a context that would not involve heavy regulation for business. Once this was decided it was inevitable that the burden of rearmament would be borne by labour and that business would reap the benefits as labour privileges were revoked and labour agitation suppressed. The state suppressed labour agitation and destroyed the Matignon agreement primarily because it saw these as necessary measures if France was to be rearmed. Similarly the easy survival of capitalism in 1944 and 1945 owed much to international factors. The Gaullist state protected industrialists from the reforming intentions of the Resistance because the state wished to raise production in order to pursue an international struggle.

It is not our intention here to suggest any definitive explanation for the actions of the French state between 1936 and 1945. To some extent all three of the explanations mentioned above are relevant. Indeed to some extent they are interdependent. The complexity of forces behind state action can be illustrated by examining one incident that paved the way for the reversal of Popular Front labour legislation: Blum's resignation in June 1937. The resignation could easily be explained in functionalist terms that place the emphasis on the role of investor confidence; Blum resigned in the midst of a financial crisis and after the senate had refused to pass his bill imposing certain financial regulations. However, the fact that Blum was so concerned about the financial situation was largely due to the international situation, which suggests a 'realist' interpretation. Finally, an 'instrumentalist' might plausibly argue that Blum was acting within constraints imposed by the class interests of the senate and of his own advisers, who had ruled out measures such as exchange controls. Most importantly of all it should be remembered that none of these theoretical approaches can completely explain the actions

[35] Zeitlin, 'Shop Floor Bargaining and the State'.

of politicians and civil servants; Blum's resignation owed something to purely personal factors of exhaustion, frustration and concern for his sick wife.

It is right that the main part of this book should finish with a reminder of how international affairs overshadowed French life during this period. For much of the study has concentrated upon internal affairs. It has discussed relations of the *patronat* with other social groups and with the government. Such an approach has made French business seem very politically successful: it got the better of the working-class movement in the period that followed the Matignon settlement and it won its struggle with the Vichy government in the period following the armistice. However, both these victories owed more to events outside France than to the internal power of the *patronat*. International events might just as easily have served to damage the *patronat*. Suppose, for example, that the Germans had signed a compromise peace with Britain in 1940. This would have allowed the winding down of the German war economy, thus rendering much French heavy industrial production surplus to requirement and allowing German industrialists to dispose of a rival. Suppose that Stalin had not dissolved the comintern and dissuaded Western Communist parties from revolutionary strategies in the wake of German retreat. This would have made the *patronat* far more vulnerable at the liberation.

Furthermore, by concentrating on political struggles within France, this study has implied that French business did well during the period under discussion. War, defeat and occupation allowed the *patronat* to gain political advantages within France but these advantages must have seemed trivial alongside the direct personal and economic harm that was done to French businessmen. Industrialists suffered the humiliation and indignation of defeat in 1940; they saw their factories bombed; they were obliged to live on turnips and wear wooden shoes; they watched their sons being deported to work in Germany; a few of them finished up in the cellar of Gestapo headquarters, or in Dachau. Members of the French *patronat* had a highly developed sense of their own importance; men like Camille Cavalier or Lucien Arbel could expect to be treated like feudal overlords in their own fiefdoms. But their power in France as a whole was dependent upon international events and France itself was a minor power whose fate depended on the attitude of other nations. Between 1936 and 1945 the *patrons* were forcibly reminded that they were only bit players in a sub-plot of the main film.

Chapter 15

Conclusions

Vichy and social revenge

Did the *patronat* see the Vichy regime as an opportunity to reverse the labour victory of 1936? It has been argued here that business did seek to overturn that labour victory. The Matignon accords were signed not because the controlling group in the business movement found them acceptable but because it found the consequences of not signing them unacceptable. Even before the signature of the accords business leaders were planning a mobilization that would overthrow them and the circumstances that had made them necessary. Because of the pivotal political role of the Radical party that mobilization focused on the *classes moyennes*, who were seen to constitute the electoral base of that party. Heavy industry sought alliances with the representatives of that class, or rather with those who claimed to represent that class. However, the destruction of the Popular Front and the labour legislation that had been imposed after Matignon had little to do with the great mobilization of the *classes moyennes*. It was achieved on the one hand by the state, which was motivated by the need to make the economy more efficient in order to be ready for war, and on the other hand by individual employers acting to restore authority within their own company. The suppression of working-class organization and Popular Front labour legislation had occurred before the fall of France. This suppression had brought changes to the tactics of the group that controlled the business movement. These changes were marked by the Majestic accords, which were an armistice in the class war, and by the abandonment of those social allies who had proved useful in 1936 and 1937.

The fact that industry had already achieved its social aims before the fall of France meant that it took little interest in the projects of the Vichy regime. Many of those with whom heavy industry had been allied now became vociferous Vichy supporters, but these men were now quite separate from heavy industry and indeed often very hostile to it. The reversal of social alliances was completed by the fact that the conditions of the war economy, and the desire to buy off social revenge at the liberation, led many industrialists to seek better relations with the working class. The separation between industry and Vichy was further increased by businessmen's desire to distance themselves from what was soon seen as a doomed regime.

None of this means that there was no relation between business politics in the 1930s and Vichy. The business mobilization of the 1930s paved the way for Vichy in a number of ways. The ideology of Vichy with its corporatism, its attempt to appeal to the *classes moyennes* and its anti-marxism owed much to the agitation of business organizations in the aftermath of 1936. It is possible to argue that the role of business is an optional extra in any account of the rise of Nazism. No such argument is possible when dealing with the collapse of French democracy. Vichy could not have assumed the form that it did without the contribution of the business movement. However, the aims of those who controlled the French business movement were always limited and specific. They might well have described social conflict in the terms that Bismarck used to describe international conflict: 'I do not want war, I want victory.' In this context the conflict was already over before June 1940. Powerful industrialists therefore regarded the Vichy regime much as Bismarck regarded the plans of his generals to march through Vienna in 1866: as a needless and provocative display of a victory that had already been won. Vichy was a reactionary regime that arrived when there was no longer anything to react against.

Vichy and modernization

Before 1940 the French economy had been widely regarded as backward and 'malthusian'. After 1945 France made the shaky beginnings of the progress that was to make her into one of the most successful economies in Europe. Not surprisingly many historians have located the roots of this apparent transformation in the Vichy period. Indeed it is fair to say that the search for the origins of France's post-war prosperity accounts for much academic interest in Vichy. The first and most influential theory that placed Vichy in the context of French modernization was advanced by Stanley Hoffmann. He suggested that economic progress in the Third Republic had been restrained by 'the stalemate society'. This society was founded on the 'republican synthesis', an alliance between industrialists, small businessmen and the *professions libérales* to maintain the social status quo. Part of the price of this alliance was the suppression of industrial expansion that might cause social dislocation: 'the timidity of entrepreneurial drives was a prerequisite for the conciliation of the interests of the groups included within the consensus'.[1] Industry as a whole remained dominated by the values of the small family firm that put status and security above profit.

Hoffmann argues that Vichy was one of the main causes of the end of the stalemate society. He suggests that during Vichy large-scale industry broke away from its paralysing alliance with small business: 'The age-old solidarity with small business...was severely tried by the circumstances of 1940 to 1944.'[2] He also suggests that industrialists began to abandon the values of the family firm and to display a modern managerial ethic that was characterized by a willingness to collaborate among themselves and with the state.

Hoffmann's assumptions have been called into question by historians of the French economy who doubt that France's economic growth was restrained by the kind of entrepreneurial failure that he describes. Even the most casual glance at the facts suggests that Hoffmann's neat assumption that technological modernity was the product of 'modern' managerial attitudes is open to doubt. For the most technologically modern firm in France was Renault.[3] Yet in terms of values and managerial style Renault was the perfect example of an old-fashioned patrimonial firm.[4] On the other hand coal-mining was, in managerial terms, the most 'modern' sector of the French economy. There was almost complete separation of ownership and management. Furthermore, a strong 'managerial ethic' was cultivated in the mining *grandes écoles*, and the habit of co-operation within the industry and between the industry and the state had been developed over many years. Yet in technological terms the mines were fiercely resistant to modernity.[5]

This study has suggested further objections to the Hoffmannite interpretation of Vichy as a modernizing experience. Firstly, it has been suggested that the Hoffmannite view of the relations between large and small business is misconceived. It is true that large-scale industry had been allied with small business in 1936. But that alliance had been based upon manipulation of the latter by the former for a specific purpose. That purpose

---

[1] Stanley Hoffmann, 'Paradoxes of the French Political Community', in idem (ed.), *In Search of France* (Cambridge, Mass., 1962), p. 7.   [2] Ibid.

[3] Patrick Fridenson, *Histoire des usines Renault*, vol. I: *Naissance de la grande entreprise, 1898–1939* (Paris, 1972). See also Aymée Moutet, 'Patronat français et système de Taylor avant 1914: le point de vue patronal (1907–1914)', *Le mouvement social*, 93 (1975), 15–49, in which Renault's enthusiasm for American techniques of production is discussed (although it is also shown that he misunderstood those techniques).

[4] Gilbert Hatry, *Louis Renault: patron absolu* (Paris, 1982).

[5] Odette Hardy-Hémery. 'Rationalisation technique et rationalisation du travail à la Compagnie des Mines d'Anzin, 1927–1983', *Le mouvement social*, 72 (July–Sept. 1970), 3–48, at p. 40. It is a measure of the confusion implicit in Hoffmann's arguments that he describes the leader of the French coal industry as a representative of 'certain traditional, patrimonial entreprises' (Hoffmann, 'Paradoxes of the French Political Community', p. 39 and note 31).

had been achieved before the fall of France, and heavy industry had already discarded small business representatives before the establishment of the Vichy regime.

Secondly, the industries that flourished in the occupation were not those that propelled France's take-off in the post-war period. Lévy-Leboyer has suggested that the breakthrough that the French economy made after 1945 was a matter of marketing rather than production. The wartime economy with its emphasis on heavy industry selling their produce to the German military machine in a time of extreme shortage can hardly have encouraged marketing skills. Indeed it might well be argued that the war exacerbated the effects of the depression in throwing the French economy back on to heavy industry and delaying the establishment of a consumer society.[6] The discontinuity between wartime and post-war industry can be underlined with a glance at economic geography. Whilst the Nord and Pas-de-Calais, which was central to the wartime economy, is now the French 'rustbelt', areas like Lyon and Haute Savoie are now among the most prosperous in France.

Thirdly, the Vichy period did not teach industrialists to co-operate with each other or with the state. Beneath the air of order which was transmitted by the Vichy industrial bodies the conflicts that had existed within the old industrial federations were perpetuated. Indeed the ferocity of such conflicts was increased because industrialists were struggling with each other for raw materials and labour, and because they no longer needed to unite against an organized working class. Industrialists were sharply alienated from the Vichy state. Only a small and unrepresentative section of business was interested in Vichy's schemes for a new organization of the economy. The majority of industrialists were only too aware that the conditions of the war were temporary, and that they would not provide a stable foundation for long-term plans. If Vichy was too late to provide industry with social revenge for 1936, it was too early to provide the modernized economy of the post-war period.

Postscript. Modernization after 1945: the Vichy legacy?

It has been suggested above that some influential interpretations of the modernization of the French economy fail to match the facts of French history between 1936 and 1945. However, many interpretations of Vichy have also been founded on a mistaken view of post-war history. A brief glance at the French economy after 1945 will make some of these

---

[6] Maurice Lévy-Leboyer, 'The Large Corporation in Modern France', in A. Chandler and H. Daems (eds.), *Managerial Hierarchies: Comparative Perspectives on the Rise of Modern Industrial Enterprise* (Cambridge, Mass., 1980), pp. 117–161, at p. 160.

misunderstandings clear and perhaps suggest a new hypothesis about the relationship between Vichy and modernization.

Large-scale business and the modernization of France

It is not hard to trace the origins of the Hoffmannite assumption that big business was a necessary precondition of modernization. Hoffmann wrote in the early 1960s at a time when American economic success seemed to be beyond doubt. It was widely assumed that imitation of the American economy was the only route to prosperity.[7] Indeed in the period after 1945 America had consciously sought to impose its economic structure on European countries. Under these circumstances it is not surprising that many historians adopted America as a paradigm of economic development in much the same way as the 'whig' historians once adopted Britain as a paradigm of political development. Ehrmann,[8] Maier[9] and Fridenson[10] have all been heavily influenced by lessons drawn from America. Paxton assumes that modernization and Americanization are almost synonymous.[11]

At first, events did seem to justify the assumption that the French economic development would centre on big business. In the immediate aftermath of the occupation the large-scale heavy industries that had benefited from the war economy continued to play a key role. Furthermore, French businessmen proved willing converts to the economic faith that was proselytized by America. The study trip to the United States had been an institution of French business life since the 1920s. Between 1945 and 1953 it became an obsession.[12] One commentator wrote: 'Pilgrimages are organized to those sacred shores where productivity was first revealed to men.'[13]

---

[7] European historians who feel that the domination of the study of twentieth-century France operated by American scholars amounts to 'intellectual imperialism' may be amused to note that the series editor of the book in which Hoffmann floated his influential ideas was Henry Kissinger.

[8] Henry Ehrmann, *Organized Business in France* (Princeton, N.J., 1957), p. xi: 'I have formulated many of my questions analogously to those which have proven useful for the analysis of group activities in the United States.'

[9] Charles Maier, *Recasting Bourgeois Europe* (Princeton, N.J., 1975). Maier is less explicit about the American origins of his models, but the message is clear enough from the books cited on page 8.

[10] Patrick Fridenson, *Histoire des usines Renault*, vol. I: *Naissance de la grande entreprise, 1898–1939* (Paris, 1972), p. 10: 'aux Etats Unis dont les études historiques sur l'automobile font pour nous jurisprudence'.

[11] Robert Paxton, *Vichy France: Old Guard and New Order, 1940–1944* (New York, 1972), p. 257.

[12] Richard F. Kuisel, 'L'American Way of Life et les missions françaises de productivité', *Vingtième siècle. Revue d'histoire*, 17 (1988), 21–38. Kuisel reports that these missions reached a peak in 1953 when a total of 2,700 men visited America in 300 missions. Of those who participated in these visits 45 per cent were bosses (25 per cent were workers and 30 per cent were civil servants).

[13] F. L. Closon, cited in Paxton, *Vichy France*, p. 356.

However, this situation did not last. French businessmen began to grow out of their obsession with the American model of development, and from 1953 onwards the frequency of visits to the USA declined.[14] As was suggested in chapter 13, this decline may, in part, have been due to the fact that the French bourgeoisie felt less in need of foreign protection against domestic enemies; it may also have been due to the increasing awareness that industrial modernization could be attained within France's traditional social structure. Small business has remained an important element in the French economy. This has been due, in part, to special political factors in France. Small business has continued to exercise considerable electoral influence which has earned it the protection of the state. Furthermore, the capacity of small enterprises to evade labour regulations has given them an advantage over their larger competitors.[15] Indeed in recent years historians have begun to revise their deterministic assumptions about the links between small business and economic progress. Dualist economists have argued that even highly advanced economies require a residue of small enterprises to offer an element of flexibility.[16] Others have suggested that, in fact, sophisticated techniques of production can be accommodated within small enterprises.[17]

Industry and the state

The second important misconception about French post-war history is that this period has seen close collaboration between large-scale industry and the state. It is widely argued that French post-war prosperity has been founded on an apolitical 'technocratic' consensus about how the economy should be run. Big business managers are seen as part of this consensus. However, closer examination shows that the consensus has been conspicuously lacking in the post-war French economy. Successive plans were the focus for fierce dispute between different interest groups, and subtle coercion rather than collaboration has characterized the state's relations with industry.[18]

The idea of the technocratic consensus between industry and the state hinges on the assumption that decisions relating to industry are taken on a

[14] Kuisel, 'L'American Way of Life'.
[15] See Suzanne Berger in S. Berger and M. J. Piore, *Dualism and Discontinuity in Industrial Societies* (Cambridge, 1980).
[16] S. Berger and M. J. Piore cite the literature on the subject.
[17] Charles Sabel and Jonathan Zeitlin, 'Historical Alternatives to Mass Production: Politics, Markets and Technology in Nineteenth Century Industrialization', *Past and Present*, 108 (1985), 133–76.
[18] An example of such coercion is the 'exceptionalism' practised by French civil servants who deliberately impose unworkable regulations upon industry which is then obliged to offer concessions to the administration in an effort to secure exemption from these rules. See Peter A. Hall, *Governing the Economy* (Cambridge, 1986), p. 162.

non-political basis that involves the objective assessment of economic consequences. But in fact the drive of the French state for modernity has been propelled by largely non-economic motives. The great showcases of French modernization – the TGV, the space programme, Concorde[19] – spring as much from a Gaullist desire to assert French 'grandeur' as from a cool assessment of profit and loss. Indeed it is tempting to suggest that, far from aping the 'managerial instrumentalism' of big business, the French state has adopted the non-economic values of small-scale patrimonial enterprises. Just as small business often used economic activity as an instrument with which to assert social status, the French state has used economic activity as an instrument with which to assert international status. The economic ethos of the French state since 1945 has been far removed from that of large-scale industry. This can be illustrated by a comparison with Great Britain. In the 1960s it was fashionable for Conservative ministers to refer to 'Great Britain Limited'; if one of de Gaulle's ministers had talked about 'La France Société Anonyme' the General would have put him on trial for treason.

The modernization of the French economy stimulated by the state and the survival of small business have been closely linked. For the state – mindful of electoral considerations – has paid considerable attention to the interests of small business.[20] Similarly, small business organizations have come to embrace the possibilities opened up by new technology.[21] All this suggests a new interpretation of modernization. Modernization has not been based on an alliance of big business and the state in the 'apolitical' realm of technocracy. Rather it has been based on a highly political alliance between a modernizing state and traditional sectors in the French economy.

This hints at a new relation between Vichy and the modernization of France. For, at Vichy, the modernizers had been surprisingly close to the preoccupations of those who sought to defend small business and the traditional social structure of France. Both the traditionalists and the modernizers had been alienated from large-scale industry. It has been suggested that Gingembre, the small business leader from the 1930s who allied with the 'technocratic' Bichelonne during the Vichy period, and who subsequently argued that the defence of small business could be combined with technological modernity, illustrates the union which sometimes occurred between these two strands at Vichy. Of course in a war economy it had been impossible to implement either the traditional or the modernizing vision. But after the war things were very different. Gingembre had a

---

[19] It is revealing that the French regard Concorde as a success because it has earned prestige while the English regard it as a failure because it has lost money.

[20] See Suzanne Berger in Berger and Piore, *Dualism and Discontinuity in Industrial Societies*.

[21] Sylvie Guillaume, 'Léon Gingembre défenseur des PME', *Vingtième siècle. Revue d'histoire*, 15 (1987), 69–81.

conspicuously successful career in post-war France; a recent article described him as one of the faces of French modernization.[22] Perhaps the real legacy of Vichy was not the triumph of modernization over tradition, but the fusion of the two.

[22] Ibid.

Appendix 1

A Who's Who of industrial leadership 1936–1945

Gérard Bardet   Educated Louis le Grand, the Ecole Polytechnique and the Ecole des Mines. A founder of 'X crise'. President of the CII and then secretary of the CSEIC.

Jacques Barnaud   Educated Ecole Polytechnique. Inspecteur des Finances. Worked for Worms bank, 1928–39. Involved in *Nouveaux Cahiers* group. Head of cabinet of minister of labour, 21 July 1940 to 23 February 1941. Delegate-general for Franco-German relations from 18 April 1942.

René Belin   Born 1898. Member of directing committee of CGT 1933. Minister of labour, 14 July 1940 to 23 February 1942.

Aymé Bernard   Born 1893. Trained as lawyer at Lyon University. Delegate-general of AICA, 1920–44 and of the FAR. Treasurer of the CNE from 1936. Vice-president of the CGPF, 1936–40. Member of the Conseil Supérieur de l'Economie Industrielle et Commerciale, 1941–44.

Jean Bichelonne   Born 1904. Educated at Ecole Polytechnique (X grand major) and Ecole des Mines. Member of cabinet of minister of public works, 1 October 1937 to 12 March 1938. Head of cabinet of minister of armament, 14 September 1939 to 16 June 1940. Head of technical services at secretariat for industry, 16 June 1940 to 26 June 1940. Secretary-general for commerce and industry, 18 July 1940 to 23 April 1942. Secretary of state for industrial production from 23 April 1942. Minister of industrial production from 18 November 1942. Died 1945.

Yves Bouthillier   Born 1901. Educated Ecole Centrale. Inspector des finances. Director-general of the budget, 1935. Director of finances for the department of the Seine, 1936–38. Secretary-general of finances from 1 November 1938. Minister of finances, 16 June 1940 to 18 April 1942.

Paul Brenot   Retired Colonel. President of Chambre Syndicale des Industries Radio Electriques. Founder of CPAS.

Pierre-Ernest Dalbouze   Born 1872. Educated Ecole Centrale. Director of engineering firm. Member of board of Fives et Lille company from 1933. President of Syndicat des Industries Mécaniques de France and Fédération des Syndicats de la Construction Mécanique, Electrique et Métallurgique from 1919. President of 12th group CGPF. Member of board of *Journée Industrielle*. President Chamber of Commerce of Paris from January 1936 and of APCC from February 1936. Signatory of Matignon. Died 27 November 1936.

Léon Daum   Born 1887. Educated Ecole Polytechnique. Director of mines in the Sarre. Apparently put forward as a possible minister of labour and industrial production in 1940.

Raoul Dautry   Born 1881. Educated Ecole Polytechnique. Director of the Transatlantique 1932, SNCF 1936. Minister of armament 1939–40. Held no official position under Vichy and kept only two of his directorships, but preserved extensive informal contacts.

Henry Davezac   Born 1898. Educated Institution Saint-Joseph de Périgueux. Cours des Comptes. Became a leader of the syndicate of the electrical construction industry 1927. Involved in *Nouveaux Cahiers* group and CPAS.

Marcel Déat   Born 1894. Educated *école normale*. Socialist leader. Created 'Néo Socialistes' in 1933. Founded Rassemblement National Populaire in 1941. Minister of labour, March 1944 to June 1944.

Auguste Detoeuf   Educated Ecole Polytechnique. Director Alsthom. Involved in Redressement Français. Founder of *Nouveaux Cahiers*. President of CO for the electrical industry under Vichy.

René Duchemin   Born 1875. Educated local school. Founder of Union des Industries Chimiques. President of Kuhlmann from 1925. President of CGPF 1926 to 1936. Signatory of Matignon. President of CO for chemical industry under Vichy. Reprimanded for collaboration in 1944.

Edouard Duhem   President of Confédération Nationale des Groupements Commerciaux de la France et des Colonies. Vice-president of CNE from 1936. Member of Bureau of CGPF from 1936 to 1940.

André Fabre   Secretary of COH.

Louis Germain Martin   Born 1897. Trained as a lawyer. Journalist and academic. Radical deputy and minister of finances. President of CPAS, 27 January 1937 to 1940.

Claude Gignoux   Born 1890. Trained as a lawyer and academic. Editor of *Journée Industrielle*, 1925–28. Deputy, 1928–32. Under-secretary of finances, 1931. Editor of *Journée Industrielle*, 1932–6. President of Fédération des Industriels et Commerçants Français. President of the CGPF, 1936–40. Member of Conseil National (and president of its economic commission), 1941–4.

Léon Gingembre   Born 1900. Trained as lawyer. Legal adviser to Paris Chamber of Commerce. Member of PMIC section of CGPF, 1937–9. Cabinet of minister of industrial production from 18 November 1943. Secretary to Comité d'Etudes de la Petite et Moyenne Entreprise. Member of Commission Ricard. Delegate-general of Confédération Générale de la Petite et Moyenne Entreprise, 1944–62; President, 1962–83.

François Laederich   Textile manufacturer. President of textile syndicate. President of CO for textile industry until ejected by Germans. Vigorous Vichy supporter.

Hubert Lagardelle   Born 1882. Socialist leader. Minister of labour, 26 March 1943 to 19 November 1944.

Lambert Ribot   Born 1888. Delegate-general of Comité des Forges. Member of Bureau International du Travail. Held no post under Vichy.

François Lehideux   Born 1902. Nephew-in-law of Louis Renault. Worked for Renault, 1935–9. President of CO for motor manufacture. Secretary, Commission pour la Lutte contre la Chômage. Secretary of Délégation Générale à l'Equipement National. Secretary of state for industrial production, 18 July 1941 to 4 April 1942.

Jacques Lente   Secretary of UIMM. Member of Comité de l'Organisation Professionnelle.

Aimé Lepercq   Born 1889. Employed by Schneider in Czechoslovakia. President of the COH until August 1943. Member of OCM from December 1942. Arrested, February 1944. Minister of finances in provisional government. Died November 1944.

George Mauss   President of Fédération des Commerçants Détaillants. Member of Bureau of CGPF, 1936–40. Held no office under Vichy.

Pierre Nicolle   President of syndicate of vendors of artificial flowers. Founded Comité du Salut Economique, 1933. Associated with FAR from 1936. Present at Vichy, 1940–44. Member of PMIC section of CGPF and Comité d'Etudes de la Petite et Moyenne Entreprise.

Painvin   Manager of Kuhlman chemicals firm. President of CO for chemicals industry. Active in Paris Chamber of Commerce and Vichy industrial committees.

Baron Petiet   Leader of syndicate of motor manufacturers. Head of social section of CGPF from September 1936. Acting president of CGPF, 1940.

Henri de Peyerimhoff   Born 1871. Trained as lawyer. Member of Conseil d'Etat. President of Comité des Houillères, 1925–40. Member of Bureau of CGPF. Member of Bureau of CNE.

Félix Prax   Born 1875. President of Marseille Chamber of Commerce, 1934. Vice-president of CNE from 1936.

Pierre Pucheu   Born 1900. Educated *école normale*. Worked Pont-à-Mousson, steel marketing syndicate (not the Comité des Forges) and Japy Frères. Member of PPF. Associated with Redressement Français. President of CO for the mechanical industry. Secretary of state for industrial production, 24 February 1941 to 18 July 1941. Minister of the interior, 18 July 1941 to 4 May 1942.

Louis Renault   Born 1877. Founded company 1898. Supporter of CPAS. Arrested for collaboration in 1944. Died in prison.

René Richemond   President of GIMMCP. Signatory of Matignon accords.

Jules Verger   Electrical entrepreneur. Member of CPAS. Promoter of Association Professionnelle Mixte. Member of PMIC section of CGPF. Member of Comité d'Organisation Professionnelle. Member of Comité d'Etudes de la Petite et Moyenne Entreprise.

Jacques Warnier   Textile industrialist from Reims. Prominent campaigner for corporatism and *Charte du Travail*. Supporter of Vichy.

François de Wendel   Iron-master. President of Comité des Forges. Deputy for Fédération Républicain seen as arch representative of 'the two hundred families'.

Appendix 2

Note sent to Lambert Ribot on 3 June 1936

Context

This note is to be found in the archives of Raoul Dautry (307 AP 83). In the top right-hand corner is written (in an almost illegible hand) 'remis à Lambert Ribot 3 June 1936'. In the top left-hand corner is written the word Bozzi. The archivist has clearly assumed that the note came from Bozzi (who was a manufacturer of rolling stock) and the note is catalogued under his name. In fact the wording of the note implies that it was written by someone who was a member of the Conseil de Direction du Comité des Forges, and therefore not Bozzi. It seems much more likely that Bozzi merely forwarded the note to Dautry – who was his colleague in the rail industry. What is clear is that the note was drafted by someone who expected his opinions to be taken seriously in the inner circle of the French business establishment. Indeed the note anticipates the negotiations and concessions which were to lead to the Matignon accords so precisely that it seems likely that it was this note which stimulated Lambert Ribot to contact Blum two days later. This document has been translated word for word; no attempt has been made to alter the rather awkward punctuation of the original.

Text

As for myself, I maintain that the *patronat* is paying for its inertia during the last elections and I would suggest that we start preparing today, that is to say right away, for the elections of 1940, because the current position will allow our adversaries to fight more effectively, as they hold the levers of command and because of that four years of hard work seems to be in order if the *patronat* wishes to avoid being wiped out not over time but straight away.

In certain meetings last-ditch resistance has been discussed. I would support this line, if those who propose outright resistance could guarantee to me that the forthcoming Government when faced with this resistance would not support the Communist party which it needs for its majority or if I could be sure that in the face of an almost general call to arms [*un look-out presque général*], the radical socialists would leave the government for a government of national unity [*un Ministère de concentration*].

I suppose that the future head of Government will opt for the easy solution : to give satisfaction to the communists and I point out that all the workers' demands which are put forward, in all France what's more, in the same format, which indicates the collusion of a political party, must not be rejected as a whole when one can be almost sure that those charged with keeping order have, themselves, hopes for the improvement of their material and moral conditions.

Sacrifices of various kinds must be proposed, not by different Syndicates and Unions, but by the whole of the French *patronat* – for that section that concerns us – that is to say by the managing committee of the Comité des Forges.

I would suggest that sacrifices be proposed frankly, and applied faithfully and that they should take account of the following general conditions :

1 The two or three people from our *Patronat* should have face-to-face meeting with 2 or 3 people representing the working class, having the power to oblige their comrades to accept the propositions discussed in common and above all to get them accepted.

We would reserve the right to resume our liberty, if the workers having delegated their powers should not accept the conditions accepted by their representatives.

2 We should propose to the workers a first level of concessions for a period of a year, in such a manner as to allow the two opposing parties to take account of the influence of the application of these decisions and to prepare a second stage, if it is necessary, in a calm mood.

3 Personally, I reckon that certain claims of a non material nature, affecting less our prices than claims that can be expressed in figures, in certain industries, in terms of failures to gain or formidable losses.

During the first stage of concessions we would not object if a workers' delegate in each factory, paid according to his capacities, should be received by the management when he should have requests from his comrades to transmit.

It could be acceptable that in factories having more than 5,000 workers, there should be 2 or 3 delegates to whom I should happily give a small office at the factory exit to allow them to receive their comrades.

This abandon of a section of employers' control might seem enormous today; it would be still greater tomorrow, if we do nothing.

4 Personally, I see no problem in giving 8 days of paid holidays to workers, on condition that it should be an obligation imposed by a decision of Parliament, in such a way, that if the general economy cannot support the sacrifice, Parliament should be responsible.

These are, I think, the two claims that are dearest to the heart of the working masses and, as I said earlier, it would be better in the present political circumstances, to give a first level of satisfaction while having the time needed to study in calm the claims, that are often exaggerated, of a few troublemakers.

Bibliography

Archival Sources

Paris, Archives Nationales

Prime Minister's Office

2 AG 586
2 AG 1927

Ministry of the Interior

F 7 1398

Ministry of Agriculture

F 10 5098

Ministry of Industrial Production

F 12 9953
F 12 1001
F 12 10033
F 12 10043
F 12 10102
F 12 10156

Ministry of Labour

F 22 1578
F 22 1836
F 22 1839

Délégation générale aux relations économiques franco allemandes. (Complete cartons of documents in this series are not issued; readers must request individual dossiers by title.)

F 37 7   Account of meetings at délégation générale du gouvernement français.
F 37 16   Correspondence with COA (April 1941–November 1942)
F 37 27   Studies of the advantages of Franco-German collaboration
F 37 31   Coal, October 1940–February 1943.

F 37 39   Nord and Pas-de-Calais, July 1940–February 1942; miners' strike in
          Nord and Pas-de-Calais, June and July 1941
F 37 46   Salaries
F 37 48   Relève, March 1941–June 1943, labour
F 37 77   *Conseil consultatif* of Centre d'Information Interprofessionnelle

Bichelonne Cosmi Papers

72 AJ 1926
72 AJ 1927
72 AJ 1929
72 AJ 1930
72 AJ 1931
72 AJ 1932

Association de l'Industrie et de l'Agriculture Françaises

27 AS 2
27 AS 4

Groupement des Industries Métallurgiques Mécaniques et Connexes de la Région
Parisienne

39 AS 209
39 AS 213
39 AS 836
39 AS 851
39 AS 852
39 AS 853
39 AS 854
39 AS 861
39 AS 941
39 AS 960
39 AS 964
39 AS 965

Comité des Houillères and Comité d'Organisation de l'Industrie des
Combustibles des Minéraux Solides

40 AS 2
40 AS 43
40 AS 44
40 AS 46
40 AS 47
40 AS 78
40 AS 95

Office Central de Répartition des Produits Industriels

68 AJ 130
68 AJ 131
68 AJ 1001

Jacques Warnier Papers

57 AS 2
57 AS 3
57 AS 12
57 AS 13
57 AS 15
57 AS 21
57 AS 22

Conseil National du Patronat Français

72 AS 6
72 AS 7
72 AS 8
72 AS 9

Etablissements Arbel

70 AQ 300
70 AQ 420
70 AQ 428
70 AQ 430
70 AQ 431
70 AQ 436
70 AQ 442
70 AQ 444

Fives-Lille

198 AQ 14
198 AQ 54

Renault

91 AQ 1/2
91 AQ 4
91 AQ 16
91 AQ 65
91 AQ 78
91 AQ 84

Compagnie des Mines de Blanzy

92 AQ 27

Compagnie des Mines d'Anzin

AN 109 MI 5

Jean Coutrot Papers

468 AP 8

Raoul Dautry Papers

307 AP 83

307 AP 140
307 AP 157

Louis Marin papers

317 AP 87/88

Private sources

Jacques Lecompte Boinet, diaries 1940–46, kindly lent to the author by Madame Lecompte Boinet

Lyon, Archives du Rhone

4 236, Prefect's report 1937

Paris Chamber of Commerce

Transcripts of meetings, June 1936 to 1940
1862, carton marked Comité National d'Entente (actually contains papers on both CNE and *comité d'étude pour la PMI*)

Paris, Institut d'Histoire Sociale

Belin papers, contained in two unmarked files
Villey report of 1944, in file marked CNPF

Lyon, Chamber of Commerce

Transcript of meetings, June 1936–September 1939

Blois, Pont-à-Mousson archives
41952
41604
41721

Printed Primary Sources

Assemblée Nationale, Première Législature, Session de 1947, *Rapport fait au nom de la commission chargée d'enquêter sur les événéments survenus en France de 1933 à 1945*, vol. VII.
Belin, René *Du secrétariat de la CGT au gouvernement de Vichy*, Paris, 1978.
Benoist Méchin, Jacques, *De la défaite au désastre*, 2 vols., Paris, 1984.
Bernard, Aymé, *L'entreprise et ses hommes*, Paris, 1962.
Bouthillier, Yves, *Le drame de Vichy*, 2 vols., Paris, 1950.
Documents, bulletin of AICA. No complete run of this is available. Scattered issues from 1939 can be found in AN, 39 AS 420. Issues from 1940 to 1947 are available in the Rhône archives in the economic periodicals. It should be noted

that this bulletin changes its title several times; pre-war issues are usually entitled 'Bulletin et documents'.

Hoover Institute, *La vie de la France sous l'occupation*, 3 vols., Paris, 1959.

Journée Officiel de la République Française. Annexe. Documents. 1935–1940.

Nicolle, Pierre, *Cinquante mois d'armistice, Vichy, 2 juillet 1940–26 août 1944: journal d'un témoin*, 2 vols., Paris, 1947.

Nicolle, Pierre, *L'organisation corporative*, Paris, 1934.

Nouveaux Cahiers, 1937.

Paillard, Jean, *La révolution corporative spontanée*, Paris, 1979.

Picard, François, *L'épopée de Renault*, Paris, 1976.

Potton, Alain, *On a trouvé un chef*, Lyon, 1937.

Pucheu, Pierre, *Ma vie*, Paris, 1948.

Rist, Charles, *Une saison gâtée: journal de la guerre et de l'occupation, 1939–1945*, ed. Jean-Noel Jeanneney, Paris, 1983.

Villiers, George, *Témoignages*, Paris, 1978.

Secondary works

Abraham, David, *The Collapse of the Weimar Republic*, Princeton, N.J., 1982.

Asselain, Jean Charles, 'Une erreur de politique économique: la loi des quarante heures de 1936', *Revue économique*, 25 (1974), 672–705.

Badie, Bertrand, 'Les grèves du Front populaire aux usines Renault', *Le mouvement sociale*, 81 (1972), 69–109.

Barnet, Corelli, *The Audit of War: The Illusion and Reality of Britain as a Great Nation*. London, 1986.

Bauchard, Philippe, *Les technocrates et le pouvoir*, Paris, 1966.

Baudaint, Alain, *Pont-à-Mousson (1919–1939): stratégies industrielles d'une dynastie lorraine*, Paris, 1980.

Berger, S. and M. J. Piore, *Dualism and Discontinuity in Industrial Societies*, Cambridge, 1980.

Berghahn, V. R., *The Americanization of West German Industry, 1945–1973*, Leamington Spa, 1986.

Block, Fred, 'The Ruling Class Does Not Rule: Notes on the Marxist Theory of the State', *Socialist Revolution*, 33 (1977) 6–28.

Boltanski, Luc, *The Making of a Class: Cadres in French Society*, Cambridge, 1987.

Bourdé, Guy, *La défaite du front populaire*, Paris, 1977.

Brady, David, *Business as a System of Power*, New York, 1943.

Caplan, Jane, 'Theories of Fascism: Nicos Poulantzas as Historian', *History Workshop*, no. 3 (Spring 1977), 83–100.

Chevigard, Marie Genevie and Nicole Faure, 'Système de valeurs et de références dans la presse féminine', in R. Rémond and J. Bourdin (eds.), *La France et les Français en 1938–1939*, Paris, 1978.

Cohen, Jon, 'Was Italian Fascism a Developmental Dictatorship?', *Economic History Review*, 12 (1988), 95–113.

Collins, Robert, *The Business Response to Keynes*, New York, 1982.

Colton, Joel, *Compulsory Labor Arbitration in France, 1936–1939*, New York, 1951.

Coston, *Les deux cents familles au pouvoir*, Paris, 1977.

Dejonghe, Etienne, 'Les houillères du Nord et Pas-de-Calais à l'épreuve: 1944–1947', *Revue du Nord*, 227 (1975), 643–67.

Dejonghe, Etienne, 'Les problèmes sociaux dans les entreprises houillères du Nord et du Pas-de-Calais durant la seconde guerre mondiale', *Revue d'histoire moderne et contemporaine*, 18 (1971), 124–44.

Dejonghe, Etienne, 'Chronique de la grève des mineurs du Nord/Pas-de-Calais (27 mai–6 juin 1941)', *Revue du Nord*, 69 (1987), 323–45.

Dessirier, J., 'L'économie française devant la dévaluation monétaire: secteurs "abrités" et "non abrités" retour vers l'équilibre', *Revue d'économie politique*, 50 (1936), 1527–87.

Duchemin, R., *L'organisation syndicale patronale en France*, Paris, 1940.

Ehrmann, Henry, *Organized Business in France*, Princeton, N.J., 1957.

Ehrmann, Henry, *French Labor from the Popular Front to the Liberation*, New York, 1947.

Les entreprises français pendant la seconde guerre mondiale, conference held at Centre d'Etudes Pédagoiques, Sèvres, 25/26 November 1986. The text of talks given at this conference can be found at the Institut d'Histoire du Temps Présents.

Feldman, Gerald, 'Big Business and the Kapp Putsch', *Central European History*, 4 (1971), 99–130.

Feldman, Gerald, *Iron and Steel in the German Inflation 1916–1923*, Princeton, N.J., 1977.

Feldman, Gerald and Ulrick, Nockeu, 'Trade Associations and Economic Power: Interest Group Development in the German Iron and Steel Industries, 1900–1933', *Business History Review*, 49 (1975), 413–45.

Frankenstein, Robert, *Le prix du réarmement français, 1935–1939*, Paris, 1982.

Fridenson, Patrick, *Histoire des usines Renault*, vol. I: *Naissance de la grande entreprise, 1898–1939*, Paris, 1972.

Fridenson, Patrick, 'Le patronat français', in R. Rémond and J. Bourdin (eds.), *La France et les Français en 1938–1939*, Paris, 1978.

Fridenson, Patrick (ed.), *L'autre front*, Paris, 1977.

Fridenson, Patrick and André Straus (eds.), *Le capitalisme français 19e–20e siècle: blocages et dynamismes d'une croissance*, Paris, 1987.

Gignoux, Claude, *L'économie française 1919–1939*, Paris, 1943.

Gillingham, R., *Belgian Business in the Nazi New Order*, Brussels, 1977.

Guerin, Daniel, *Fascism and Big Business*, London, 1973.

Guillaume, Sylvie, 'Léon Gingembre défenseur des PME', *Vingtième siècle. Revue d'histoire*, 15 (1987), 69–81.

Hall, Peter A., *Governing the Economy*, Cambridge, 1986.

Halls, W. D., *The Youth of Vichy France*, Oxford, 1981.

Handler, Edward and John Mulkern, *Business in Politics: The Campaign Strategies of Corporate Political Action Committees*, Lexington, Ky, 1982.

Hardy-Hémery, Odette, 'Rationalisation technique et rationalisation du travail à la Compagnie des Mines d'Anzin, 1927–1938', *Le mouvement social*, 72 (July–Sept. 1970), 3–48.

Hatry, Gilbert, *Louis Renault: patron absolu*, Paris, 1982.

Hayes, Peter, *Industry and Ideology: IG Farben in the Nazi Era*, Cambridge, 1987.

Hoffmann, Stanley, 'Paradoxes of the French Political Community', in S. Hoffmann (ed.), *In Search of France*, Cambridge, Mass., 1962.

Jackel, Ebhard, *La France dans l'Europe de Hitler*, Paris, 1968.

Jackson, Julian, *The Politics of Depression in France*, Cambridge, 1985.

Jeanneney, Jean-Noel, *L'argent cache: milieux d'affaires et pouvoirs politiques dans la France du XXème siècle*, Paris, 1981.

Jeanneney, Jean-Noel, *François de Wendel en République: l'argent et le pouvoir, 1914–1940*, 3 vols., Paris, 1975.

Jones, Adrian, 'Illusions of Sovereignty: Business and the Organization of Committees in Vichy France', *Social History*, 2 (1986), 1–33.

Jones, Joseph, 'Vichy France and Post-war Economic Modernization: The Case of Shopkeepers', *French Historical Studies*, 12 (1982), 541–63.

Julliard, Jacques, 'La Charte du Travail', in FNSP, *Le gouvernement de Vichy 1940–1942*, Paris, 1972.

Kedward, H. R., 'Patriots and Patriotism in Vichy France', *Transactions of the Royal Historical Society*, 32 (1982), 175–92.

Kolboom, Ingo, *La revanche des patrons: le patronat français face au front populaire*, Paris, 1986.

Kolboom, Ingo, 'Patronat et cadres: la contribution patronale à la formation du groupe des cadres (1936–1938)', *Le mouvement social*, 121 (1982), 71–95.

Kourchid, Olivier, *Production industrielle et travail sous l'occupation: les mines de Lens et les mineurs 1940–1944*, Paris, 1986.

Kriegel, Annie, *Aux origines du communisme française, 1914–1920, contribution à l'histoire du mouvement ouvrier français*, Paris, 1964.

Kuisel, Richard F., *Ernest Mercier: French Technocrat*, Berkeley, Calif., 1967.

Kuisel, Richard F., *Capitalism and the State in Modern France: Renovation and Economic Management in the Twentieth Century*, Cambridge, 1981.

Kuisel, Richard F., 'Auguste Detoeuf, Conscience of French Industry 1926–1947', *International Review of Social History*, 20 (1975), 149–74.

Kuisel, Richard F., 'L'American Way of Life et les missions françaises de productivité', *Vingtième siècle. Revue d'histoire*, 17 (1988), 21–38.

Larmour, Peter, *The French Radical Party in the 1930s*, Stanford, Calif., 1964.

Landes, David, *The Unbound Prometheus*, Cambridge, 1969.

Larkin, Maurice, *France since the Popular Front*, Oxford, 1987.

Lévy-Leboyer, Maurice, 'Le patronat français 1912–1973', in Lévy-Leboyer (ed.), *Le patronat de la seconde industrialisation*, Paris, 1979.

Lottman, Herbert, *The People's Anger: Justice and Revenge in Post Liberation France*, London, 1986.

Luirard, Monique, *La région stéphanoise dans la guerre et dans la paix 1936–1951*, Saint-Etienne, 1980.

Maier, Charles, *Reconstructing Bourgeois Europe*, Princeton, N.J., 1975.

Mason, T. 'The Primacy of Politics', in S. J. Woolf (ed.), *The Nature of Fascism*, London, 1969.

Mason, T., 'Labour in the Third Reich', *Past and Present*, 33 (1966), 112–41.

Miliband, R., *The State in Capitalist Society*, London, 1969.

Milward, Alan S., *The New Order and the French Economy*, Oxford, 1970.

Mioche, Philippe, *Le plan Monnet: genèse et élaboration, 1941–1947*, Paris, 1987.

Mioche, Philippe, 'Aux origines du plan Monnet: les discours et les contenus dans les premiers plans français (1941–1947), *Revue historique*, 265 (1981), 407–36.

Moutet, Aymée, 'Patronat français et système de Taylor avant 1914: le point de vue patronal (1907–1914)', *Le mouvement sociale*, 93 (1975), 15–49.

Muller, Klaus Jurgen, 'French Fascism and Modernization', *Journal of Contemporary History*, 3 (1976), 76–107.

Natali, Jacques, 'L'occupant allemand à Lyon de 1942 à 1944 d'après les sources allemandes', *Cahiers d'histoire*, 22 (Lyon, 1977), 441–64.

Nord, Philip, *Paris Shopkeepers and the Politics of Resentment*, Princeton, N.J., 1986.

Overy, Richard, 'Heavy Industry and the State in Nazi Germany: The Reichewerke Crisis', *European History Quarterly*, 3 (1985), 1312–40.

Paxton, Robert, *Vichy France: Old Guard and New Order, 1940–1944*, New York, 1972.

Poulantzas, Nicos, *Fascism and Dictatorship*, London, 1974.

Rousso, Henri, 'L'organisation industrielle de Vichy', *Revue d'histoire de la deuxième guerre mondiale*, 116 (1979), 27–44.

Rousso, Henry, 'Les élites économiques dans les années quarante', *Mélanges de l'Ecole Française de Rome*, 95 (1982–3), 29–49.

Rousso, Henri, 'L'aryanisation économique, Vichy, l'occupant et la spoliation des juifs', '*YOD*', nos. 15 and 16 (1982).

Sarti, R., *Fascism and Industrial Leadership in Italy 1919–1940*, Berkeley, Calif., 1971.

Sauvy, Alfred, *La vie économique des Français de 1939 à 1945*, Paris, 1978.

Soucy, R., *French Fascism: The First Wave*, New Haven, Conn., 1986.

Thepot, André 'Les ingénieurs du corps des mines', in M. Levy-Leboyer (ed.), *Le patronat de la seconde industrialisation*, Paris, 1979.

Thullier, J., 'Aspects de la crise industrielle dans la région Nord/Pas de Calais sous l'occupation allemande, *Revue du Nord*, no. 2 spécial hors de série (1987), 419–67.

Turner, Henry A., 'Big Business and the Rise of Hitler', *American Historical Review*, 75 (1969), 56–70.

Turner, Henry A., 'Hitler's Secret Pamphlet for Industrialists, 1927,' *Journal of Modern History*, 40 (1968), 348–72.

Turner, Henry A., 'The *Ruhrlade* Secret Cabinet of Heavy Industry in the Weimar Republic', *Central European History*, 3 (1970), 195–228.

Turner, Henry A., *German Big Business and the Rise of Hitler*, Oxford, 1985.

Vinen, Richard, 'The French Coal Industry during the Occupation', *Historical Journal*, 33 (1990), 105–30.

Weber, Henri, *Le parti des patrons: le CNPF (1946–1986)*, Paris, 1986.

Wilson, G. K., *Business and Politics*, London, 1985.

Woolf, Stuart, 'Did a Fascist Economy Exist?', in Woolf (ed.), *The Nature of Fascism*, London, 1968.

Young, Robert, *In Command of France. French Foreign Policy and Military Planning 1933–1940*, Cambridge, Mass., 1978.

Zdateny, Steven M., 'The Artisanat in France: An Economic Portrait, 1900–1956', *French Historical Studies*, 13 (1984), 415–40.

Zeitlin, Jonathan, 'Shop Floor Bargaining and the State: A Contradictory Relationship', in S. Tolliday and J. Zeitlin (eds.), *Shop Floor Bargaining and the State*, Cambridge, 1985.

Unpublished dissertations

Holter, Darryl, 'Miners against the State: French Miners and the Nationalization of Coalmining 1944–1949', unpublished PhD. thesis, University of Madison, Wisconsin, 1980.

Passmore, Kevin, 'Conservative Politics and the Crisis of the Third Republic: 1928–1939', unpublished manuscript in possession of author.

Rossiter, Adrian, 'Corporatist Experiments in Republican France, 1916–1939', unpublished D.Phil. thesis, University of Oxford, 1986.

Index